W9-BCY-710

DATE DUE

JUL 2003

Cy Feuer

I Got the Show
Right Here

**The Amazing, True Story of
How an Obscure Brooklyn Horn
Player Became the Last Great
Broadway Showman**

**Producer of *Guys & Dolls, How to Succeed
in Business Without Really Trying, Can-Can,*
and Many, Many More Legendary Shows**

With Ken Gross

Simon & Schuster
New York London Toronto Sydney Singapore

SIMON & SCHUSTER
Rockefeller Center
1230 Avenue of the Americas
New York, NY 10020

SIMON & SCHUSTER and colophon are registered trademarks of Simon & Schuster, Inc.
For information regarding special discounts for bulk purchases,
please contact Simon & Schuster Special Sales at
1-800-456-6798 or business@simonandschuster.com

Manufactured in the United States of America
10 9 8 7 6 5 4 3 2 1
Library of Congress Cataloging-in-Publication Data is available.
ISBN 0-7432-3611-4

To Posy, a woman who, when we stayed at The Imperial Hotel in Vienna, referred to it as "The Heil Hilton." I salute you. And to my sons, Bob and Jed, especially Jed, who patiently served as my eyes and pen during the editing process, spending an unbearable number of hours as I picked at everything.

June 11, 2002

I Got the Show Right Here

Prologue

I'm five feet five. Not what you would describe as a giant. I used to be taller. But that's what happens when you hit ninety. You lose some bone mass. You also lose some memory. And you lose all your friends. All the people who knew you when you were putting together what have become classic Broadway shows—*Guys & Dolls, Where's Charley?, How to Succeed in Business Without Really Trying, Can-Can, Silk Stockings* . . . They're all dead, the people who remember me as five feet seven. A really big man.

I'm not complaining. Yeah, well, maybe I am. My wife, Posy, and I think of ourselves as being alone on an island. Where the hell did everyone go? Frank Loesser's gone, and Abe Burrows and George Abbott and Billy Rose and Cole Porter and Bob Fosse and Ray Bolger and Ernie Martin. Especially Ernie. He was my partner. He knew the story. And it's a pretty good story, how I got to be a bigshot Broadway producer. There's nobody left who knows the whole story, not even me.

It's not like you have a whole, fully wound memory that unspools when you try to let it play. It's more like a broken reel. Scenes pop up on the screen, incidents float loose in changeable decades—I don't know when the hell some things happened. I remember playing sandlot polo in Hollywood, but was that before the war? When was I in Paris with Fosse trying to sign up Max Schell, was that during Kennedy? When did Sam Goldwyn stand by the barbecue pit, posing with that mitt on his hand, making believe he was cooking, when the butler really handled the food? Was that after he bought *Guys & Dolls?*

It's work, getting it all straight.

There's one moment during the day when I almost get it right. Every night I get drunk. At my age, it only takes one drink. I really look forward to that drink. I used to favor wine, flattering myself that I could appreciate bouquet and all the rest; now I find that I like the taste of whiskey. I sip it, sit back, and feel the blood rush through my head, blowing away the dust, clearing it up . . .

Part I

Brooklyn with a "V"

Chapter One

I *can,* with a pretty high degree of accuracy, reconstruct the essential flavor of my life. I can remember the conspicuous events, the exotic places, the remarkable characters, the moods, the textures—the actual taste of my days. I know pretty much how things turned out the way they did. And why. In fact, when I think about it, I can recall almost everything, albeit with a kind of dim and jumbled clarity. It's all there—I'm just a little weak on specifics.

I believe that this fuzzy retrospective is nature's way of filtering the water. Who wants to relive every boring incident? But there are moments—jolts of remembrance that come back to life, even now, half a century later. For instance (and this may not even qualify as a solid fact in the encyclopedic sense), I can remember with precision the actual shock of opening night of *Guys & Dolls* in the autumn of 1950. I was sitting out front with Posy when the orchestra began the overture. Suddenly, the audience exploded with applause. All they heard were a few notes; all they saw was a dropped curtain, but they went wild. Somehow, they knew something big was about to take place. I turned to my wife and said, "They were waiting for us."

Well, it appears that I am going to write a book, after all. I will try to lay it out with some lucidity, and I will try not to repeat myself; but at my age I can't promise. This material has been floating around in my head for a long time. So give or take a few facts, and with some unavoidable digressions, this will be the highly colored and close-to-authentic version of my career as a big-shot Broadway producer.

Bear with me.

*   *   *

I am, by nature, averse to emotional skylarking (that sort of thing, I have always maintained, belongs on the stage); however, there was an event that transformed my life completely. It happened on a recording stage in Hollywood where I had come by way of Brooklyn to seek, if not glory, at least a good night's sleep.

Thus, without too much ado, we plunge into my first digression.

I was raised in Brooklyn, a low-skyline borough of New York City, home to many urban rustics. My debut, if you want to pinpoint it historically, was on January 15 of 1911, which was somewhere between the Spanish-American War and World War I. Brooklyn (pronounced with a *V* by the natives, as in Bvooklyn) is a small-town cousin to Manhattan, which, by contrast, is tall and glamorous and pretty tough on cocky kids who try to elbow their way into the big time. Which appears to have been my intention from a very early age. I was convinced by my mother's unshakable certainty that mine was a singular and glorious destiny. My talent, such as it was, lay in music. So my mother stole time from her job as an underpaid saleslady in a dress shop and dragged me to all the great bandleaders and trumpet masters of the day who were somehow persuaded by her indefatigable gumption into listening to me play. I never heard anyone use the word genius in connection with what I was doing, but neither did they discourage my efforts.

Well, the truth is they couldn't. Maybe I didn't have to be a world-class trumpet player, but I had to succeed. I had no choice. Someone had to be the head of the family. It became clear to me at a very early age that I was chosen.

*   *   *

My father, Herman, was a vague, almost nonexistent presence in my childhood. I knew him mainly as a lump under a blanket who came out for air from time to time, mostly to go off to work. Not that I ever remember seeing him emerge. He was the general manager of a Yiddish theater on Second Avenue on the Lower East Side.

I do not remember seeing him at the dinner table, or walking around the house in his underwear, or even in a suit. There is simply no physical image that springs to mind when it comes to my father. I do have one specific memory. We were in a restaurant, and when it was my father's turn to order I heard him say to the waiter, "I'll have the chicken soup, with evidence." I liked that. There was some nice nasty sarcasm in that order. But that's about all I have to go on.

I cannot even picture his face. I have an old photograph of him and my mother—very formal—taken at some important function. That photograph is my only proof that he knew my mother personally.

He died of cancer when I was thirteen. I don't remember any illness, any air of doom, or even any lingering sense of sorrow. I remember sitting in the parlor, unable to work up any emotion. None. So I put on Offenbach's opera *Orpheus in the Underworld,* which always moved me, and thus wept for my father. (Even then I was boosting the drama with background music.) I don't remember a funeral or a burial—although I'm certain that both took place because I kept getting bills from the cemetery for maintenance—but everything else about him is gone. He was known to Stan and me as the myth. My mother was the heroine.

If all this sounds cold, it is, perhaps because of his frustratingly blurry legacy, plus the fact that, in the end, he left me holding the bag. After Chaim (my father's Yiddish name) died, I became the head of the family. This did not happen overnight, or after prolonged and reasonable discussions. It took place gradually, over some months, and came with a kind of natural inevitability. My father was gone. There was a leadership vacuum. Someone had to bring more money into the house. Someone had to make important decisions. Someone had to be in charge. It fell to me. And everyone seemed to accept it.

We could not afford to live on my mother's small salary as a saleslady in a dress shop. The rent, food, clothing—all of it—took at least fifty dollars a week. She earned half that. So I turned professional before I was fifteen. I found that I could make enough money playing trumpet on clubdates over a long weekend to balance the books.

*   *   *

As it turned out, the trumpet was our meal ticket for quite a while. I do not credit my father for my choice of a musical career. For one thing, there wasn't enough intimate contact between us for that kind of influence; he might as well have been a tailor for all the vocational transaction that took place between us. Whatever else I didn't get, I didn't get a taste for show business from him.

No, the motivating force in my younger years was my mother, Ann. No matter who was bringing in the money, she kept the four-room walk-up in the Flatbush section of Brooklyn spotless and tastefully furnished. She kept me and my younger brother, Stan, adequately fed, stylishly dressed, and deeply motivated. Her faith in me, in particular, was boundless and, when I think about it, frightening. She thought that I could do anything and be anything. The fear of disappointing her obviously fueled my ambition to succeed.

It was my mother, in a shrewd leap of imagination, who picked the trumpet as the instrument for me. However, that comes after a long and odd digression. It begins with my cousin Lester, who had a very bad temper. I witnessed it firsthand when his younger brother, Norman, locked himself in the bathroom to escape Lester's wrath. The bathroom had one of those frosted-glass doors and Lester—a spirited youth who was exactly my age—smashed his way in. He didn't do anything much to Norman; apparently breaking the glass was enough for Lester. Nevertheless, I admired his determination to terrorize his kid brother, who was the exact same age as Stan, my kid brother. In my daily physical battles with Stan, I never was able to break his will, much less a frosted-glass door.

With that kind of severe mentoring, I had no choice but to follow Lester into the Boy Scouts, even if it was an inconvenient arrangement. Lester lived near Prospect Park and I lived four elevated subway stops away in Flatbush. But so what? I took a certain amount of pride in doing the difficult and unpredictable. Of course, Lester soon lost interest and dropped out of scouting, but I remained a loyal member of Boy Scout Troop 255.

I loved the uniforms and the merit badges and the sense of impending adventure. Communing with nature, learning wood crafts, applying tourniquets, becoming self-reliant—all this appealed to me. And all of these arts would be tested on that grand scouting rite of passage, our first overnight hike. I was twelve years old when we boarded the subway in Brooklyn with our uniforms and equipment; I might as well have been sailing off to Europe on the *Normandie*. We rode up to 242nd Street in (for us) the strange and uncharted reaches of the far north Bronx. Our troop of six valiant scouts then trekked north until we reached the wild woods of Yonkers where, in a baggy fashion, we pitched our tents. It was raining when we reached the campgrounds and got set up so we couldn't start a fire. But we were hungry, and we used our Boy Scout resourcefulness, plus an authentic Boy Scout six-blade knife, to open our provisions—cold cans of franks and beans. Giddy with delight at our brave trek, we dined under the leaky tents in the rough pastures of the city's suburbs.

Unfortunately, one of the troopers, a kid named Billy, got a belly-ache from the cold food eaten straight out of the can. Like good Boy Scouts, we did not panic. We checked the manual, which informed us that Billy had been poisoned. The antidote for poison was milk. So we poured a quart of milk down poor Billy's gullet, which apparently made him more poisoned. That's when we panicked. We made our way back to the subway, rode two and half hours back to Brooklyn, and dumped Billy on his family's doorstep. Then we scattered.

That experience did not discourage me from scouting. Belly-aches and cold franks and beans notwithstanding, I liked almost everything about the Boy Scouts. I liked going down to Fifth Avenue and 23rd Street, the headquarters for Boy Scout paraphernalia, and browsing through the equipment, uniforms, and gadgets. All those canteens, knives, and shiny mess kits were intriguing.

But if there was one thing that really got my attention it was the bugle. There was always a bugle around a Boy Scout troop. No matter where you went, there was one on the wall. Of course, nobody could blow the damn thing. The most you could get, even after a huge effort, was a pretty screechy, pint-sized sound. But if you were a Boy Scout troop, you had to have a bugle. It stirred thoughts of Rudyard Kipling, taps, high drama. I kept trying to produce something musical out of it, but I got nowhere. Finally, after a lot of effort, I learned how to pump out a few legitimate notes.

I couldn't mount a cavalry charge, but I produced something recognizable. That only encouraged me, and I informed my mother that I wanted to take lessons. My father was still alive at the time, but in my house, if I wanted something, I appealed to my mother. She was my advocate. We didn't have much money, and she wouldn't spend it on lessons for a bugle—a relatively useless device—but she said that she would pay for lessons on a trumpet—a more practical instrument. You could get four lessons for ten dollars in those days. That's how I got started on the trumpet.

*   *   *

By the time I entered high school, my life was in chaos. My father had died, leaving us financially adrift, and I knew that it was my job to fix it. With no experience and few resources, I did my best, within my own limits. According to strict district lines, I should have been enrolled at Erasmus Hall High School. Instead, for some peculiar reason, I demanded a transfer to New Utrecht High School. The academic standing of one was roughly the same as the other (not that it mattered to a student of my low standing). But I got my way and entered New Utrecht High School where I played in the band. The only interesting aspect of my high school career was the casual jostle between myself and another student, Abe Burrows. He had his own musical gifts, which consisted mostly of enthusiasm. He played a ragged piano and wrote gag lyrics for popular tunes. But apart from that, no one would have picked him for an enormous talent. Not until we met again in Hollywood and I hired him to write the book for *Guys & Dolls.*

The rest of my high school career fades into unimportant memories. I worked out some of my excess energy on the football field. I considered myself a beefy guy in high school, but it was mostly fat. I never played in a varsity game. I was the tackling dummy. At every practice I was the offensive right guard who took great pun-

ishment from the defensive players. This was old-fashioned football in which the really big kids on the starting varsity team came
at you full force, without mercy. I would end up on my backside after every play. It did not take me long to realize that I was just a
piece of meat. It was frustrating and futile so I quit.

I took up lacrosse—at least they gave me a stick. Then one day I
realized that I wasn't very good at lacrosse either, so I quit sports
altogether.

I was no better in the classroom. I had no interest in mathemat-
ics or science. These things had no meaning in my life. So I quit
high school. I wanted to devote myself to something relevant, like
making money. This revealed to me a lifelong trait: I couldn't just
go along; I couldn't follow the expected rules, play the predictable
game for the sake of ease or expectations. Work or play had to
make some sense, or else I walked away. I was a quitter, but in a
good way.

Chapter Two

Noneof this should be construed as any kind of surrender. On the contrary, I was on fire with ambition. By my early teens I had convinced myself that any further public education was a complete waste of time, and that my energy would be put to better use in the practical world. So I turned professional.

Although my level of musical skill was not high, I was able to find work pretty easily. My first paying job was playing trumpet on the back of a political campaign truck. That's how the political candidates drew a crowd in those days. They stuck a few guys on the flatbed of a truck—a drummer, a clarinet player, a trombone player, and a trumpet player. Lots of brass, lots of noise. The truck was lit up bright with red, white, and blue bunting and had a big sign on the side: VOTE FOR SO AND SO.

We'd drive slowly up and down Flatbush Avenue, the band banging away, playing the loudest upbeat music we could—John Philip Sousa marches, "Alexander's Ragtime Band," "Sweet Sue"— and pretty soon we'd get a following. There was always an audience in the street. This was a time when life was lived on the street; people were outdoors. This was before television. We'd drive around awhile and then we'd pull over, making sure that we were in front of a big open space, large enough to handle a crowd, and then the candidate himself would step up on the back of the truck, wearing a big boater and a big smile, stretching out his arms to show what a great guy he was.

I don't remember if these guys were Democrats or Republicans, or what the political message was, usually something about helping the downtrodden, taking care of people in trouble, looking after the workingman—bread and butter stuff. Come to think of it, they must have been Democrats. I don't think Republicans had any kind of serious following in Brooklyn, not in working-stiff, blue-collar neighborhoods. They paid us five bucks a night to play, which was a big help in my depleted household. And the way life works is that one thing led to another. It was a much smaller world then.

You play on the back of a campaign truck and someone tells someone else. Pretty soon somebody's offering you steadier work, which is how I came to Eddie Schloss. Eddie was a smooth character who started a pickup band to play at affairs or in small clubs. Eddie would go to the publisher and get a standard songbook with stock arrangements for a small group of musicians. We'd play out of the songbook, modern, jazzy, and standard tunes—"Pack Up All My Cares and Woes," "Down by the Old Mill Stream," "K-k-k-Katy," "I Dream of Jeannie," "Muskrat Rumble," "Black Bottom," "St. Louis Blues," "Sugarfoot Stomp". . . . You played by the numbers. Once, someone else took over the band—an Italian guy —who said, "The next set we're gonna play one-oh-eight, one-oh-nine, one-oh-ten, and one-oh-eleven."

Eddie played piano and was very good-looking. He was seven or eight years older than I and had the girls hanging around the band like the groupies do today. It was exciting and I grew up fast. Pretty girls drawn to hot young musicians—I guess that's eternal. There was one, Helen, who was vivid and funny and good-looking, and I had a crush on her. It came to nothing because she was somebody else's girl. My timing was always off when it came to Helen. The next time I ran into her she was Nat Perrin's wife. He was the guy who created Sergeant Bilko on television.

I had some close friends in our pickup band. There was Sid Sternstein (known as "Murphy" for reasons that will become even more murky later), a fiddle player; Artie Orloff, who played banjo; and Al Bernstein who played the tenor saxophone. We all started off in Brooklyn, scuffling for adventure and money, and we'd all meet again in California. It was a small, tight, and comfortable world. Eddie would book us into catering halls and between sets we could eat our fill. The bootleggers left little bottles of bathtub gin on the buffet tables, and I remember taking a swallow, not realizing the potency of the drink. It felt like the top of my head was gone. You couldn't drink that stuff and play, so I quit drinking it. We needed the money too much to risk the paycheck. You could pick up enough jobs at fifteen or twenty dollars apiece to bring home fifty dollars for a weekend, which for us was a living wage.

I was not lazy when it came to music. I practiced for a couple of hours every day. But I knew that something was missing. I was good, maybe even talented, but I had no foundation. I knew that I needed professional training if I was going to advance beyond club dates. That's when my mother started taking me around, begging conductors to listen to me.

I had one contact of my own. Bert Panino was a friend from high school. He played the trumpet. A nice kid. He was uncle to Francis Ford Coppola and Talia Shire and later claimed that I dated their mother, although I don't remember that. Bert and I were in the orchestra at New Utrecht High School. Once, before I quit school, we were playing against DeWitt Clinton High School band in the Bronx. Schools used to have competitions in those days. Well, Bert had just gotten a brand new French Besson trumpet from his father—expensive instrument, maybe two hundred dollars—and he dropped it on the subway on the way home and dented the surface. The poor kid was terrified. "My father's gonna kill me"—that sort of thing. I told him not to worry, that it was only a slight dent, and no one would notice. Well, no one noticed, or at least no one made a fuss. When I needed some help, he introduced me to his uncle, a talented flutist. He listened to me play and told my mother that I had promise.

My mother always had to have a second opinion, and maybe even a third if she didn't like the first two. There used to be band concerts in the park in those days—all wind instruments and no strings, symphonic bands. Edwin Franko Goldman led one of the orchestras in the bandshell in Central Park. He had white hair and wore a buff uniform, and the bandshell orchestra would play military airs. My mother somehow made contact and took me to his Park Avenue apartment. I played for him, and he listened and considered it very carefully and said that in his opinion—his deeply considered opinion—I should take lessons.

Next we even went to see Max Schlossberg, the legendary teacher at The Juilliard School of Music. There came a time when all four trumpeters of the New York Philharmonic Orchestra were former students of Maestro Schlossberg. Like the others, he listened to me and was also impressed by my playing, but suggested that I continue my education.

That's when I decided to go back to school. I took a variety of tests, obtained letters of recommendation, and my mother crusaded in her relentless fashion, until finally I was enrolled in The Juilliard School of Music in Manhattan where I flourished. At least studying music seemed to suit me. The discipline never bothered me. Unlike high school, this was relevant to my life.

*   *   *

During the summers, I took a job at the Echo Lake Tavern in the Adirondack Mountains. The tavern was owned by a tough guy named Mo (you had to be a tough guy named Mo to keep all those rampant kids who worked for him in line). At night I played in the band and during the day I was an assistant lifeguard. It was one of those primitive mountain colonies where the sexes were divided— men and women in separate bungalows. The single girls came up in droves to find husbands. There were also a lot of married women with kids who came up to find adventure. The husbands worked in the city during the week and came up on the weekend. During the week, some of these lonely wives would take some guy from the band out into the woods where they would try not to catch poison oak. That was the big fear—no one wanted to catch poison oak or, worse, be caught by a jealous husband.

The waiters were all college guys and we all bunked together in a big barn. It was great in the evening, listening to these really intelligent guys discuss the state of the universe, philosophy, and the hot new girls coming up from the city. I must say that the new theories about social democracy and the fear about the rise of fascism, and the measure of industrial output in a totalitarian versus freemarket state took a backseat to the weekly ascent of the new stock of available women. I mean, they were serious young men, concerned about literature and social justice and geopolitical affairs, but let's face it; they were young and the sap was rising. We'd pick up the weekly arrival of young women at the Lake George train station seven miles away from Echo Lake, and everyone wanted to be on the truck to handle their baggage and get the first shot at the good-looking ones.

I will say that I had my share of encounters. I would take out a canoe and a blanket and one of the crop of available girls. We would cross the lake and find a secluded spot under a shady tree, and it was there, in the idyllic setting of evergreens and lavender, that I learned the ways of nature. I got my room and board and a small salary, and between the smart college boys and the savvy city girls, I got a first-rate education.

*   *   *

I graduated from Juilliard in 1932, equipped with a weighty and rounded schooling in all the forms of classical and popular music. I could compose, arrange, and play, all with rare artistry and distinctive technical skill, or so I insisted. I exuded an artificially inflated confidence because I had some secret doubts about my natural gifts. I could do it all and do it well, but there were students who were more naturally gifted. My success, I know now, was because I worked harder than everyone else.

Thus, with my qualified gifts and my complicated agenda—the need to support the family and to establish myself—I set off to conquer the world. Soon, after some demanding auditions and some even more demanding interviews (unlike today, you had to be of good character—sober—to play in a band), I landed what was in those days a well-paying job at about a hundred dollars a week playing trumpet in the pit of the Roxy Theater on West 47th Street. This was a lot of money during the Great Depression.

The Roxy was an old movie palace. You could seat six thousand people in the auditorium. The dancers—a corps of ballet dancers—were called the Roxyettes, and when the Rockefellers built Radio City Music Hall in 1932, they installed their own corps of dancers and called them the Rockettes.

Radio City Music Hall not only bought the idea of a corps de ballet, along with a very similar name for its dancers, it also lured me away. I got a raise and was doing four shows a day for $150 a week. Radio City Music Hall was a little more elegant than the Roxy. We all had to wear tuxedo pants and white shirts and a black velvet jacket with black satin facing. And I tell you that when ninety guys in tuxes came rising out of the pit on that big elevator, with all the lights flashing, it was thrilling. In between shows, when the movie played, I'd put my instrument in a locker, hang up that beautiful velvet jacket, go out and get something to eat, take a walk, breathe in that very strong show-business air, and feel terrific. There were lots of girls, there were great restaurants, and there was the sense that life was endless and sweet.

After the last show we would pile into a car and drive out of town, where the latest hot band was playing at the Glen Island Casino, the "in" club in Westchester. There would be some of the guys from the band and some of the girls from the Rockettes or the corps de ballet, and invariably there was some disorderly conduct that took place in the back of those roadsters.

Naturally, no matter how great life is, you hit some bumps along the way. One night, I came back late from my break. Well, you couldn't be late for a show because once they hit the downbeat and the orchestra started up on that elevator, anyone not on the bandstand was out. I grabbed my horn and ran and jumped onto the elevator. The guys pulled me up while the orchestra was going into the *1812 Overture,* which is very loud and very distracting. I hoped it was loud enough and distracting enough for the conductor to miss my grand entrance. So we rise up into the light, and I'm in my seat trying to look small, and playing like mad and I feel the heat of the conductor's eyes. He's glaring at me. I can feel the daggers. Apparently he noticed me. And he seemed very upset. When I look down to avert his gaze I realize that there are eighty-nine guys in black velvet dinner jackets and one dumb dope in very loud brown tweed. After the set the conductor wouldn't talk to me. He raged and sputtered backstage to managers, to scenery, to heaven, but he wouldn't address me personally. I was too lowly. A fourth trumpet cannot be addressed in person by the lofty maestro. Second, I had committed a very grave sin, worse than a sour note. I had ruined the visual impression. Finally, the stage manager came over to me and delivered the message. He said I was not fired, which was all I was worried about, but that this would never happen again. I agreed wholeheartedly.

* * *

Meanwhile, I was so overcome by my own achievement in getting this fine job that I rashly decided to move my mother and younger brother, Stan, into Manhattan. Now, with my big salary, my mother retired as a saleslady, and I became the official and sole head of the family with all the honors and pressures that went with the job. My kid brother graduated high school and asked me what he was going to be in life. I said, without too much thought, an engineer. I didn't even know what the hell an engineer was, except that it was something important and it involved arithmetic. It sounded right. He said okay and began attending City College with engineering in mind. I moved my mother and Stan into an apartment in a big building on West 72nd Street, not far from Central Park. This was a mistake. I was accustomed to short Brooklyn brownstones, close to the sidewalk. Like me. I did not anticipate the dramatic difference this move was going to have on my future.

In fact, the move was the cause of my breakdown. No one knew it at the time, but I had a mental breakdown. We were living on the tenth floor of this building near the park and after about a year I began to dread going to bed at night. I had a recurring dream. The only thing that I remember about the dream was that it centered on a string of pearls. The pearls were on a chair, placed in such a way that they kept falling off. Every night the string of pearls slid off the chair, slipping slowly, brought down by the weight of the other pearls. Inexorably down. It doesn't take Freud to figure out that I was unsettled by the literal and figurative heights in my new life. But this was before psychiatry, at least before psychiatry in our family. There was nobody I could go to, nobody I could talk to. That dream scared the hell out of me. It scared me to the point that I couldn't go to sleep at night. It went on for six months. I had to do something.

In those days, the country was crawling with big bands going from one town to another. You got on a train, played in some hick town for a few nights, then moved on to the next town. Guys were always dropping in and out of bands so there was always an opening. When I heard that Leon Belasco was looking for a first trumpet for one of his road trips, I went to see him. Now, Belasco was a Russian and very tall. He played the romantic violin. A very high-class bandleader. His orchestra played on the roof of the glamorous St. Moritz Hotel, one of those radio orchestras, coming to you straight from the roof of the St. Moritz Hotel in midtown Manhattan: Leon Belasco and his Society Orchestra.

I didn't have to audition because I came highly recommended, but I had to go see him in his suite at the St. Moritz. He was getting dressed, putting on the tails and the white tie and silk slippers. I can still see those fancy slippers and how impressed I was by the high style and dignity of the man.

I got the job and quit Radio City Music Hall, and we went on the road. It was impulsive, but I was always impulsive. I had enough money so that my mother and Stan didn't have to worry about the rent or food. And I'd be making good money on the road. And the train took me to Burbank, California. I never quite realized what the country was like until this trip. It was big and it was thrilling. When we got to Burbank, I looked around—there was nothing there higher than two stories. For the first time I saw the sky. Really saw it. God, there was a sky! In New York, the sky was this little sliver of blue that you got a peek at every now and then. Even in the Adirondack Mountains, I didn't take time to notice.

I never stopped appreciating it.

We had a ten-week contract at the Airport Gardens in Burbank. This was a country club setting and it was ideal. A bunch of guys in the band rented an apartment on Beachwood Drive in Holly-wood for fifty dollars a week. We bought a Pontiac roadster for $150, and we drove to the beach and we drove to work and we had a helluva time. The pressures of the responsibilities I had assumed were, I suppose, a factor in what I call my mental breakdown. That, and the effects of the dizzying heights I literally could not sustain. But in any event, the move to California worked. I never had that dream about the pearls again. I've lived many places, even at great heights. But the pearls never slipped off the chair again.

At the end of the ten weeks, we were booked into Minneapolis. The guys were getting on the train, set to go, and I backed out. I was going to stay in California. I couldn't give it up—the night's sleep.

Chapter Three

By rights I should have been nervous about my situation, which, from a purely technical standpoint, looked pretty shaky. I had no job, no prospects. I didn't even know anybody in the entire city, not one person. I realized as I watched the train pulling out of the station with my friends waving good-bye that I had no one left to talk to. It's a very strange feeling not having someone to talk to. I was three thousand miles from home, which in those days was a lot farther than it is today. It took four days to get to California by car. I might as well have been on the moon.

And yet I felt liberated. I can't completely explain it. The sky, the space, the air—everything opened up for me. It was remarkable. The only material thing I owned was the car. The guys gave it to me and told me to pay them back when I could, which meant forget about it. I checked into a cheap hotel and found someone to talk to—the clerk. He was a young guy and I don't know what we talked about; but we talked and that felt good. You can't be completely isolated in a crowded city. You need to communicate.

I had one tangible productive thing: a horn. A trade. I went down to the union, Local 47, and they told me that although I was a member in good standing and they would transfer my membership to California, I couldn't work for six months. When I asked why, they explained it with a kind of bare-knuckle logic. They had enough trumpet players in California. They didn't need another guy coming in from New York, taking a job. So I would have to wait six months, by which time I would either have given up and gone home, or starved to death. Either way I wasn't gonna put a California horn player out of work. It was a very shrewd system.

So I was out of business. And still I wasn't worried. I wasn't even particularly angry. It made a certain kind of protectionist sense. The union was looking out for its own.

There was one other trick I had up my sleeve (more of an asset than a trick): my sunny disposition. I am by nature an optimist. I always had a lot of confidence, a lot of energy. I do not mention this immodestly, or with any particular pride. I just offer it as an explanation to account for the customary welcome I received. Doors were open to me. No one wants to be around someone habitually gloomy. And I wasn't brought down by being unable to work. It is not my nature. I bump up against something and I try to find a way around it. I don't spend a lot of time bellyaching about it. I was convinced that this interruption was all part of some larger adventure. My attitude remained that everything will work out, sooner or later.

And so, without giving it the proper, modern title, without even plotting it out, I began my own random system of networking. It was an old and common practice. People who came from Europe had the names of people from the same town stitched into their clothing. A custom as old as a wandering Jew. When you landed in some distant place, you had a name, someone to make you feel less strange. An arranged friend. When I left New York, one of the guys in the band gave me the name of someone who ran a small chain of movie theaters. He was another transplanted New Yorker and we would have that in common. Bernie somebody. An older man, but what the hell. Someone who had a familiar frame of reference. Bernie somebody invited me to his home, introduced me to his family, and fed me a nice Jewish meal. Then he tried to fix me up. Not with a girl—I had access to lots of girls; they grew like oranges in California. He wanted to introduce me to someone who could possibly help me get a job. Someone with connections in show business. A guy my own age.

Rodney Pantages was in his twenties—my age—but apart from that we didn't seem to have that much in common. For one thing, he was rich. Heir to the fabulous Pantages Theater fortune. Really rich. Nevertheless, Rodney and I became friends. And we became friends instantly. Sometimes it works like that. You just hit it off. The difference in our cash assets didn't matter. When I mentioned to Rodney that I was out of work, he said, "That's terrific; that's just perfect. This will come in very handy." Then he asked me if I played squash, which was like asking me if I spoke French. I laughed and said, "No, but I play handball." "Great," he said, "if you can play handball you can play squash."

I did not quite get it—his delight at my misfortune. But it turned out that Rodney had reserved the squash court at the Hollywood Athletic Club for four o'clock every day. That's a tough time to make a squash date. You can't find a partner. Most people are out working. Not me. I'm unemployed—perfect.

Rodney was a pretty good athlete and a very aggressive squash player. He taught me how to play and he regularly beat the hell out of me. He was unmerciful. I finally got good enough to give him a game, but he still beat me. And I enjoyed playing. There was something very charming about Rodney. He was fun to be around. He had a forty-foot boat and took me sailing. It was a beautiful boat; he taught me how to sail and I developed a real love for the water. We'd sail to Catalina and meet his wife and kids who were staying there on the island. We'd have dinner at the club and listen to Little Jack Little, who was not much of a band leader. A little corny, like Guy Lombardo. He didn't go in for swing, which was the popular music among young people. However, it turned out that the manager of the band was in my class at Juilliard. We had a big reunion and he asked me what I was doing. I told him and he said that it just so happens that he can throw me some work writing arrangements at fifty bucks apiece, which is easy for me, given my training.

*   *   *

At last I had some income. I had been borrowing money from Rodney—a hundred here, a fifty there—but I made certain to pay him back. I didn't want that to interfere with the friendship. Writing arrangements saved me from dipping into my friend's pocket. Still, there wasn't much work. I was living pretty well, but I wasn't making enough to send back home to New York. My mother and Stan were living off the fifteen hundred dollars I left behind, but I was getting a little uneasy. What happens when that runs out? As head of the family I was obliged to earn enough to support my mother and brother. From the moment I stepped off the train in Burbank, my intention was to bring them out to California. That would be cheaper and more sensible than keeping two households. I had written to my mother, describing the beauty and ease of California. I knew that Stan and she would take to it. I would find a house and we would all live together. I wasn't exactly sure how I would accomplish all this, but that was the plan, and my mother wrote back and declared that Stan and she were ready to go West.

Once again I fell into another bucket of pure luck. Rodney was kind of in the picture business. He—or his father—owned a lot of theaters, so one could say that he was in the retail end of show business. This put him in contact with a lot of people in the wholesale end of the game. One of them was a New York–based friend who happened to be a recording company executive. He was coming to California to make some records. The friend worked for Republic Pictures. Republic made a lot of movies with Gene Autry and Roy Rogers—big singing movie stars. In order to exploit its singing stars, Republic bought a record company, Brunswick Records. To promote their pictures, the stars would record the songs. The problem was that Rodney's friend had no idea how to make records. He was strictly an East Coast businessman. He hired people in California who knew how to make records. And it just so happened that he was looking for someone to record the stars.

So Rodney introduced me to his friend, who was understandably skeptical about hiring this sailing bum to make recordings. But Rodney vouched for me and that was enough. I couldn't play in the musical group to back up the singers because the union wouldn't let me, but I could write arrangements, I could rent a recording studio, and I could hire all the technical help I needed to make the records. In short, I offered to become Brunswick's California music department. He agreed and just that easily I was in business. I didn't question these things because, at the time, I had a Panglossian blindness to the casual opportunities that opened up before me.

* * *

I had no trouble figuring out where to find the musicians. After all, I know musicians; I know that they're likely to be short of cash and eager to make a buck. I went down to the hotels where the big bands were playing and waited outside for the break, since I couldn't afford the cover charge for admission to the ballrooms. And when the guys in the band came out for a smoke, I grabbed the band contractor (every band has a union contractor) and made him the offer. I was paying fifty dollars apiece, which was decent money. The contractors jumped at it. Then I rented a recording studio, hired technicians, wrote some arrangements, and the making of the records was easy. It all fell into place, naturally, as if I were walking through some scripted plan.

One thing always seemed to lead to another. And the recording gig led me to a weekly paycheck. Since I was working for Brunswick, which was owned by Republic Pictures, the name of Cy Feuer as musical director appeared on a lot of record labels. And when the head of the music department at Republic retired, my name was high on the list of possible replacements, which is how I became music director of Republic Pictures—a big job at a little studio.

But now I had a weekly paycheck of $350 and the flush confidence to send for my family.

*   *   *

At the time I was sharing a house on Serrano Drive with three other guys. It was a bungalow with a lot of bedrooms and we got it cheap. I had managed to recreate the Brooklyn atmosphere under one roof. One of the guys was Sid Sidney, one of the fiddlers from the Eddie Schloss band in Brooklyn. His name was really Sid Sternstein, but he once had a high school football coach who couldn't pronounce Sternstein. "From now on you're Murphy," declared the coach. And for a while he was Murphy. But he didn't feel like a Murphy. On the other hand, he was in show business and didn't want to go back to the difficult-to-pronounce Sternstein. So when he got to Hollywood he changed his name to Sid Sidney, which had a certain sliding harmony and was, I suppose, some kind of compromise.

The second guy in the house was another refugee from the old band, Artie Orloff, a banjo player. Then there was Albie Schaff who went to Yale and was a ridiculous snob. He was strictly Ivy League.

He had a law degree, smoked a pipe, and was a script writer. Albie had style, although there were people who thought he had too much style. He drove around town in an early Rolls Royce; it was so old that it had a right-hand drive and the gear shift on the running board. He wore an Inverness Cape and a collapsible top hat and scared the hell out of pedestrians. He looked like Dracula.

The house was filled with visiting future luminaries. Musicians, writers, actors, hotshots. Nat Perrin (Bilko creator) was in our group. George Antheil. Jule Styne. Frank Loesser. Some of these guys weren't just aspiring—they were getting fifteen hundred, two thousand a week from the studios. This was big money. The atmosphere was collegial, lighthearted. In fact, it was so lively and friendly that we tended to attract a certain number of pilot fish—opportunists who smelled opportunity. It was inevitable with such a concentration of talent.

One guy in particular whom I remember was Jerry Wald. He would later become a big shot and head a studio. He hung around the house and stole writers, got some hungry author to knock out a script, then put his own name on it. He had two of the most talented writers in town under his own personal contract—Phil and Julie Epstein. They were twins, and very gifted. Julie was one of the sweetest, funniest guys I ever met. He lit up a room when he came in. Never got the full credit for his work. One of his screenplays was *Casablanca*.

It was a busy and crowded house, and when my mother and brother entered it, they fell right into the happy spirit of the place. Stan became one of the guys and my mother became the house mother to this great clatter of young men on the verge of . . . something.

Chapter Four

It's hard to exaggerate the impact that California had on the entire Feuer clan. We arrived like starving Russian peasants set loose in Utopia.

Stan received a fellowship to Cal Tech where he did very well and got very involved in tennis. It was a big craze for New York Jews. Outdoor exercise, nice white outfits. It seemed to fit into the open-air lifestyle. And he did indeed become an engineer, according to my makeshift plan.

My mother entered show business. She tried to become one of the uppity Selznick mothers. There was a claque of them, socially conscious women—mostly widows—who spent the morning talking on the phone, bragging about their sons, getting all dressed up, and then meeting for fancy luncheons in the beautiful homes in Beverly Hills. They played Mah-Jongg and a killer game of one-up-manship—whose son was doing better. Oh, my son wrote a wonderful screenplay. My son conducted an entire orchestra. My son directed John Wayne. But no one could top Mrs. Selznick, whose son, David, was the golden prince. She had the showstopper. My son produced *Gone With the Wind*. Tiers and hierarchies of the Hollywood mothers—that was real class warfare.

My mother was right in there, slugging it out, fighting for her Cy's place in the sons. Once we were at a barbecue; the men were over by the food and the mothers were by the pool. There were a lot of mothers and a lot of sons. Then there came from the men a burst of raucous laughter. My mother came running over from the pool and demanded, "What did Cy say?"

All those transplanted palm trees and transplanted East Coast Jews were right at home on the western fringe of America. We joined clubs, we socialized, and we acted as if we really belonged. We imported fancy smoked sturgeon, we learned to play tennis and polo as well as squash, and we kept alive the bitter shtetl wit and pitiless skepticism that has nourished our Jewish souls and saved our Jewish hides for five thousand years. We gorged on the delicious quips that flew back and forth at the Hillcrest Country Club (the alternative to the gentile clubs that ostracized Jews). Someone didn't like Frank Loesser's wife and said she was the evil of the two Loessers. Georgie Jessel, noting the fat content of the corned beef served from Willoshen's deli, muttered that it killed more Jews than Hitler. Maybe he didn't say it—maybe it was the writer Everett Freeman—but Jessel was very funny. Once, coming back on a train from New York, he brought a four-foot package of smoked salmon and sturgeon that began to spoil and really stunk up the sleeping car. When the porter asked him what was in the box, he said, "Oh, that was my uncle Max, the midget, who died in New York. I'm taking him back to California for burial."

It was a splendid Diaspora. We surrounded ourselves with the familiar. People. Food. Yiddish waggery. It was New York on the road. Wonderful, but somewhere in the back of my mind I must have known that it was all make believe; I could never entirely overlook the fact that this was a land of movie sets. Sunsets were painted by an art department. Landscapes were perfected by a human hand. It was not really real. You could lift a big rock with your bare hands. It was made out of papier-mâché. So while I could enjoy a sweet, honey-dipped life and appreciate the cleaner, less cluttered atmosphere, I don't know that I ever really trusted Hollywood. Not completely. After all, I was also in the business of creating moods, conjuring up emotion. It was my job to pump music into an acted-out, artificial movie scene.

It was not all bon mots and afternoons playing polo. There was the production end of the business. I scored a truckload of pictures between 1938 and 1948. It was hard work. I got there early and stayed late and made certain that the music was appropriate, technically perfect. If it had to be done over ten times, I would do the work. I was never lazy, never afraid to get sweaty. I always believed in going all out. But now that I think back on it, there was something not quite committed, not quite credible about what I was doing. There began to take shape, in the back of my mind, a suspicion of something . . . missing. Could I move over to a major studio and be the musical director of, say, Warner Bros.? I didn't think so. Perhaps I had reached the far limits of my abilities.

Not that I realized it openly. If you asked me when I was going through it, when I was in my late twenties, I would have said that I was working at full throttle, doing the meaningful labor indicated by my talent and training, and that I had found a home in California and the movie business. I was the musical director on a bunch of films, some of which were not bad. *Shine on Harvest Moon; The Fighting Devil Dogs*—classic B movies—nothing to be ashamed of. However, it was a kind of drudgery. Glamorous factory work. And I surely was aware of it. In fact, I was—without even knowing it—preparing myself for something else. Something that fit my real strength.

*   *   *

I was working toward my doctorate in an exotic niche of the show-business world: the musical. Consciously and unconsciously, I was placing myself into an art form that would occupy my life. There were great opportunities on the Hollywood lots, friendships to be enlarged, lessons to be learned, tastes to be educated. It was not insignificant that I met Frank Loesser in Hollywood. He was at Paramount while I was at Republic, but there was a lot of cross-pollination among musicians. Frank and I knew each other from the early days when we were broke, living on borrowed money.

I start with Frank Loesser.

I needed a pianist. Somebody recommended this little chatterbox who turned out to be Jule Styne (whose real name was Julius Kerwin Stein). Jule had been working at 20th Century-Fox as a rehearsal pianist. I hired him for $150 a week and explained the rules: he had to play for anything I wanted—rehearsals, auditions, etc. He also had to be prepared to go on location and check synch—that is, be a shitkicker. That's what we called the guys who went out on location. And there were a lot of location shoots because we made a lot of Westerns: six Gene Autry and eight Roy Rogers musicals every year. So we were constantly out in the desert.

Jule grabbed the job, with the stipulation that he could write any original songs that had to be written and placed with the publisher. Okay, but they belong to the studio. You're under contract. I was a stickler for following the rules, within reason. I could bend when I had to. For instance, when I had to audition a teenage soprano. They wanted her to sing "Tales in the Vienna Woods." I looked at the music, and the lyrics were in German. "Christ," I said, "if this isn't in the public domain we're going to pay a hell of a royalty. So I changed the lyrics. Actually, what I did was change the letters—the Rs to Bs, the Ls to Ms, the Cs to Ds. It was gibberish, but it sounded great. The Germans thought it was Czech, and the Czechs thought it was Bulgarian—who knows? I told the soprano, "Learn this," and it was actually in the movie. The singer was Deanna Durbin, who became famous for a duet with Judy Garland in a short subject *Every Sunday*. She also starred in a bunch of movies, with titles like *One Hundred Men and a Girl* and *Three Smart Girls Grow Up*.

Jule was the pianist for that audition and turned out to be a barrel of fun, a helluva piano player, and full of energy. I always looked for energy. He was also a double-talking madman. You never knew what the hell he was saying, but he always had a mouthful to say. Whenever we had a song to write, I'd buy him a lyric writer for twenty-five bucks and we'd have a song. We worked on a shoestring.

And Jule's a trooper. He went out on location and did the job and never complained. He always came back with a story, some of which I actually understood. One of my favorites was when he went out on location with Jimmy Durante, who was making some dumb musical. Durante was a very skittish character, very urban and unaccustomed to the wilderness. Also, he was very funny. So he got out into the desert, looked around at the sun and the sky, took a deep breath of fresh air, and said, "How long has DIS been going on?"

Jule fit right in at Republic and he was always in my office, pushing the envelope, trying to get ahead. Well, we all were. But we were limited by the B-picture budgets. We finally got a picture that had a little budget to it—a musical. It was about the navy. A lot of songs about the navy. I think it was called *Pride of the Navy*. So, since we had some money to play around with Jule says, why don't we borrow Frank Loesser? I'd love to write with him.

Frank was at Paramount. In those days it was easy to borrow writers. They were like horses. So I called Louie Lipstone, the head of the music department at Paramount, and I arranged to borrow Frank for four weeks at $350 a week. "That way," I said by way of incentive, "he's off your payroll. You save $350 a week." Louie saw the advantage and turned Frank over to me for four weeks.

The next call I got was from Frank, who started off by calling me a male genital organ, then a son of a bitch, and it went downhill from there. "You should have called me first," he said, really pissed, which is how he spent a lot of his time. "Do you know who I'm writing with now? I'm writing with Hoagy Carmichael."

For the next four weeks I told him, you're going to be writing with a terrific pianist named Jule Styne.

"Who the hell is Jule Styne?"

He's very good.

"I don't give a shit whether or not he's good; I'm writing lyrics with the best in the business!"

He had a point. Not that I could have admitted it. He came over to confront me and we had lunch instead. I figure that if he were going to kill me, I want witnesses. Frank was a little guy, but he had a commanding presence.

Well, he cooled off, and when he finally came to work at Republic, when he actually sat down with Jule and saw what he could do, he became mild as milk. Frank's got a nose. He can tell when he's in the presence of talent. Suddenly, Frank was having fun and not trying to kill me anymore. They didn't produce a very memorable score for that picture. The only thing I remember, because it was a terrible picture, is a gag song that they wrote:

> *The admiral married Minnie,*
> *Ahoy Minnie.*
> *Oh, the admiral married Minnie J. McGee.*

The admiral married Minnie,
Ahoy Minnie,
But I wonder if he knew
What she did for you and you and you and you.
And me.

Typical Frank Loesser. Of course it never made it into the picture.

About a week after we finished the picture I got a call from Louie Lipstone at Paramount. He wanted to borrow Jule Styne. I had to laugh. Now they're inseparable. Frank wanted to work with Jule.

For the picture called *Sweater Girl,* they insisted on coming to my office and playing the score for me. I didn't understand why, at first. Jule played the piano and Frank sang, and one tune sounded very familiar. I realized it was something that Jule had already written. He wrote it at Republic. A guy named Eddie Chirkos had written a different lyric. But the music belonged to the studio. That was the deal. I didn't say anything. Frank and Jule thought they put it over on me, but as we walked out into the parking lot, I said, "Listen, fellas, it's fine with me if you steal the tune, but you better make it up with Eddie Chirkos."

Apparently they did because that tune became very popular. It's still around, with Frank's lyrics:

I don't want to walk without you baby
Walk without my arm about you baby
I thought the day you left me behind,
I take a stroll
And get you right off my mind
But now I find that I don't want to walk without the
Sunshine

Why'd you have to turn off all that sunshine
Oh, baby please come back
Or you'll break my heart to me
'Cause I don't want to walk without you no siree.

You know, later we worked together on *Where's Charley?*, *Guys & Dolls*, and *How to Succeed in Business Without Really Trying*, and the relationship was always the same. Loesser spent his whole life calling me a prick and then changing his mind. I really admired the guy.

Chapter Five

Working at a movie studio is not like holding down a job in a factory. There is a certain atmosphere of high glamour. The director looks like he knows what he's doing. The carpenters and electricians seem unusually competent. The actors are all handsome and the actresses are all beautiful. And you're making motion pictures.

Then one day, not too much later in your career, say a week, it's just like going to work in a factory. The only difference is that this factory turns out movies. Sure, you turn a corner and bump into John Wayne (which actually happened to me; I came up to his belt buckle), but it's still a job and you have to do your work. After awhile you're just not blinded by all that sparkle and glow. However, in some respects the advantages are obvious. For a single guy, the selection of companions is pretty good.

I refer now to 1940, when I was twenty-nine, no longer a boy, not yet a malingerer in the marriage game. It was a funny period in my life. I was not looking for a big-time love affair. I never had any thoughts about marriage. I had too much responsibility. I had my mother to support, a career to keep afloat, and creeping doubts about my ultimate talent. No, marriage was remote and full of problems. I just wanted to get laid, which, in the land of eager young things, was never a problem.

I refer to basic biology. If I worked for a big corporation, I'd be flirting with the secretaries. This being a movie studio, I talked to the actresses. It was a natural inclination. I'd have to go around to the sets and see what was shooting. It was part of my job. I had to stay in touch so that I could get an idea about the music that would have to be scored. I was also pretty sociable and I liked to chat with my fellow workers.

On one particular set there was a very pretty blonde. She wasn't a star, just another young girl trying to break into the business. She had a small part in a small forgotten production. Her name was Florence Rice, and she was the daughter of Grantland Rice, the great sports columnist who wrote so poetically about fist fights and football games and horse racing and golf heroes. I have been told that he was the first famous sportswriter. His daughter was very nice and we hit it off. I'd go to the set and we'd spend time between shots or during a lunch break talking about the business. What the hell else did we have in common?

One day I stopped in at another set where they were shooting a picture called *Sis Hopkins*. In it was this twenty-two-year-old kid—another Brooklyn transplant—who had come out to Hollywood a few years earlier to test for *Gone With the Wind*. She came very close to getting the part of Scarlett O'Hara. It would have made her an instant star. But the part went to Vivien Leigh. It would take this kid a little longer, but she was gonna be a star, no doubt about that. All you had to do was look at her. She took my breath away. She had that glorious red hair and green eyes and luminous skin. She was radiant. This was Susan Hayward. Funny thing, she had a sister who was almost a look-alike. They could have been twins. Same red hair, same green eyes, almost identical features. They just didn't look as good on the sister. But Susan . . . my God! A knockout.

Susan was very nice, in a tough, scrappy kinda way. She liked me, I thought, because we had that same Brooklyn edge. She didn't take any crap and neither did I. She'd been in a few movies since she came to town—clunkers—but it was only a matter of time.

I didn't think too much about it. I talked to her and we got along; and then I went about my business. It didn't cross my mind that she would be interested in me. It was different with Florence. I thought I had a shot with her. I stopped by both sets. I wanted to see Susan because she was so good to look at, and I was making a play for Florence.

That went on for a few days, and then one day I was sitting with Florence between shots when my assistant, Ralph, came over.

"I gotta talk to you," he said. "You've got a problem."

He told me that he was under strict orders to deliver a message from Susan Hayward, word for word, to me personally. "She said that if you don't get your ass over to the stage she's walking off the picture."

I was astonished. I had no idea I got that far with her. This was a glamorous and beautiful woman, five notches above my usual objective.

"What are you talking about, what do you mean, she's gonna walk off the picture?"

He said, "Cy, I'm telling you to go over there because there's gonna be trouble."

So I went over and she was sitting there looking at me and she was mad. "What are you doing on that other stage with that blonde?"

I said, "What are you talking about?"

She said, "You know what I'm talking about."

There we were, having an argument. "Okay, I'm here now." I tried to mollify her.

"I'm finished shooting at six. Pick me up."

That's how it began.

*   *   *

We became a couple. And it wasn't easy. For one thing we both lived with our mothers. We had no place to go. We could arrange some long weekends in Santa Barbara, where it was pretty nice. But on a day-to-day basis we were like high school kids on a date, making out in the backseat of a car. It was great. I felt myself losing control in a way that I never did before. Girls were soft companions who would come in and out of my life without disturbing the rhythms. Susan disturbed the universe. I couldn't take my eyes off of her and I couldn't stop thinking about her. This was very unusual for me.

And we had fun. One night we had dinner at the Coconut Grove. I picked her up and she was lovely, in a silk dress, and bright with enthusiasm. She had qualities I really liked—energy and enthusiasm. We went to dinner and were dancing when she saw Louie Lipstone from Paramount across the room sitting with his wife.

"Oh, I have to say hello," she said, breaking away, rushing across the floor.

His back was to us and she came up behind him and grabbed him. As he turned his face a little we both saw that it wasn't Louie Lipstone, but another guy with that dumpy Louie Lipstone look. He was sitting across the table from a real battle-ax who was glaring at us—and at the poor Lipstone look-alike.

"Sir," I said as we backed away, "I'll thank you to not look so much like Louie Lipstone in front of my girl."

Of course, being with Susan was fun, but it was also pretty

tough. She was dedicated to her career. And that aggressive quality, which would come out in her acting later, was always apparent. Any little thing could set her off. We were going out one night for dinner, and I had to stop in at a party that was being thrown by one of the studio executives.

"You didn't tell me about the party," she complained when I picked her up.

"I thought I did."

"You didn't tell me."

"I'm telling you now."

"I don't want to go to a party."

"What's the big deal? We stop off, put in an appearance, then go to dinner."

"I don't want to go. Don't make me do this."

"Well, I have to go."

She was fuming. And sullen. We got to the house and she made straight for the liquor. Now, Susan was not a drinker, but she started chugging straight whiskey. One, two, three, four. I saw this from across the room, and I rushed over and took her outside before she started a scene. The liquor hadn't hit her yet, but she was a little loose in the joints.

"Where the hell are you taking me?"

That was a good question. I couldn't deliver her to her mother in this condition. I couldn't take her to my house because my mother would insist that I marry her. I couldn't take her out to dinner because the gossips would see her loaded. So I poured her into the car and drove down to the beach and pumped her full of coffee and hamburgers. I waited until she was able to stand up and then I took her home.

* * *

Our love affair—that's what it was—went on for a year. I thought about marriage, but I never got any further than thinking. The relationship blew hot and cold; but it was always interesting, and we never had an actual breakup. It was a drift. Maybe we recognized that we both had different careers to attend to. But in fact, for a long time I was crazy about her.

Being in love is like waking up with a cold. That's all you think about, there's nothing else on your mind. Then, one day, you wake up without a cold and life goes on.

Chapter Six

As I juggled my personal and professional life, it was in the context of the studio. In those days, before the war, movie studios were run like sovereign states. One guy was in charge. Period. Republic Pictures was a small kingdom, cranking out B pictures and horse operas, and Herb Yates, the owner, was an absolute ruler.

As monarchs go, he wasn't bad, but like all rulers, even the good ones, he had his iron-willed whims.

It is not easy for someone to move from the hard-nosed world of business into the high-strung universe of entertainment. There are matters of temperament to deal with. But Herb managed the bumpy transition better than most. When I first came to Republic in 1938, Herb was in his late fifties; we called him "the old man." When you're young everyone past youth is old. The old man started out in the tobacco business. He worked his way up from an office boy to sales manager of the American Tobacco Company. But when the Supreme Court dissolved the tobacco trust in 1911, Herb eased his way out. He invested some money with the notorious silent film star Fatty Arbuckle in a technical process for making film. The profits were so good that he began buying small studios, eventually consolidating them into Republic.

His specialty at Republic was the "horse opera," the singing Western. And he had under contract Gene Autry, the biggest singing cowboy of them all. Autry did tremendous business for Herb Yates, and one day in 1937, his agent demanded a raise. Autry was already under a seven-year contract, and Herb couldn't see any reason to reopen negotiations just because his hired hand was making him a lot of money. That was the hard-shell autocrat in him. Well, Gene Autry took a pretty tough stand and said he wouldn't make any more movies until he got a raise. Herb put him on suspension. That's how the studios played the game; they starved you back to work.

"I made Autry and I'll make somebody else," Herb vowed to Mo Siegal, who was the head of the studio, and very nervous about this turn of events. He didn't think you could mass produce singing cowboys.

"Who's that guy over there?" demanded Herb, pointing to a kid holding a guitar. He was one of The Sons of the Pioneers, a very popular musical group featured in a lot of Westerns. "Put him in the next Autry film."

The kid with the guitar was Roy Rogers, who went on to make a lot more money for Herb and earn the title, "The King of the Cowboys." So Herb wound up getting Gene Autry and Roy Rogers for Republic by his thick-headed, stubborn streak. And, clearly, he had an eye for talent.

*   *   *

It wasn't always reliable. Herb had a romantic side, which is probably what drew him into the motion-picture business in the first place. He had this thing for Vera Hruba Ralston. She was an ice-skating champion from Czechoslovakia who was the runner-up to Sonja Henie in the 1936 Olympics. I will not be the first to remark on the fact that she was also the runner-up to Sonja Henie's rich movie career. But Herb, the son of a Bible salesman from Brooklyn, who already had a wife and four kids, fell head over heels for Vera and devoted a big portion of his life to trying to make her a movie star. He never did. But not for lack of effort. He put her in a lot of pictures, he ran way over budgets, but she remained a dim reflection of Sonja Henie.

Billy Wilder once told me something that explains star quality. It's a matter of flesh. The camera chooses some flesh. It's that simple. Marilyn Monroe had camera flesh. So did Marion Davies, although she didn't have any talent. Alice Faye, the shop girl's dream, photographed beautifully, in a cheap kind of way. It goes without saying that Susan Hayward had it. But the camera just didn't care for Vera Ralston, in spite of Herb. He did everything humanly possible to make it happen. He had skating scenes written into her pictures and starred her with John Wayne, who had plenty of flesh, and even that didn't help. She didn't have camera flesh.

In any event, the point is that Herb Yates fell blindly in love with her and stayed in love with her for the rest of his life. He would later divorce his wife and marry her. It was kinda sweet. She was forty years younger than he was, but there was true love between them. No doubt about it.

In the early flush of his obsession, Herb built a magnificent recording stage, with absolutely no thought about the cost. It was the most up-to-date, state-of-the-art, modern recording stage constructed in Hollywood. He put it up on the old Mack Sennett lot, which was where Republic had its studios. The recording stage consisted of one huge, block-long building with every known gadget and gizmo for recording music. And on the back third of this recording stage he built an ice rink. And the ice rink had a floor over it so that you could cover it and use it for a platform. But when you drew it back, it was an ice rink. Not the size of the rinks that we use in the pictures. A personal rink.

And that was for Vera. She would practice there every evening. You could see her gracefully circling the rink; it was quite something to watch. One day I was in my office and Herb came in and said that he wanted me to record some waltzes.

"What kind of waltzes," I asked?

"Well," he says, "some waltzes. You know, waltzes."

I said, "Like Strauss waltzes?" And I hummed something.

"Yes," he said, "some of those."

"How many?"

"I don't know. It's up to you. Give me half a dozen waltzes."

I had, at that time, a forty-piece orchestra under contract to the studio. There are books with waltzes for orchestras. You don't have to orchestrate them. You turn a page and there's a waltz, you turn another page and there's another waltz. So I handed out the books and the orchestra played, one after another, and finally, the concertmaster comes over to me and lifts his eyebrows. He wants to know what the hell is going on. We're not scoring a movie.

I couldn't tell him what it was for. I said, "Don't give me any guff, just play the damn waltzes." We put it on a reel, which requires a playback operator to cue up the music. We didn't have an electronic system in those days.

One night, not long afterward, I worked late. It was ten o'clock on a very pleasant evening, and I had that virtuous kind of fatigue you get after a hard day's work. I took my time as I walked to the parking lot. Then I noticed a light far down at the end of the lot, near the loading dock of the new recording stage. As I watched the light, I heard my waltzes coming from the stage. I knew that nothing was shooting so I walked over and stood in the dark, looking onto the lighted stage. The floor had been drawn back exposing the ice rink. There they were, the two of them, Herb and Vera, both wearing matching houndstooth suits, his with knickers, hers with slacks, skating around the ice rink, hand in hand. Behind them was a screen and up high was the operator, playing the waltzes. Finally, the music stopped and they sat down on a bench and had a cigarette. He used a cricket clicker as a signal and the waltzes started up again. Around they went, hand in hand. It was very old-fashioned, very romantic, and very private. I slipped away in the dark.

* * *

I found that I had to keep myself very busy to stay trim in Holly-wood. In the mornings I went out riding in the Hollywood Hills. Riding hard along the firebreaks. I played sandlot polo with a group of Jews (Jews on horseback, what a scene!), and I kept my polo gear in the office so I could get some exercise in the after-noons. I stayed in good shape in those days, skiing and riding and walking as much as I could. But I was also coming face-to-face with a pretty rough truth.

My work was a great exertion. When I scored a movie, it was an effort. I had to strain to dream up a decent score. I had to try five different ways before it worked. I loved it because I valued exer-tion—I gave that effort some credit for worth. If you paid for it with sweat, something was worth more. So I didn't mind working hard and I loved the idea of being a musician. This is what I told myself.

The truth was that I feared I had no great musical gifts. I had long since come to the conclusion that I was a second-rate trumpet player. I couldn't do what the other guys could do. Other guys could just take the horn out of the bag and play it. I had to practice hours a day to stay competent. Getting into Juilliard, and all through my Juilliard career, I knew it, although the admission, the conscious acknowledgment of my limitation, wasn't possible. My point was that I did it. I got into Juilliard; I learned arranging and orchestration by dint of sheer perspiration. When I started to write and arrange, I did it. But that, too, was hard work. I did it well, but it was very difficult.

The light began to dawn when I ran into Victor Young. He was a Hungarian composer, a cocky little guy with a big cigar. He was famous in Hollywood. Well, he wrote "Tea for Two," for instance, so his musical gifts were never in doubt. He was at Paramount, but I used him now and then, as I used Loesser. He came over and conducted his own stuff, and he was great with the musicians. They loved the guy. They recognized talent.

Every week, Victor had the guys over to his house for a game of hearts, which is like a half-assed version of bridge. I came to one of the games and Victor was there, with his feisty spirit, yelling at everyone, criticizing the way people played their hands, and turning every now and then to work on a musical score. It didn't even require his full attention. That was frightening. George Antheil could write a score while holding a conversation and playing chess. I had to lock myself in a room and concentrate like crazy to score a picture. These guys did it without breaking a sweat.

Never mind. I can still produce quality work, I told myself, even if mine requires more exertion. I was looking for something upon which to test myself. We made a movie about World War I called *Women at War,* which required a lot of music. Altogether, about fifty minutes of music, which is about the length of a Schubert symphony. So there was a tremendous score to be written, and I said, boy, I'm going to do all of it myself; I'm going to compose it, orchestrate it, and conduct it. It took me awhile, but I was satisfied. I thought it was some piece of work. Then there were going to be three days of recording. And I thought the whole thing was brilliant.

I brought the orchestra to this magnificent stage—forty-five pieces—and we recorded for six hours a day. It was late afternoon on the second day and I gave the guys a break—we were all kind of tired. I was all by myself on this dark stage, and I called up to the operators to play the cue. I wanted to test the music against the picture, to see that everything was in synch. I sat on a high conductor's stool. I watched the movie for a while and suddenly I became detached.

It felt as if I had moved out of my own body. I was listening to this music as if it were written and conducted by someone else. My critical self had taken over. And I came to a terrible conclusion.

It was second-rate.

I had complete detachment from the work and was operating on my musical judgment, which is good, and I saw that my musical talent wasn't. I was just listening to it, not even evaluating it, just reacting. And I said to myself, "This is my best shot and the stuff is no good." There were no inspired passages, no flights of original musicality, no shock of talent.

It was something that I had secretly suspected and feared. The other guys, like Victor Young, Styne, Loesser, and George Antheil had a different ear. They heard the music before they wrote it down. That was their secret. The music was already inside their heads. They heard it. But I had to put it down on paper first. I couldn't hear it in my head.

It was a blow. I had worked so hard, tried so hard. All that effort to end up second-rate!

I was sitting on the same stage where I had watched Herb and Vera make perfect circles. Maybe I was influenced by that exquisite, perfect memory; maybe I saw that Susan's promise would outshine my own; maybe all those things combined to force me to face the fact of my own mediocrity. In any event, I decided right then that I was going to quit.

It was a relief.

Part II

"No Whistling"

Chapter Seven

*I*t was a great and glorious moment. I was about to take charge of my own fate, alter the course of my life, turn the world upside down . . . only something else came up. World War II.

It is hard now to convey just how great that upheaval was. One minute it was every man for himself, everyone devoted to a private and personal destiny. Then, in a thunderclap, we were at war. We were also angry and frightened. And in all these elements we were united—the whole country. It was that sudden and that plain.

December 7, 1941 . . .

*   *   *

The California Dons were playing . . . somebody. It was the beginning of professional football. College football was more popular then, with the built-in rooting section of alumni. But these guys had graduated and still wanted to play; here they were at a high school stadium on Melrose Avenue in Los Angeles and the game was just getting started when the announcement came over a loudspeaker. "The Japanese have just bombed Pearl Harbor."

Nobody knew where the hell Pearl Harbor was; nobody knew

what had happened there—the extent of the attack. But we all knew that we were at war. The game stopped cold, the players stood dumbstruck in the middle of the field, and we all filed out of the stands like a whisper.

We were transformed overnight. Our cozy world was over for the duration. We knew it without speaking a word, with a kind of idiot insight. No one had to give speeches or pull us along or work us over. It was as if we had just been waiting. That same night there were blackouts. And soon there were air raid wardens, and fire wardens. You put a hood over the headlight of your car so that the beam pointed down and couldn't be seen from the air. You closed the blackout curtains and followed the rules. Nobody wanted to screw up.

California may have felt it a little closer. There was a great fear that the Japanese fleet was gonna come right up to the coast and attack us. The sky was filled with searchlights looking for Japanese planes. A lot of it was silly, but underneath was that real sense of nervous certainty: now life was serious.

We all went down to the draft board and registered. My brother, Stan, was an engineer for Lockheed Aircraft—an essential civilian category—so he was automatically deferred, but I was 1-A. When I went for my physical, it was funny because there were all these Hollywood wise guys, and the sergeant was some crusty old regular army grunt, going through the military drill on how to fill out the forms properly. "Now, I want youse guys to put down your last name first, then your middle initial, then your first name. You got that? Last name first, then the middle initial, and then your first name. Let me repeat myself, last name first. Then the middle initial. And last, the first name. Everybody got it straight? Last name. Middle Initial. First name. Any questions?"

A hand went up, grasping for us all, the prophetic and eye-opening recognition of where we were headed and whose hands we would be in for God-knows-how-long: "Hey, Sarge, where do we go to surrender?"

*   *   *

Unless you had a punctured organ or a missing limb, you were going into a uniform. And it didn't seem unreasonable. The only room for maneuver was which branch of the service you were going to end up in. Herb's son, Doug Yates, was called up immediately. He'd been through ROTC at an Ivy League college and had a reserve commission as a second lieutenant in the army. They jumped him to first lieutenant and appointed him a film specialist in the Signal Corps. We were pretty good friends and he called me and said he could use me to run the sound division of a lab making training films for the Air Corps. The draft board already had its eye on a spot for me in the infantry, where I stood a very good chance of getting shot. However, Doug needed me, and if he insisted on putting me to work in some cushy stateside film lab, and getting me a commission, well, what could I do—I was a patriot— I'd just have to get shot some other time.

Doug started on the paperwork to get my commission so that he could take me to Dayton, Ohio, where the Signal Corps was building a lab. I broke the news to the draft board; I told them I had a better offer.

Assembling a film lab in a remote outpost in Ohio was not such a crackpot idea. It actually made sense, in a zigzag kind of army way. When I look back on it, that's how a lot of things got done during the war, with a kind of oblique but shrewd logic. It only seemed absurd, no doubt to confuse the enemy.

The obvious thing would be to put a film lab in Hollywood where they already had all the technicians and experts. But the air bases were in Ohio. Wright Field and Patterson Field were loaded with planes and hot young test pilots, just what you need to make training films. It would have been a lot harder to move the air fields to Hollywood than ship the technicians to Dayton. There seemed to be an underlying sanity to the way we fought that war.

Meanwhile, the army was taking a long time coming through with my commission, and the draft board—no doubt concerned that it would lose a crack at me—was hot on my heels, demanding that I either get my commission or it would take matters into its own hands. This was in March of '42. I had just turned thirty-one. So Doug said to come on out to Ohio as a civilian. He'd put me to work in the labs and that way the paper work would sail through.

And that's what I did and that's how it worked. I drove to Dayton, took a room at the YMCA, and began work at the lab on Wright Field for $150 a week. You could live off the fat of the land on that kind of money. In fact, when I got my commission that summer, I made $135 a month and I still lived like a prince. I never ate army chow if I could help it, and I had a charming social life in Dayton. A uniform went a long way toward breaking the ice when it came to meeting women, getting seats in a restaurant, or tickets to a show.

There was also the comforting presence of a lot of pals from Hollywood at the lab. I didn't go through that disorienting loneliness that most soldiers experience when they're thrown into a crowd of rough strangers. Nevertheless, I didn't just go from Brooks Brothers to army pinks. There were reminders that something big had changed.

*   *   *

One night after work a bunch of us were in a bar in Dayton and something was playing on a jukebox. Harry James. I was alert. You can't mistake that slow, sweet horn that he blew. "Fellas! Fellas! Listen!"

I got off the stool and then started to laugh. A few months earlier we were in Hollywood and Jule Styne got sick of hearing all these classical melodies being turned into pop songs—Rachmaninoff, Mozart, Beethoven (they only stole from the greats). So, as a kind of inside joke, he put together this very fast, jazzy tune that made insinuated fun of that devious traffic and put it into one of those long-forgotten college pictures. Here was Harry James playing it on the jukebox in a real slow, pop style: "It seems to me I've heard that song before." It was a strange and funny moment and it hit me there in the bar, hearing that particularly familiar tune, that I wasn't in Hollywood pulling musical pranks anymore.

*   *   *

Our colonel, whose name is adrift somewhere in my jumbled memory, was a sweet guy. He was regular army, a West Point graduate, and had a legitimate claim to fame. At the turn of the century our colonel helped lay the Atlantic cable. But he lacked a lethal air so he remained in the Signal Corps, running the base in Dayton. He never really stood a chance of leading men into battle, but he made the best of things and he was kinda cute. He had a little mustache and he fancied himself a literary type. He sent little epigrams to magazines such as *Punch* and *Judge,* and from time to time they would get printed.

He was a friendly guy and he invited Everett Freeman, who had some pretty good credits as a producer, and screenwriter (*You Can't Cheat an Honest Man, Jim Thorpe—All-American*), Charles Grayson (screenwriter for *The Boys from Syracuse*), and me over to his house for drinks late one afternoon. He had one of those old stone colonial brick houses that were put up for the commanding officer on army bases. You couldn't get whiskey during the war so he served us some sherry. It was very sweet, and after one glass, I was through. Not Grayson and Freeman. They tried to keep up with the old man, but the colonel really knocked it back and he finally just keeled over and passed out. We tried not to notice, but there he was, out cold on the floor of the den. So we picked him up and carried him into his bedroom and put him to sleep. The next day, he was a little sheepish, but he made a great comeback. He said to us, "You know, a gentleman can only display his weakness to people he holds in high regard." An epigram. He probably had that published in *Punch* under a cartoon of an unconscious colonel being carried to bed by three nervous lieutenants.

The duty at the lab was pretty good, mostly because the colonel was a reasonable guy and the lab was run by professionals. Sound guys, cutters, editors—pros who worked on the soundstages of every big Hollywood studio. They knew what they were doing. But the army made a huge mistake in where it positioned the lab. It was right next to the test site for new propellers. These propellers were put on a stand and run all day long, full throttle, to see how much stress they could take. *Rrrrmmmmm!* That was fine in the morning, when you're fresh. But the army hadn't calculated on this type of audience. We were big eaters. One of the guys had a rich uncle who gave him a magnificent Packard Pierce Arrow limousine, which seated seven people. We would arrive to work in it and at noon we'd drive back into Dayton where we would load up on a big lunch. Then we would pack ourselves back into the car and head back to the lab where the propellers were still running— *RRRRRMMMMMMMMM!* Only now it sounded like snoring, and with all that food rumbling in our bellies and that lulling hum in the background, we would invariably fall asleep at our desks. If you walked through that lab at naptime, there were rows and rows of sleeping officers with DO NOT DISTURB signs around their necks.

We were a disgrace, militarily speaking. One young lieutenant, skinny little kid, a writer, had to pull officer of the day, which meant that he had to wear a loaded sidearm. Well, the routine was that when you turned over the duty to the next man, you handed an empty weapon to the guy who relieved you. The way you did that was to remove the clip of ammunition, then clear the chamber, then pull the trigger to show that the weapon was empty. Well, this poor kid forgot to remove the clip so that when he cleared the chamber, he actually put a round in it. The result was that when he pulled the trigger to show the gun was empty, he killed the ceiling. It was funny and we tried to overlook harmless mishaps. We were, after all, a civilian army.

All you had to do was to look at the company of enlisted men attached to us. Company C consisted of sad-sack writers, producers, musicians—anything but soldiers. These were accomplished, talented guys who didn't want a commission out of principal, or reverse class snobbery. William Saroyan was a buck private. He was given an assignment to write something about a physical director and he made a surreal comedy out of it. After that the army left him alone. Good guys, but a horrible sight on parade. I'd review them and pronounce them, "a fine body of men."

*   *   *

One day, we got a new executive officer. A major. He'd worked for a news service as a photographer in Chicago and was a reserve officer. He thought he was an expert on talent and the military. A true horse's ass. He wanted more discipline. More army. So he made rules. No more smoking inside the lab. And no whistling. So I gave the men a ten-minute smoke break every hour followed by a twenty-minute whistle break.

But with all the slacking off, we did the job—we made training films: *How to Ditch, Care and Maintenance of the Shimmy Damper Accumulator* (one of my big hits). I'd gone back to Hollywood where the Signal Corps had a huge stockpile of "wild tracks" (different sounds to suit any occasion—gunshots, explosions, screams) at The Hal E. Roach Studios, which was called Fort Roach. The executive officer, Ronald Reagan, was a very nice guy I knew from the old days. I found him to be a thoroughly decent and easygoing fella, and he helped me get the stock material I needed to make the training films. (Little did I realize at the time, how much I would despise what he eventually represented.) If, for example, you needed the sound of a fighter plane coming in to attack, you could pull out some old footage from *Wings*. We had a big inventory of wild tracks.

However, they didn't always work. You couldn't fool the pilots. They knew the sound of their own engines. If you tried to use the sound of a P-47 and showed a picture of a P-13, they'd laugh at the film. They'd dismiss the whole training film as a fraud. You had to have the right engine sound to go with the footage, which meant that we had to go out and get fresh sound tracks to match the right sound with the right plane.

By now I was captain and full of big-shot captain confidence. I was about to confront a kind of guerrilla action that would take me down a peg.

To make a particular training film I needed the sound of a B-13. This is a two-seater aircraft with an open cockpit and a sliding canopy. Bright and early one morning I sent the crew down to the South Dayton Airport, a small civilian airport, to wait for me. They would record the sound of the plane. I went to Wright Field where I requisitioned a B-13 complete with a pilot. There were always a lot of test pilots hanging around the orderly room. The guy assigned to me was one of those lazy, dumb lieutenants who didn't appreciate playing chauffeur to some dilettante feather merchant. He was a hot pilot and would have preferred combat, even in

Ohio. I could sense the resentment when we were suiting up to get ready for the flight. It was cold in those open cockpits and you had to wrap yourself in a lot of cold-weather flying gear. Then, when you were stuffed like Santa Claus, you had to strap on a parachute. You couldn't go airborne without a chute.

It took me a little longer than my pilot to get into the gear and he grabbed the last comfortable seat parachute, the kind you sit on. I was stuck with a backpack parachute, the type that makes sitting in a tight cockpit almost impossible. It was like having a huge hump on my back. When we got into the air, this airhead pilot asked me over the intercom: "By the way, Captain, where we going?"

"The flight plan says South Dayton Airport," I replied.

"Uh, where is South Dayton Airport?"

"Go south, you asshole!"

We couldn't find it. So we opened the canopy and rolled the plane from side to side so we could see over the wings. It took some time and effort, with cold air blasting in my face and the backpack chute breaking my spine as I twisted from side to side to try to find the landing strip, but we eventually found it. All that twisting and squirming apparently undid the lacing in the back of my chute and the silk began to leak out. When we landed, I got out of the plane to give instructions to the sound crew before we would take off again and make the sound passes around the field. I noticed the parachute trailing out of the backpack like the train of a bridal gown. If it had come apart and unraveled in the air, I would have been dragged out of the plane and killed.

"That coulda been real serious," said the pilot with a smug smile. "Well, guess I'll head home."

We were supposed to spend the day circling the field so that the sound crew could record the engine of a B-13. The pilot began to climb back into the plane.

"Where the hell are you going?"

"Sorry, Captain, I can't carry you without a parachute. That's regulations. So long."

It was a pretty good lesson in tactical defense. You have to watch all the flanks—and especially your rear—if you're gonna beat the assholes.

Chapter Eight

By the winter of 1943 the war was over. Not that little scuffle with the Axis. No, I speak of that really big bloodbath between the United States Army and the Air Corps.

Like so many wars, this one was all a matter of pride. The Air Corps men wanted star billing in the war. Apparently, they didn't trust the Signal Corps camera crews to favor their good side in the close-ups. This was when the Air Corps was still a branch of the army, before it became the U.S. Air Force, a separate service. The army, operating in the horse-and-buggy age of public relations, was outclassed by the fly-guy glamour of the Air Corps. The army was lucky to get a few measly camera crews. If they pressed it, the Air Corps men probably could have gotten their own makeup department.

As it was, the Signal Corps film labs in Ohio were disbanded and the personnel scattered east and west. Most of the guys took Horace Greeley's advice and went west; they were shipped to Fort Roach in Hollywood and stayed in the Signal Corps. In an augur of what was to come, I went east. I passed into the Army Air Corps in New York City, where I served on Park Avenue. Bold duty.

* * *

If Dayton, Ohio, provided a low-key kind of welcome for the military, New York City had all the bands out. It felt like you were always in the middle of a ticker tape parade. The best restaurants, Broadway, women—all of it belonged to servicemen. By the third year of the war, it was clear that we were going to win and the gloomy pessimism of 1942 and 1943 had been replaced by a mood of restrained exhilaration. There were still battle casualties, there was still Hitler and the Japanese, but the outcome was certain and the sense of relief and impending victory was like wine.

There was no period of adjustment for me as I stepped off the *Superchief* at Grand Central Station. I felt completely at home in New York City. I was stationed in an office building across from an old armory on 34th Street and I took an apartment with my old pal Art Lewis on East 73rd Street off Lexington Avenue. Once again, my ass had landed in butter. I had plenty of dough. I had my friends. We ate at Joe & Rose. And my job had meaning. I had to screen the raw combat footage that came back from Europe. I took the material straight from the air crews that flew into battle with the bombers, along with the gun-camera footage from the fighter planes, and sent them to the Pentagon and to the newsreels. I also kept quite an inventory of stock footage, which came in handy later.

At home, the apartment was always filled with pretty women and young men dressed like soldiers. If there was rationing, it didn't seem to affect us. There were always steaks to be had. And my roommate was ideal. Art Lewis, whose father ran a production company in Hollywood, had been in the executive end of the movie business before the war. He was in the same sort of vague line of work in the army, producing training films for the Signal Corps at a studio in Astoria, Queens. He bathed regularly, made very little noise, and was always game.

One night over dinner with a big gang at the restaurant Longchamps, I met Posy Greenberg. She was young and spunky. She was also divorced and had a three-year-old son named Bob. She lived in Forest Hills with a bunch of her sisters, and I found myself riding the subways back and forth to Forest Hills with this captivating little woman who chattered on in the most sensible, beguiling way about a range of matters that were outside the reach of most women her age. She had wit, humor, and a lot of energy, which always meant a lot to me. Nonetheless, we never made plans. No one thought too far ahead. I was a soldier, we were at war, and all thoughts about the future were deferred. But unbeknownst to me, an attachment was being fused behind my back.

In any event, Posy and I became a couple. Most of the guys were coupled up. Charley Grayson brought his brand new wife, Dorothy, from Dayton. She was as cute as a button, and he was crazy about her. They took an apartment in our building on the third or fourth floor. Maybe it was the switch from the Ohio diet to the fancier New York City cuisine, but Charley suffered a common war wound: hemorrhoids. He had to go in for one of those minor operations that are both painful and embarrassing. The hospital had been turned over to the army and Charley was in a ward reserved for Jews. It wasn't specifically segregated, but it turned out that way. Most of the patients were suffering from obesity or hemorrhoids and they were almost all Jews. The next ward over was for alcoholics. Not a Jew in the place. The manner of our overindulgence, it seems, was culturally distinctive.

When we went to visit Charley he asked us to check in on Dorothy. He hadn't heard from her for a while and he was afraid that she was overcome by his infirmity, or shame. He gave me the key. So Art Lewis and I went up to their apartment and knocked on the door; there was no answer. I used the key and we tiptoed through the rooms, quietly calling her name and then something struck me: it didn't seem like a woman lived there. There were all of Charley's uniforms. But there were no female clothes in the closet. No makeup on the vanity. No lotions in the bathroom. No delicate toiletries hanging from the shower rod. On the dresser, however, there was an ominous envelope with Charley's name on it. That cute little button was missing. Dorothy ran off with John Sturges, a big, tall, lanky drink of water who wanted to be like John Huston. He even joined Huston's wartime crew to film the famous combat footage *The Battle for San Pietro*. In any event, she divorced Charley and married Sturges, who went on to become a terrifically accomplished but inexplicably uncelebrated director in Hollywood. He made some pretty good movies: *The Great Escape, McQ, The Magnificent Seven, Bad Day at Black Rock, Gunfight at the O.K. Corral*. Strangely enough, there were no grudges, no aftermath. We all remained lifelong friends.

*   *   *

Among the leftover eccentrics who came from Dayton to New York with me was a singular character named Ben Grauman Cohen. Ben was the nephew of Sid Grauman, the owner of the world famous Grauman's Chinese Theatre in Hollywood. As a result of growing up amidst the splendors of movie royalty, Ben was afflicted with a disease common to such an uncommon crowd. He was like a child when it came to money. He didn't know where it came from, he didn't know how to acquire it, and he certainly didn't know how to hold on to it. He did, however, have a true genius for spending it.

One morning the phone rang in my apartment on 73rd Street. It was Ben. He wanted to borrow a hundred dollars. It was urgent. OK, I gave him the cash. Later that day, he called my office to invite me over to his place for drinks. There were already a bunch of guys drinking and eating when I got there. It seems that Ben needed the loan to throw a party for me and eight other guys.

When we first got to New York it was cold and we needed to buy trenchcoats. I wanted to pick one up at the PX at Governor's Island for thirty-five dollars, but Ben was horrified by the idea. He wanted his trenchcoat from Saks Fifth Avenue, the preferred supplier for the well-to-do army. So we went to Saks where he picked up his trenchcoat for $150. The trouble was he didn't have $150 and he had no prospects of getting that much money. He told the salesman to put it on his account. This was before the days of credit cards and revolving accounts. You were supposed to pay cash or settle your account when the bill arrived. When I pointed this out to Ben, he waved me off.

"Don't worry," said Ben, "I do a lot of business with Saks. When I get the money I'll pay the bill. Meanwhile, I need a trenchcoat." You couldn't really get too mad at Ben; he didn't understand complicated financial operations, like paying your bills. He was married to a Cuban girl named Josephine who would rattle off her exasperation in Spanish. After the war, Ben went broke many times, investing in a three-wheeled car or some other harebrained scheme, and Josephine stuck by him, rattling off her woes in Spanish.

In spite of everything—or maybe because of everything—we had fun. There was that live-for-today mood that put trouble in perspective. And it was an erudite and witty band of guys: Frank Loesser, Everett Freeman, Charley Grayson. One guy, Leonard Spiegelgass, a major, was being shipped out. Leonard, who would later write the screenplays for *I Was a Male War Bride*, *Gypsy*, and *A Majority of One*, among a bunch of other terrific movies, was gay. This was not a big deal to us; we were, after all, artists. However, Leonard made an art of his inclination. There he was in front of a mirror trying on his battlefield equipment—the sidearm, the web belt, the helmet liner—getting ready for combat. When he was satisfied, he turned smartly and said: "Now, then, which way is the war?"

On a summer afternoon, sitting pretty, we were across from the Plaza Hotel, having lunch at the old Savoy, which was a pretty good place to have lunch. One of the writers had just come out of basic training—he was a private; we didn't take rank too seriously—and he had to go to the bathroom. He stood up and said to this crowded table of officers, "Would a couple of you mind coming with me to the bathroom? I can't pee alone anymore."

In spite of all that, we took the war very seriously. We picked our spots, but we wouldn't goof off when it counted.

*   *   *

After about eight months in New York, late in 1944, I got a call from Arnold Belgarde, another captain I knew from Ohio, who was now stationed at the Pentagon. Arnold was attached to the film headquarters of the Army Air Corps. "Great news—I just got you transferred to the Pentagon. You'll be executive officer of the Air Corps film division. There's a majority in it."

Arnold's judgment was seriously impaired. First, I had no desire to be a major. Being a captain was just about right—enough rank to hold off the savages, but not enough to cause any real damage. Second, I didn't want to leave New York. I was very comfortable in my East Side life. When I protested, Arnold said it was too late, orders had been cut. Why was he quitting this ideal job, I demanded? He said he wanted to see some action. He wanted to fight. And where was he going to take on the enemy? Alaska. He was completely unimpressed with the fact that there was not much war going on in Alaska. Nevertheless, it was done; I was transferred.

* * *

As it turned out, Washington was fine. Again, I found a house with a bunch of other officers. It was one of those rotating wartime apartments where, when one guy was shipped out, someone else moved in. It was a pretty good deal. Posy even came down four or five times. But it couldn't last. In the spring of 1945, just as the war in Europe was grinding to an end, Franklin Roosevelt died. I was listening to the radio when the new president made his first address and my head snapped in recognition of the voice. "My God," I blurted out. "Gene Autry is president!" It was a relief that it was really Harry Truman.

Not much later, some three-star general came up with the bright idea that all officers in the Pentagon under the age of thirty-five who had not been overseas should be shipped out as soon as possible. I came in just under the wire. My commanding officer offered me a choice. I could become executive officer of a film unit on Saipan or I could join a combat camera crew in Europe. He gave me twenty-four hours to think it over. Some of the hairy veterans wise in the ways of the army gave me firm advice. Pass up Saipan. Demand combat.

"If you pick Saipan, they'll ship you out tomorrow," one old soldier explained. "But if you ask for a combat assignment, first of all, they'll really be impressed. Then you'll have to go to gunnery school for six weeks. It'll take another month to qualify as a gunner. After that the paperwork will take another few months. By then the war will be over."

It was that infallible zigzag army logic. Of course, the veterans were right. The colonel was touched by my patriotic zeal. He clapped me on the back, welcoming me to the fellowship of public-spirited lunacy. While my orders were being cut, a major came in with a request for a film about his general, who was with the Eighth Air Force in England. The general had something to do with strategic bombing, something about which I was completely ignorant. I decided to educate myself. This was to lead to my last great army adventure.

I knew nothing about strategic bombing. I didn't even know where to begin to prepare a report. So I looked up strategic bombing in the Pentagon telephone directory. A secretary answered the phone and became silent when I asked if I had the right number. Then a bird colonel got on the phone and demanded to know who I was and how the hell I got the number. I explained that it was listed in the Pentagon directory. He was amazed. Then he ordered me and my commanding officer up to his office immediately.

I could tell that it was serious business because his office had plush carpeting. Sitting there was this full-bird colonel and a two-star general. They questioned me about my assignment. Who sent me to spy on them? What did I know about strategic bombing? Then, from another office came a civilian. An undersecretary of war, it turned out. He was interested in the fact that I was with the Air Corps film headquarters. A second civilian, someone from an insurance company who was going to make a damage assessment of strategic bombing in Europe, said it might be a good idea to have film to go with his strategic bombing survey.

"Who do we have who could handle such a mission?" asked the general.

All eyes turned to me. I was ordered to be ready to fly out in four hours. "But I have no clean underwear," I protested. By that afternoon, I was at the airfield, ready to go. One of those legendary gruff army sergeants wouldn't let me board the C-47 until I watched a forty-five-minute training film *How to Ditch.* I explained that I had personally made the film, but the sergeant wasn't impressed. No one was going over the Atlantic without watching the film in his presence.

* * *

After rattling around inside that primitive DC-3 for twenty-nine hours, I landed at an airfield outside of London with my unclean laundry stuffed into my B-4 bag. London smelled fragrant. There was no central heating and everyone burned cannel coal, which is an oily form of shale and leaves a very pungent odor behind. I loved it. The whole place struck me as very foreign. Not like now, when you can't tell where you land because the same chain stores are everywhere. In 1945, England was a foreign country. It was Sherlock Holmes and Charles Dickens. You drove on the other side of the road, the cockney dialects were impossible to understand (as were some of the upper-class accents). You could see the bomb damage. London had really been at war. There was true rationing, and the only place to get a good meal was at the officer's mess in the Dorchester Hotel. The big banquet rooms were laid out like a cafeteria and the English girls would swoon when you took them to dinner at the officer's mess.

I reported to General Orville Anderson, who was high up in the Eighth Air Force, but he had no idea what to do with me. He told me to go about my business; that is, don't bother him. General Anderson had his own B-17, two pilots, and a WAC secretary and not much to do. I moved into a house on Baker Street with the pilots and the WAC, and on the days when the general wasn't using his plane, which was almost always, we would fly to Brussels for lunch, or Paris for the hell of it. There was a piano in the house and one of the pilots was an aspiring pianist. He played for me and, as I recall, wasn't bad, although I have no idea what became of him.

In Paris I ran into David Miller, a director I knew from Hollywood, who invited me to his home—that is, the house he had requisitioned in Paris—which was filled with pretty young French girls. There was a garden that came with the house, along with the cook. I was joyriding through postwar Europe and stopped for a week or two with Miller in that idyllic house in Paris.

At some point, I tried to get to work on the assignment—filming the damage from strategic bombing. There were combat film crews waiting for reassignment all over the place and I used one crew to shoot some footage of Berlin. I was shocked, making passes over the city, at the damage, at the sheer violence of our bombing raids. Driving into Berlin, it was impossible to find an address. Everything had been obliterated. The city had been flattened and it had a dark and menacing feel. One evening, I went to dinner and had to return to Bachelor Officer's Quarters across a deserted park. *Stars and Stripes* had been warning against "Werewolves," packs of avenging Nazis. Crossing that Berlin park as darkness fell was the one time in all the war that I was truly frightened. I took out my .45, cocked it, and made my way from tree to tree until I got back to the BOQ.

I had a jeep and a driver (officers were not allowed to drive themselves) and we went into Third Army territory—General George S. Patton country. We were stopped by two huge M.P.s, who made us get out of the jeep, put on neckties, helmet liners, and wipe our combat boots clean. Patton would've made a great Nazi. The driver was an Italian kid from Brooklyn. He just came off of a three-day pass in Rome where, after an all-night binge with a prostitute, he got into line with a bunch of other GIs. He thought it was either a chow line or a pro line (a postcoital prophylaxis) and he could use one or both. Only it turned out to be a line of soldiers waiting outside the Vatican, which is how he got his accidental audience with the pope. He didn't know whether to feel bad or blessed.

One day we were in Munich and drove a few miles outside of town to Dachau. We could smell it before we could see it. A mile away from the camp there was a Gothic depiction of two thirty-foot-high German soldiers. Then the green and wooden barracks of the camp came into view. There were a few survivors in striped prison rags wandering the grounds in a pointless daze. The gas chambers were all cleaned up, except for the fact that you could see the marks on the walls where people had tried to claw their way out.

The Germans were, in their own way, apologetic. Everywhere I went, in my high captain's uniform, I was treated with great respect and told of their sympathetic suffering. Oh, they all said, my great uncle was a Jew. Some third cousin or fourth aunt—a Jew. They all had a Jew hiding somewhere in the family closet. Maybe some of those distant relatives had left their fingerprints on the walls of the gas chambers at Dachau.

It was time to go home. There was no need to make a film. We had all the footage from the combat crews on file. I went back to the Pentagon and slapped together some footage and handed it to an indifferent colonel who was also just waiting to get discharged. I was processed out of the army and headed back to California.

Chapter Nine

*B*y *late 1945* I had resumed my old life, but with some slight modifications. I was married.

This was a direct result of postwar panic on my part. When I got out of the army, I tried to contact Posy, but her sisters told me she'd moved to California. This set off emotional havoc. At the time, I thought it was leftover irritation with the Germans, coupled with pique over the fact that she didn't leave a forwarding address, but I now recognize the whole business as amateur jealousy. The fear of losing her, plus the completely opposite apprehension of getting tied down, kept me up at night. I didn't know which misgiving was stronger.

The thing that worried me most was the fact that I knew she got along—too well—with my friends. Art Lewis was a hound when it came to women and I naturally assumed the worst. (This calls for a slight digression. Art Lewis got out of the army early and was back in California long before I was discharged. He had several months to beat my time. How he managed to get an early discharge is one of those magical army parables that gives a man hope. One day in the middle of the war he went to the Pentagon office that handled discharges and casually asked the officer at the desk, "How do you get discharged?" He was told to fill out a form, then come back after lunch. When he returned, he was a civilian and went back to California.) So Art and Posy were alone together in the same state while I was counting bricks in Germany. Naturally, when I finally got my own separation from the army and tracked her down, I decided in a very cold-blooded and calculating way that I better marry her before she got involved with somebody else. If it wasn't a moist, romantic decision, it was at least the act of a mature grown-up.

Besides, marriage seemed to be trendy. All the old bachelors were marching down the aisle. Stan married a girl named Margot Kramer and the family split up, both of us moving to apartments and homes of our own. We had a couple of wedding luncheons at a restaurant owned by Preston Sturges at the end of Sunset Strip.

I was relieved to be out of the army, but apprehensive about getting my old job back. In my absence the music department at Republic Pictures had been run by Walter Scharf, a very talented composer (who would go on to have a pretty impressive career). Walter gallantly stepped down when I returned.

Nevertheless, the work at the studio was incomplete, unsatisfying. Somewhere in the back of my mind I was restless for something I couldn't even name. I have heard women say that they can feel the biological clock ticking away their reproductive life span. So it was with me and my professional life span. I felt a clock ticking.

And then I met Ernie Martin.

*   *   *

We were drawn together at yet another cocktail party (all life seemed to pirouette around that social custom—people standing in awkward clusters, holding glasses of mixed drinks, and making pale imitations of the Round Table conversations). And we were a custom-made match. Ernie was tall; I was short. He was charming;

I was blunt. He was Savile Row; I was Brooks Brothers. He was in his mid-twenties; I was ten years older. He was tough . . . well, I was tough, too. The perfect yin and yang.

We began to talk, in that first noisy, overheated, and completely unreserved exchange, about Broadway. He was the head of comedy programming for KNX, CBS's flagship radio station in Los Angeles, but he spent a lot of time in New York meeting with Bill Paley. He was Paley's fair-haired boy. In his spare time, Ernie went to the theater. When I was stationed in New York, I, too, spent a lot of time going to the theater. And the thing I remember—the thing we both agreed upon instantly—was that the musical theater was a ridiculously silly art form. Archaic. It struck us both as pipsqueak entertainment.

For example, when I was stationed in New York, I went to see a musical called *Something for the Boys*, a wartime comedy starring Ethel Merman. And believe me when Ethel Merman starred in a musical comedy, she let you know about it. Every time she had to do a number everyone else had to back off and let her take sole possession of the stage. No one else could share the same atmosphere. The "book," or plot, for this particular show had absolutely no logical meaning. The story was that she had gone to the dentist and he had filled her teeth with something radioactive, which enabled her to pick up enemy broadcasts. So she became a spy. The songs had nothing to do with the plot; they just gave her an opportunity to perform. This was the musical theater.

This was also the golden age of the Hollywood musical. The talent was all migrating west. Hollywood was overcrowded with musical geniuses. Ernie and I agreed that our only chance to make our mark lay in going in the other direction. Compared to the sophisticated business of making a complicated movie musical, a cockamamie Broadway musical had to be a cinch for a couple of hotshots like us.

This conversation between us did not take place at a single cocktail party. We spoke of it at the Beverly Hills Tennis Club, during dinner dates with our wives, and most of all while riding horseback along the firebreaks in the Santa Monica Mountains. Ernie loved riding and we would rent a few saddle horses in the afternoon and talk about our plan while cantering in the hills above Hollywood. An inspiring setting.

It took a while to evolve, but Ernie really did have a plan. He began working on it long before I came into the picture. It started out as a dreamy and impractical proposition. But that was Ernie's strength—the cloudy, shapeless concept that had no true mass. He needed me to set the thing in motion, to lay the practical groundwork, to do what had to be done to bring the ghost to life.

*   *   *

Ernie's daydream started with Ira Gershwin at Santa Anita Racetrack, which is where they both spent a lot of time. Ernie's father was a handicapper, so he had the track in his blood. Ernie and Ira would meet in the clubhouse of the Santa Anita track where Ernie, with his infinite charm, lulled Ira into joining his scheme.

"I'd like to make a musical out of *An American in Paris,*" Ernie declared out of the blue.

Ira, who owned the rights to it replied, "Fine." He was only being polite.

"I'd like to take it to Broadway."

"Go right ahead."

What did Ira have to lose? He signed no paper, made no deal. And he kept his charming young friend happy.

Ernie, on the other hand, being the irrepressible optimist, now operated under the completely preposterous conviction that he owned the rights to a musical show called *An American in Paris,* of which there was none.

To Ernie, the agreement was signed in blood. On his next trip to New York City, he went to see a show called *Three to Make Ready,* starring Ray Bolger, who was at the time a very big star. After the show, Ernie went backstage and informed Bolger that he had locked up the rights to the musical play *An American in Paris* and he wanted Bolger to star in the production. Bolger, who also did not sign any papers and was suitably impressed by this spirited young man, also said, "Fine."

Without any real commitments, Ernie was now the proud owner of a nonexistent show starring a completely uncommitted star. This was show business without a net.

He needed a lawyer to cement the deal. He asked his patron Bill Paley to recommend the best show-business lawyer in New York. Paley said there was only one person to consult under such dubious circumstances: Howard Reinheimer. Somehow, Ernie beguiled his way into the famous attorney's office, who agreed to represent this phantom project.

Like Professor Harold Hill in *The Music Man,* Ernie convinced himself he had a show. He convinced us right onto Broadway.

The reality was that we went about it with an intense and detailed immersion. First of all, both being in show business, we knew something about the basic ingredients. We pored over all the contracts (Actors' Equity, Dramatists Guild, American Federation of Musicians, etc.), even including the boilerplate: what guarantees had to be offered principal performers, how much rehearsal time was required before taking a production on the road, and on and on. We went to school on the subject.

While Ernie investigated the tactical requirements, I went to work on *An American in Paris.* However, no matter how hard I tried, I couldn't make it work. *An American in Paris* had no story, I couldn't dream one up, and Ray Bolger did not lend himself to whatever role didn't exist in the first place.

Then Howard Reinheimer came to our rescue. Over the years Howard had tried for one or another client to obtain the rights to an English play called *Charley's Aunt*. It was a Victorian farce first performed in London in 1892 and was regularly revived and produced by stock and amateur companies, which threw off an annual income of fifty thousand pounds a year for the heirs of its author, Brandon Thomas. The heirs—Amy, Sylvia, and Jevon Brandon-Thomas—had invariably refused to risk the income on a musical version of the play. However, that was before the Ray Bolger factor. *The Wizard of Oz*, in which he played the scarecrow, was still fresh in England, and Bolger was a major star. His participation might make all the difference. Nevertheless, it would not be an easy thing to sell.

Someone, we decided, would have to go to England and convince the heirs to let us turn their cash cow into a musical show. That same someone would have to quit his job, since this campaign would take some time, and devote himself wholeheartedly to the project. Once again, as it happened in the Office of the Undersecretary of War for Air, all eyes settled on me. I knew England well enough to get around, and it made sense for me to quit my job since I could always piece together an income by getting small freelance composing assignments for radio programs thrown my way by Ernie at CBS.

Still, there was one other colossal problem. The play didn't work as a musical. Ray Bolger's part was not big enough. I went to work on the manuscript.

The story takes place at Oxford University in 1898, a period of ridiculous Victorian prudery. Two young students, Jack and Charley, have invited their girlfriends to attend an overnight varsity show festival. This is only possible during this starched, mannered age because Charley's aunt is expected to act as chaperone. When Charley's aunt sends word that she will be unable to attend, the plans are in ruins. Then Lord Fancourt Babberley, a neighbor from across the hall, enters to show off his costume as a Victorian dowager. This inspires the notion of using Lord Fancourt as Charley's aunt, which leads to endless gender confusion (a thing the English are especially fond of) and wholesome titillation.

Now the problem: Assuming that Bolger plays the lead—Lord Fancourt Babberley—how would he perform his athletic dance routines swaddled in the skirts of a Victorian dress? He couldn't. And yet I had to have him in that dress; the picture of him as a painfully unfeminine woman was essential to the comic core of the play. But I also had to get him out of that damn dress so that he could dance. The solution was pretty risky: I killed Lord Fancourt Babberley, the lead character. Charley would play both roles—himself and his own aunt. This would lead to an infinite variety of complications and setups and awkward situations. When Charley was in the room, the aunt was offstage resting; when the aunt was present, Charley was gone. His girlfriend, Amy, would ask plaintively, "Where's Charley?" Hence the new title, plus the new structure.

It was the winter of 1947 when I finished the revised version of the manuscript and prepared to go to England to make my pitch to the Brandon-Thomas heirs. I had enough money to finance the trip, plus some extra for emergencies. It did not seem like a risk, quitting my job and flying off to start a new career. I was still in my thirties and life still seemed in play. Everything about this move seemed natural, and we were fearless in our reckless overconfidence. It still seems unremarkable, fifty-five years later. All the chips were down—we knew that—but we had nothing to lose. We were determined to become Broadway producers and that's what we did.

*   *   *

I stopped in New York and saw Howard Reinheimer, who called a solicitor in London to arrange a meeting. I bought a new $125 suit at Brooks Brothers and flew back to the city that had the familiar smell of musky coal.

I stayed at Claridge's and, upon the advice of Howard Reinheimer, stopped off to visit a legendary character named Louis Dreyfuss. Louis Dreyfuss and his brother Max were in the music publishing business. That is a low-life kind of business, but these guys were gentlemen, so much so that all the great talent went to them to be published. The result was that, like any successful enterprise, they had been swallowed up by Warner Bros. in the 1930s. The deal was that they could no longer publish music of artists they had groomed within the United States. But the contract didn't say anything about England. So while Max stayed in the states, Louis moved to England and worked his way back into the music publishing business. Once their contracts ran out, the artists wanted to be published by Louis Dreyfuss. I could see why. Warner Bros. was a cold corporation and Dreyfuss was this wonderfully warm character with a bowler on his head. He was a big mug and he welcomed Americans, especially an American with music credentials. He had a shop on New Bond Street with a piano and he made me feel welcome while I was waiting for an answer from the heirs. We went riding and ate kippers and then went to town and caroused till all hours of the night. I was soothed and made patient by Louis, in this strange and foreign city.

Eventually I met with two sets of lawyers and turned over a copy of the revised manuscript to Amy and Sylvia and Jevon. The heirs, who were in the income business, took it very seriously. Amy Brandon-Thomas, who was the oldest of the children and lived in a fourteenth-century cottage outside of London, was a flamboyant woman in an eccentric, gentle sort of way, and she saw the benefits of the musical from the start, then brought the others along.

After a week or so the answer came. The Brandon-Thomases agreed to the deal on three conditions: first, that Ray Bolger would star in it; second, that it be presented on Broadway in a first-class theater; and third, that the revised version of the play be attached to the contract and be the basis of the musical. There was something else, something I hesitate to even mention, but it bears mentioning. Amy had a figurine that was made in 1892 to commemorate the first production of *Charley's Aunt*. It's the lead character dressed up as the Victorian dowager. If you look at that figurine, I swear it is the spitting image of Ray Bolger. That's all I have to say about it, but I think maybe it influenced Amy and Sylvia and Jevon to go along with us.

To celebrate our agreement, we dined at the Royal Automobile Club, a private club thick with tradition and dark with wood. It was a magnificent room, glistening with silver and rare crystal. The service was great, the atmosphere was bright, and I was happy. They passed around great platters of food and I, in a moment of exuberance, piled my plate high with cauliflower au gratin. Typically English. They were still on rationing, and I was dumb. The main dish was duck and I took a pretty hefty portion, really filling my plate. I was hungry. We started to eat and it was terrible. The cauliflower tasted of ammonia, and the duck tasted of fish. It was sea duck. Incidentally, you had to finish everything because of the rationing, so I cleaned my plate. I was sick for a couple of days afterward, and I can taste it to this day.

When I got back to the hotel I bought a four-dollar cigar and sat in the lobby and smoked it, trying to smoke out the taste of the dinner and savor the triumph of the deal. Then I went upstairs and called Ernie.

Chapter Ten

*O*nce *again we* had come to that critical junction—a moment of truth. Put up or shut up. We now had to actually produce a musical play. Two things are essential in order to produce a musical play: music and a play. (Technically, three things, if you include money.)

Setting up the musical part was relatively easy. After all, I had been the musical director of a movie studio for a few years and knew a lot of talented people. I persuaded one of the most gifted—Harold Arlen—to write the music for *Where's Charley?* At the age of forty-two, Harold Arlen was in the midst of a brilliant career. He had composed the music for *The Wizard of Oz,* including "Over the Rainbow." This was not his only popular classic composition. He'd written the music for such songs as "Stormy Weather," "Blues in the Night," and "Let's Fall in Love." He also had some ambition to write for the stage. His personal life was somewhat bumpy (he was married to a beautiful but emotionally fragile woman), and maybe that contributed to the weighty and haunting dimensions of his compositions.

And for the lyrics I hired my feisty old pal Frank Loesser, who periodically denounced me in public. (A custom dating back to the time when I deviously hired him away from Louis Lipstone at Paramount Pictures to work with Jule Styne; he got over my high-handed methods, but he couldn't break the habit of condemning me out loud.) In spite of that, I liked Frank. He had an interesting mind, always preoccupied with minutiae. He once wrote a song about the material he found in the bottom of his pocket: "Lint!" He wrote another about a leaky faucet: "Drip, Drip, Drip," as I recall.

He and his first wife, Lynn, had an act that they would perform at parties. They sang a number he had written called, "Baby, It's Cold Outside," a great duet and the high point of every party. It appeared in an Esther Williams film, *Neptune's Daughter,* and won an Academy Award.

Frank tried to come off like a street mug. It was, no doubt, the result of his mother's belief that he had undertaken a shady career. Her other son, Arthur, was the music critic for *The Cleveland Press* and head of the piano department at the Cleveland Institute—a noble profession, compared to a seedy songwriter. For spite, Frank lived out of the side of his mouth.

The remarkable thing about Frank was that he did everything well. In addition to writing terrific songs ("Praise the Lord and Pass the Ammunition"), he was an excellent caricature artist. He even made his own furniture; he had a workshop in his basement—a lathe, everything. The one thing that he couldn't do was drive a car, which, in Los Angeles, makes life almost impossible. There was, at the time, virtually no public transportation in southern California. People would have to pick him up or go to his home. In order to pull that off he had to be a very talented guy. Mountains invariably came to Mohammed.

*   *   *

Now that the music was in good hands, we needed the play. I had sketched the outlines for the Brandon-Thomases, but someone would have to write the libretto, line by line. Ernie and I went to New York and again asked our reliable mentor and counselor, Howard Reinheimer, for advice, and he said, well, the best writer on Broadway right now is George Abbott. The sixty-year-old Abbott had a long string of credits—*Three Men on a Horse, On Your Toes, Too Many Girls*—and was a true Broadway elder. Perfect. Could we get him to write and direct our play?

Try him, suggested Reinheimer. He has an office in Rockefeller Center. Just go up there and ask him. What have you got to lose?

Being the cocky guys we were, Ernie and I went to see George Abbott—Mister Abbott, as he was called by everyone. Mister Abbott had a simple office: a secretary, a chair, and a desk behind which sat the great man himself in his tall, distant composure. He was about six feet three, and Ernie used to call him the tallest gentile on earth. Under that diffident exterior, however, beat the heart of a soft romantic. He and his assistant, Harold Prince, would, from time to time, take an afternoon off, get a couple of girls, and go ballroom dancing. You have to be capable of a sentimental swoon to do something like that.

Reinheimer had called ahead and Mister Abbott was expecting us. He treated us with the formal respect that a call from Rhineheimer demanded. But it seemed to me that this meeting was an obligation, without promise. He was completely unimpressed when we told him that we had obtained the rights to make a musical out of *Charley's Aunt.*

"I know the play," he said with a kind of unspoken caution.

We told him that we had Ray Bolger for the lead. He remained underwhelmed. Then we said that we had Harold Arlen and Frank Loesser. He nodded solemnly.

Then he delivered his opinion. This was all well and good—Bolger was a great talent, Harold Arlen was a terrific composer, Frank Loesser (whom he didn't know from Adam) could no doubt write memorable lyrics—however, there was a fatal flaw in the structure of the play. The lead character was trapped in a one-joke story line. Successful musical plays require a little more dexterity in the story line.

Now it was my turn to display aplomb. I handed him my revised manuscript.

George Abbott was finally impressed. "This will work," he said with his customary thrift. The fatal plot flaw had been cured by my combining Charley and his aunt. The great Mister Abbott agreed to write and direct our play. This was a tremendous professional validation. The imprimatur of George Abbott gave us solid professional grounding and pumped up our confidence. One giant step for Feuer and Martin.

*   *   *

It was not to be an easy alliance. As George Abbott would one day note of our collaboration: "They're captains; I'm a captain." He was right. With three captains the ship is bound to be under a certain amount of strain. Our first clash came over the title. Clearly, we couldn't use *Charley's Aunt* for the musical. We had to give the play a different name so that the public would know it was not the old Victorian farce. This preoccupied everyone for a few days until, finally, Mister Abbott made a command decision. "We'll call it *Where's Charley?*" he said. It made a lot of sense since that was the question everyone in the play keeps asking when Charley is in drag playing his own aunt.

The trouble was that we (Ernie and I) didn't like it. The title didn't jump out at us. It had no . . . music.

"Come up with something better," said Mister Abbott, and that settled that. It would be *Where's Charley?* until we found something better. No one ever did.

There arose another "name" issue. What to call George Abbott. Given his seniority and majestic manner, everyone called him Mister Abbott. Ernie and I whispered behind his back, debating sotto voce whether, since we were paying his salary, we could get away with calling him George. We didn't think so.

Then came the crisis. Harold Arlen's house in Beverly Hills burned down. He lost everything—memorabilia, possessions— and, on top of that, his wife, Anya, had a nervous breakdown. Under the circumstances, he begged off, saying that he could not write the music for the show.

We were without a composer. Frank was dying to handle it alone. He had multiple gifts and I trusted him to pull it off. If he said that he could write the words and the music for the play, he could do it.

Mister Abbott was not so certain. He would have to go out to California and meet Frank Loesser and assure himself that the music would be compatible with the book. This trip would be a heavy burden for a couple of thinly financed producers trying to put together a show on a shoestring. The contract called for us to pick up all of his expenses and Mister Abbott only traveled one way— first-class. First-class airfare, first-class hotel, first-class restaurants. We had no choice; the contract was clear, we would foot the bill.

That settled it. "From now on," I told Ernie, "I'm calling him George."

*   *   *

George checked into the posh Sunset Towers where, after meeting Frank, satisfying himself that he had a professional handling the music and giving the go-ahead, he began to write the book on a portable typewriter. He was a very conscientious, no-nonsense guy, and he went to work immediately. He had the manuscript on one side of the desk and my revisions on the other, and he would type in the changes. I got Ernie outside and said, "What do we need him for? I can type my changes in the manuscript."

Fortunately, Ernie had the sense to shut me up. Of course, we needed him. He was George Abbott, a recognized, accomplished, and polished writer and director. More than once he tolerated our childish impudence and swallowed our guff, perhaps because he recognized something valuable in our contribution—call it boundless enthusiasm. The disputes arose and fell without leaving fatal wounds. Sometimes we were right, sometimes he was right. For instance, Frank and I had an idea about how to start the play. It seems corny now that I think back, but at the time we thought it was terrific. We wanted a big opening. Everyone would come out on stage and sing a rousing opening number, "I'm on My Way." It would introduce the cast and the fact that they were on their way to Oxford.

In comparison, George's opening seemed a little pale and sluggish to us and Ernie brought this up, along with the fact that Frank and I had worked up something livelier, something with a little more bounce to get the thing started.

In his economic way, George dismissed the idea. "This is a farce," he explained. "That means you must establish the premise. Later on you may break out in song, but not before you establish the premise."

"But the opening is not funny," protested Ernie.

George Abbott paused, then said: "You must establish the premise; funny is not essential while you are doing that."

Ernie reached into his pocket and handed George a pencil. "Write funnier," he said.

I do not remember George Abbott's answer. I doubt that he said anything at all. But it must have been galling for this proud Broadway patrician to be lectured by these two brash upstarts. And I wonder now that he bore it so quietly.

*   *   *

Meanwhile, the bicoastal effort was taking a toll. Posy was far along in a pregnancy, keeping pace with the unborn musical taking shape on Broadway. We were living in California while I was traveling back and forth to New York where the show was being organized; issues were left dangling in between. In retrospect, I neglected the domestic part of my life in favor of the show business obsession. I don't know that I could have done it any other way. I knew that Posy could handle things. My son Bobby would be yanked out of one school and put in another, and when it came time to give birth, someone would pull the baby out. I trusted her. My concentration lay elsewhere. After all, it was the beginning of our odyssey.

On April 30, 1948, Posy gave birth to our son Jed at Good Samaritan Hospital in Los Angeles. It was time to make the final commitment to the new career. It was past the point where it could all fall apart. We had Frank Loesser and George Abbott and, one way or another, a show was going to be produced. Ernie Martin quit his job at CBS and we all flew back to New York. To save money, the Feuer and Martin families settled into a three-bedroom sublet on 92nd Street and Park Avenue. The apartment was owned by Artur Rodzinski, conductor and music director of the New York Philharmonic, who was away on a world tour. Posy and Ernie's wife, Nancy, got along well, so there was no domestic shock from the living arrangements. Bobby had his own bedroom. We stuck Jed in an alcove where babies did what they did—cry and sleep.

Given the chaos and noise, Ernie and I needed a place to work, an office, and there again we came up lucky. This calls for another digression. There was, in California, a theatrical booking agency, Fanchon and Marco. The two owners were former ballroom dancers who specialized in the tango and saw the end of vaudeville coming. So they booked acts to play all the great movie palaces before the start of the film. It was a common thing in those days, in the forties, to see that last burst of vaudeville glitter before a movie: magicians, dancers, soft-shoe artists, singers. Fanchon, who was the lady in the partnership, took a liking to me. She said that she had an old office in the Paramount Building on Broadway and 43rd Street that lay vacant. They seldom got back to New York, so we were welcome to use it. When we went up there, on the eighth floor of the Paramount Building, we found that Fanchon and Marco had left their initials on the door—F. & M. Feuer and Martin. That single room with two desks facing each other and a telephone became our headquarters for the time being.

All the elements were in place—music, book—except for the third ingredient, money. We hired a general manager who worked out a budget and told us that we had to raise $150,000, which seems today to be a paltry sum, but was huge then. Fortunately, we only had to raise half. Ray Bolger was married to a woman named Gwen Rickard, who had some ambition to be in the theater and wanted some official role in the production. We gave her half the show and a credit as an associate producer, which turned out to be a brilliant tactical move. This ensured the loyalty of Ray Bolger and, second, that she would raise half the money.

Gwen and Ray were becoming close friends of the family, hanging out at the apartment. Ray was great with kids and loved playing with Bobby, who was about to turn seven. Ray was a sweet and easy man and left it to Gwen to manage his career. The relation-

ship was not unlike Danny Kaye and Sylvia Fine. Although, unlike
Fine, Gwen had no real push. She was one of those people who
seems aggressive, whom you think you're not gonna like, then you
find that there's no real toughness underneath. She didn't intrude
in the development of the show; she just wanted a legitimate reason to stick around and keep an eye on things.

It was not a problem to find backers. There were lists of people
who were eager to pony up $500, $1,000, or even $1,500 to be in-
cluded in the inner circle. For their small investment they would
get bragging rights about being Broadway angels, good seats on
opening nights, and the chance to smell greasepaint. We didn't
want any substantial backers because they might want some say in
how we ran things. And, as previously noted, we already had too
many captains.

It must have seemed like a telemarketing scheme, the way we
gathered these people—dentists, lawyers, businessmen, show-
business aficionados. I made some of the calls, Ernie made some of
the calls. "We are putting on a play starring Ray Bolger and wonder
if you might be interested in joining us. . . ." We would rent out a
rehearsal room and Frank and Lynn Loesser would gather twenty
or so rich people at a time and play the score. He'd always start off
with "Once in Love with Amy," which was the showstopper. Then
we'd give them contracts and let them go home, read them, and
decide.

In the end we came up ten thousand dollars short, but Gwen
Rickard agreed to find the extra money in exchange for extra
points in the profits. We were in no position to quibble.

If we had trouble finding backers, it was because we were new. A
lot of these backers stayed with us for all our shows. They'd come
to opening night and we'd have the seating arranged so that the
important ones were down front. My favorite was Harriet Ames,

one of the Annenburg sisters. Very rich. She was married to Paul Ames, whose father bought him a seat on the stock exchange. He was fascinated by the electric typewriter and would sit in his office all day and type thank-you letters. He also fancied himself well informed on current affairs. Television had just come out and he was very impressed by this new device and had strong opinions about the influence that it was going to have on the average American family of three.

"What is the average three?" I asked when he raised this topic at dinner.

"The average American family: a man, a wife, and a maid."

Harriet, however, was the dominating influence in the family, although not in any bullying way; it was just that she made the decisions without being pushy. Her sister, Enid, who funded The New York Botanical Garden in the Bronx, was married to a great big guy named Ira Haupt. We were invited to a party at Enid's house one night and Frank Loesser asked if I was going. I said yes, and he said, "I'll meet you in front of Ira Haupt."

* * *

Meanwhile, the casting continued, as did the clash of wills. We were casting the part of the ward, a key role requiring some spirit in the performance. I arrived for a two o'clock audition at 2:04. George didn't say a word, but merely looked down at his watch disapprovingly. At the end of the day, he said he was going to cast a certain actor as the ward.

"But he's not good enough," I objected. Ernie agreed with me.

"He's the best one who showed up today," replied George.

"Then we'll try another day," I insisted, and a call went out for another round of casting. We finally did get someone who fit the role and George agreed that it was worth the effort.

*   *   *

In the production of a Broadway show there is a kind of military timetable that cannot be disregarded. First, a theater is booked. A certain date is laid down for occupation of the theater. That means that you must tabulate the five weeks of rehearsals in New York, then add in another eight weeks for run-throughs and performances in Philadelphia where all the errors must be worked out, so that you can move back into the Broadway theater on the specified date. In our case, we were booked to move into the St. James Theater on 44th Street on October 11, 1948.

That meant that by the end of May, we all heard a clock ticking. First the casting and the search for the principal players. The hiring of accountants and managers—all these details were explained and handled by George Abbott, a veteran of fractions and specifics. Ernie and I went running from place to place, behind George, absorbing, learning, putting our two cents in when it seemed sure.

The rehearsals went on in three different sites. Singers and chorus were rehearsed in one hall, with Frank overseeing that group. I can still remember his brilliant rhymes:

The New Ashmolean Marching Society and Students Conservatory Band

The new Ashmolean could have licked Napoleon
With all those deadly instruments in hand
But to me it's bully
It satisfies me fully
When I hear that thunder close at hand
of the New Ashmolean Marching Society and Students
Conservatory Band.

Where did such ideas come from? There was Frank, an unfiltered Camel cigarette dangling from his lips, writing great lyrics. I have always been astounded by a mind that can dream up such things.

Ernie would make fun of some of his stuff, call it too sentimental, and Frank would say he's in the sentimental business. Frank wrote one song, "My darling, my darling, I've fluttered and fled like a starling, . . ." and Ernie would come in singing, "My darling, my darling, I farted, and you fled like a starling. . . ."

None of that snarling had any teeth.

Meanwhile, the principal players rehearsed with George Abbott, and there was one method actor who made the mistake of asking, "What should I be thinking about during this speech?"

And George's crisp reply was "Just say it and get off."

His direction was not mean or cruel, just efficient. George was uninterested in unimportant details. There was the St. James clock ticking in the back of his mind.

There was one last member of our staff who arrived at the theater every day with a copy of *The New York Times* crossword puzzle, which he filled in with the speed of someone writing a letter. He was our choreographer, George Balanchine. I didn't realize he was GEORGE BALANCHINE, who had recently founded the New York City Ballet. I just thought he was a regular choreographer who was very quiet and staged too many dances with people holding hands and turning in and out, out and under, while they still held hands. To me it looked more like a child's game than dancing. I was wrong.

By midsummer, *Where's Charley?* had taken form and George Abbott eased up and invited us out to his country home on Long Island. Off duty, he could be very charming. I can still remember the sight of him walking the length of the pool with Posy on his shoulders. Her head remained dry as he walked into the eight-foot-deep water, holding his breath.

And then we were back to reality or, rather, the theatrical version of reality. We combined dancers, singers, and principal players and had a run-through. The costumes were ready. The sets were being loaded for shipment. Before I was quite prepared, we were taking the show to Philadelphia.

Chapter Eleven

It was August and hot, but things such as climate and comfort did not register with us. We were completely immersed in the show.

There was a rattle of excitement as we rode the train down to Philadelphia—cast and crew. We checked into the Warwick Hotel, then went down to the Forrest Theater where the sight of the scenery on the sidewalk was, by itself, strangely compelling. The sets and drops were very neatly arranged so that the pieces would go into the theater in precise, functional order. You couldn't just stack it all up and stuff it all in because then you would be hunting for something lost in the clutter. It all had to be done according to a finely worked-out plan.

What had become clear by the time we got to the out-of-town phase was the complete devotion of each unit of the crew to the success of the show and, consequently, their sheer professional mastery of the business. Henry Corbisson, the production stage manager, was the sergeant major who ran the operation with no-nonsense composure and kept everything moving. That's what the stage manager does. He has it all down on a master script—lighting cues, scenery cues, actor cues, prop cues—the whole play.

The crew expected the stage manager to do a good job. In fact, they depended on it.

You could hear Corbisson calling out his lighting cues: "Two, five, nine A . . . GO!" and a spotlight would hit a mark when a lead character entered the scene. It's all done with electronic keyboards now, but then the stage manager had to use a radio to call the spots, to change the scenery, to drop the curtains. Backstage the clearings and cavities were packed with costume racks for quick changes for actors who didn't have time to go to the dressing rooms. Tables were laid out with props. Below the stage, a whole corps of seamstresses and laundresses were prepared to fit and sew and repair anything in an emergency. Overnight, they would clean and launder costumes that had to be fresh.

Over everything, like the hum of anticipation, was the hubbub of excited young performers. Actors were clearing their throats. Dancers were stretching; singers were vocalizing. Ray was in his dressing room where he met various visiting firemen. I always got a kick out of Ray—his innocent poses. The essential point about Ray was that he had no life off the stage and fell automatically into antic character when in doubt. If an Englishman came into his dressing room, he suddenly developed an English accent. Shamelessly. When the Englishman left, he took the accent with him and Ray went back to his own voice, whatever the hell that was.

If all the backstage and onstage activity seemed chaotic and disorganized, it was a misreading of the experience. There was order and purpose to all the pandemonium; Ernie and I were being given advanced degrees in the complicated virtuosity of the theater.

After the first day—the "take-in"—the cast showed up for one more day of boning up. Dancers, singers, and actors, all on the stage of the Forrest Theater. And from another makeshift section, the road orchestra. We couldn't afford the union per diem of bringing down the whole orchestra, so we just brought the key men—

the first violin, the first trumpet, the drummer, the pianist, and the conductor. The key men would work with the road orchestra. And on that first full day, as they tuned up and began playing the music from the show, the cast could hear it from behind the practice walls. These people had been working for four or five weeks on a bare stage with just a piano player plinking out a thin tune. Now, for the first time, they heard the full orchestra, and the stage lit up with emotion. So this is what it sounds like! Some combination of pride and relief overwhelms the cast and crew—always, even when the material is bad. It's like the feeling when you walk into a theater and hear the orchestra tuning up—that expectant moment of an unopened gift. Not that I ever felt it. For me this was a business—ditch digging. I never bought that sentimental, romantic, fancy side of the theater. I was too busy digging.

*   *   *

By the third day, we were ready for the "stop-and-go" rehearsal. You start at the beginning of the show and keep going until you hit a problem. Once you run into trouble, you stop and clear it up. If someone can't make an exit because a couch is in the way, you move the couch and change the mark. If Ray Bolger can't make a change on time, you put two dressing rooms in the wings and slow something down so that he can get onstage. If a prop won't work, you get one that will. The point is, you confront every single hitch and you fix it before you move on. You are forced to do it properly. It takes four days to go from the beginning to the final curtain in the stop-and-go, but it is the most important rehearsal of the show. If you do it right, if you pay attention and fix every single problem completely, nothing should go wrong during the performance. Now you can run the show.

I was basking in the aftermath of all that sweat when Ernie called me aside. "I want you to see this with your own eyes." He dragged me out to the lobby. There was a woman buying two tickets to *Where's Charley?* Someone was actually putting up money to see our show. Amazing! It was the first time that the relationship with the audience and money was brought home to me. Working in the movies, you never actually saw the flesh of a live customer. You put out a film and somebody in Omaha bought a ticket. Ernie worked in radio and he put on shows for people he never saw. But now we were looking at real people, customers laying out hard cash to see *Where's Charley?* The reality was emotional.

* * *

After the stop-and-go, we had the dress rehearsal. That is the first true performance of the show. It comes hard after the stop-and-go because by now time is precious. A Broadway theater is waiting. Time is always too short.

This is also the first time that we put the whole thing in front of a live audience with the full orchestra, and there is an atmosphere of emotional brinksmanship. Everybody is going all out, at full speed. And everybody expects a hit. The house is packed with friendly faces—relatives of the stagehands, members of a nearby dramatic school, and lots of backers. These are people who are pulling for you and feel as if they're part of the adventure. Posy and Nancy came down for the show and we felt that we were on the threshold of something wonderful. It's always important to see the show put on in front of a live audience: we get to time the laughs, see what works and what doesn't work. And it went, as I recall, pretty smoothly.

The brain trust met afterward, as we would after all preopening performances, this time in a coffee shop, and we made small criticisms of stage business. Some things came off better than others. Nobody was crazy about the big South American production number, but it couldn't be changed. It was essential to the story. George wanted to cut one song: when Allyn Ann McLerie, who was playing the part of Amy, sang about the objects in a bachelor's room. The rest of the criticism was over minutiae. George Abbott was not a perfectionist. He settled for the best available solution and didn't hold out for the unattainable, which kept the thing moving. He said some business needed work, he fussed over a few other bits and said he would fix them, and then he left us there. He placed a dime on the table. "This is for mine," he said, referring to his coffee. It was, in a way, quintessential Abbott: utterly correct, utterly compartmentalized. He could be charming and generous when he was off duty, but he could also be fastidiously and astringently exact when he was working.

The next day was opening night. The first paying audience and, again, the emotions ran sky high. Ray worked his heart out, almost literally. After all, this was a farce, which means that there's a lot of running around, a lot of entrances and exits, a lot of falling down, leaping around, jumping up and down—all done at a very high pitch. It's very physical and very difficult. And Ray went all out. In fact, he went too far. After the show, Ernie and I went backstage and he was lying on the couch like a dead man. Gwen was standing over him, looking grave. "We should call a doctor," she said. Ray'd worked himself into a state of total exhaustion. Ernie and I just stood there, seeing our whole world moaning on the couch, and said (I think at the exact same instant), "Oh, shit!"

Opening night almost turned into closing night. To begin with, Ray was a very physical performer. Not a great dancer, he didn't have the charm or smooth, graceful form of Gene Kelly or the elegant style of Fred Astaire. But he always had a lot of energy. He was what we used to call an "eccentric" dancer. He'd do all these "rube" moves that you might expect to see in a cornball country fair, but he did them with a tuxedo on and it worked. However, on this particular night of killer high energy, it looked like he might take us with him.

As he was lying on the couch, moaning and barely conscious—Ernie and I frozen with fear—Frank comes storming into the dressing room in his usual state of gruff indignation. He starts right in, blistering this half-conscious star: "Listen, you son-of-a-bitch, how many times do I have to tell you about the tempo of that number. . . ." We were waiting for the doctor, and Gwen, the custodian of Ray Bolger's well-being, rose to the occasion. She threw Frank out of the dressing room.

The doctor showed up and pronounced Ray physically exhausted, unable to perform again. For how long? I asked.

"Indefinitely."

They took him away in an ambulance and we sat there in the dressing room, convinced that we were doomed, or worse. We turned to the only true grown-up in the bunch, George Abbott.

What do we do?

"Wait," he said with infuriating sangfroid. "He'll probably get better and come back to the show."

And if he doesn't?

Abbott shrugged. "We close the show. Ray Bolger is not just the star—he is the show."

* * *

We spent three days in Philadelphia in a state of bewildered, frenzied, and idle desolation. Reports came from the hospital that Ray was "resting," but no definite word about his return. At the theater, where the cast and crew were awaiting the verdict (while still being paid), backstage seemed like the demoralized campground of a defeated army. Actors were draped over chairs, dancers were sprawled on the floor, and stagehands were getting that disinterested glaze of mercenaries looking to enlist in a new cause. The head of steam that had been building up was fast leaking out of the company.

Meanwhile, Ernie and I were trying to find ways to console ourselves. It wasn't easy. We had six months of advance sales. That was good. However, the sales had come on the strength of Ray Bolger's name, and if he dropped out, all the tickets would have to be refunded. Posy and Nancy, unable to listen to such ping-pong peevish chatter, returned to New York. And on the third day, Ray returned to the theater. He looked fit and rested. And he acted as if nothing had happened. "Let's get to work," he said in his ebullient way.

He gave all the performances for the rest of the four-week stay in Philadelphia, and the only thing that gave Ernie and me grief was the notices. The critics were mild about the show. Oh, it'll be better in New York, we agreed. So on a Tuesday in early October we "froze" the show. No more changes until we opened in New York. That way the cast could grow comfortable in the parts without the daily fidgeting with lines and stage business. It was important to allow the performers to develop confidence in their roles.

* * *

We settled into the St. James Theater on 44th Street where, after three previews, and opening night, we were a flop. There were seven newspapers in New York City at the time and six gave us terrible reviews. Posy and Nancy had bought expensive new dresses and gone to the flower market on 28th Street and bedecked our apartment with all the blossoms in the world. There, as the flowers died, Adolph Green (who was married to the leading lady of the show, Allyn Ann McLerie) read aloud the death notices. As I recall, Brooks Atkinson's review was the murderer: "*Where's Charley?* is a rhetorical question. Where's Bolger? is more to the point." The general tone of the criticism went downhill after that.

It didn't matter. Atkinson wrote for *The New York Times* and that was the only review that counted. Walter Kerr of the *Herald Tribune* liked Bolger, but . . . well, these were not money notices. They were the notices of a failure. The one solidly good notice came from the *World Telegram* and Frank Loesser threw the guy a party.

However, once again the miracle of the buttery berth saved my butt.

On the first matinee—a Saturday—Bobby went to see the show with a school friend. They sat in the second row. Posy and I stood in the rear of the theater. During the second act, Ray performs the showstopper, "Once in Love with Amy." It is a long number with a song, some dancing, some more song, and some more dancing. After the first chorus and some dancing, Ray, as we say in the theater, "went up." He forgot the words to the song. Now, Ray was the sort of person who had very good stage presence. He could step out of character, which is what he did. He stopped the orchestra and came down front.

"Ladies and gentlemen, I forgot the words. Does anybody here know the words to this song?"

A voice came out of the dark. "I do, Ray."

He can't see because the lights are in his eyes and he laughs and says, "Then why don't you sing along with me."

Bobby, who had been listening to the demo records of the show for weeks and knew the lyrics cold, began to sing: "Oh, once in love with Amy, always in love with Amy."

By now the audience, knowing that the show is in the hands of a seven-year-old boy, is in a great mood, laughing encouragement.

They go through the number. After the performance, we take Bobby backstage and we can hear Ray yelling, blowing his gasket to the stage manager. "What the hell is going on here! Kids screwing up my number! Why the hell do they let kids in the theater in the first place."

Bobby heard Ray's outburst and stuck his head in the dressing room. "It was me, Ray."

It took him a second to comprehend. Then Ray just opened and closed his mouth like a fish. He really loved Bobby. Then he said, "Oh, shit!" and grins. "We were pretty good out there."

Later, he came to me. "You know, I think there was something to that."

"What do you mean?" I asked.

"The audience really liked that. Maybe I should try something like that again tonight."

"No," I insisted. "Not tonight. Saturday night audiences are the worst. Very unsophisticated. All tourists. Try it another night."

And that's what he did. On another night, he broke out of the character and asked the audience to sing along. He would cue them up—it's the sort of number that has gaps in which you can shout out the next lyric—and they would join in.

The reviews were deadly, but the word-of-mouth after that was terrific. And we had six months of advance sales to spread the word-of-mouth. Because of Bobby and the impromptu duet, we had gone over the heads of the critics. We had a smash hit. *Where's Charley?* ran for three years. On opening night, "Once in Love with Amy" was less than four minutes long. By the end of the run it was a twenty-minute number.

Chapter Twelve

I was flat broke. The show was a critical flop. And I was on top of the world.

There is a simple explanation for such an inappropriate reaction: it didn't feel like failure. It felt like a great victory. Everything worked out just the way we figured. We could handle Broadway. We started out to produce a Broadway play and that's just what we did. Maybe *Where's Charley?* wasn't a fabulous success with the critics, but the audiences didn't know that; they loved it. Maybe I couldn't afford to support my mother, but it was only a temporary condition; Stan could fill in the gap. The only significant fact was that we were right about how far we could take this absurd ambition. And we were just getting started.

Meanwhile, I needed an income. The money from *Where's Charley?* would not start to flow for six or seven months, not until the backers were paid off. We wouldn't see any money until the production started to show a profit.

Ernie took a job as general manager of the *Where's Charley?* company for $150 a week and I picked up freelance assignments arranging musical background for *Ford Theater of the Air* at about $350 a week.

And so life went on and our heads were up high, looking for the next show, which was certain to come along any minute. That's how it felt: they were up there in the wind, all these free-floating ideas for musicals, and we were sniffing the air, looking for something to grab on to. Sure enough, we plucked the next show right out of the sky. One day I got a call from Ernie, who was in California on some family errand, and he tells me that Nancy is in bed reading an anthology of Damon Runyon stories called *Guys & Dolls*.

"That's it," I said. I didn't have to hear any more. I had already heard the title of our next show. Ernie knew it, too. That's how it worked with us. We were in complete harmony. It had to be that way. It was essential to maintain the pact that we agreed on everything. The deal was that the "no" guy won every argument. If there was ever a disagreement about anything—the material, the project, the talent—that was the end of it; we killed it. The "no" vote rules. Otherwise you would have a half-hearted collaboration. Not that we ever spelled it out, or even said it in so many words. But it was clearly understood. Just like our partnership.

"Yeah," said Ernie from California about our next project, *Guys & Dolls,* "I think so, too."

* * *

When Ernie got back to New York we wasted no time. The mood was on us and we were hot. It couldn't wait. We found the guy who handled the Runyon estate, a theatrical agent named Robbie Lantz. Very nice man. He had an office in the fifties on Park Avenue and we went up there in our cocksure, determined way and said we wanted to make a musical out of *Guys & Dolls*.

Robbie was delighted. He was there to protect the Runyon interests, and the more interests the better.

"That's fine, fellas, which story?"

Well, here again, it could have been a snag. We didn't have a specific story. We just had the title of the book. And there was no single story in the book called "Guys & Dolls." That was just Runyon's affected way of referring to the men and women who inhabited his Broadway-gangster milieu. Of course, that was enough for us. We'd pick a story later; we knew what we wanted. It was a taste, a feel, a belief about the combination of Damon Runyon and a Broadway musical. About that there was complete certainty. We could always find an unencumbered story, that is, a story not sold to the movies.

Nevertheless, we did not yet have it.

Lantz, being an orderly, efficient man, another professional trained to specifics, pushed us.

"Pick one and we'll make a deal," he demanded.

No, we insisted. Our enthusiasm was running high, and to start chasing the right story now would slow us down.

Be practical. Let's find an available property. . . .

I had a better idea. "Draw up a contract committing us to produce a Broadway musical based upon 'X,' 'X' to be filled in later."

Done.

*   *   *

When the deal was signed (still in its vague, tender state of "X"), I called Frank Loesser with the news. "I'm in," he declared. "I love Runyon."

With his unchecked enthusiasm, Frank went straight ahead and wrote a song. He wrote it without knowing a thing about the show, the story . . . anything. He, too, was inspired by the title. It was a terrific piece of music written as a roundelay for three guys in a mildly contrapuntal form. Frank called it "A Fugue for Tinhorns," but it would later come to be titled "Can Do."

I got the horse right here, the name is Paul Revere
And here's a guy that says
If the weather's clear
Can do, can do—
This guy says the horse can do . . .

There is a kind of kinetic jolt you get when something works like that, when three guys click, all come to the same conclusions, and see the same possibilities; the accumulated energy is greater than the sum of one guy's exuberance. We were on fire.

Now we had to find a story to attach to Frank's song. It arrived sometime in the spring of 1949: "The Idyll of Miss Sarah Brown," a Runyon gem. Sergeant Sarah Brown was running the Save-a-Soul Mission, loosely based on the Salvation Army, which was particularly unsuccessful in attracting sinners in spite of the fact that it was situated in the heart of sinful Manhattan. The mission was so bad at doing good that the regional general was coming to town to decide whether to keep the mission open. When the biggest gambler in town, Sky Masterson, hears of this great moral crisis, he decides to stick in his two cents, since he has a personal interest in keeping the attractive Sergeant Sarah Brown in visual range. At a local crap game, he offers the following bet to all the players: "I will put up cash and you will put up a marker. If I lose, you win cash. If I win, you will have to attend one prayer meeting."

No true degenerate gambler could resist such a bet.

Naturally, Sky Masterson won, and the gamblers, in all their shady and colorful shapes, attended the prayer meeting while the regional general is present and the mission is saved. This puts Sergeant Sarah Brown under Sky's spell and leads to the love story: the gambler and the missionary.

The first writer who wanted to take a whack at the book was Paddy Chayefsky, who would one day become one of America's foremost social satirists, but who was, at the time, a twenty-six-year-old wunderkind who had accumulated a lot of high-quality credits as a television writer (*Philco Television Playhouse*). But in spite of all the promise and talent, Paddy was a little too intense for this particular project, and although he came back again and again, I never had the feeling that he was a serious possibility for our author. For one thing, he demanded that we let him write the music as well as the book, and no matter how many times I told him that we already had Frank Loesser and that was nonnegotiable, he kept trying to get a crack at the whole thing. There was no doubt that he had the talent and the energy to do the job; I just never believed that he was willing to submit to Damon Runyon, which is what you would have to do to write this kind of book.

* * *

There is a fuzzy period in which the progress of the show became muddled in our travels back and forth to California. We finally moved out there—this I know—for a long season of indefinite work. We rented a house in Beverly Hills and signed Jo Swerling to write the book. Paddy Chayefsky just drifted off the project; both sides lost interest in each other. There were no hard feelings, just a clear recognition on everyone's part that this wasn't going to work. He didn't have the essential Runyonesque *dese, dems,* and *dose* in his blood. We were all relieved.

Swerling, who had a big house in Malibu, had a huge string of film credits, including work on *It's a Wonderful Life, A Lady Takes a Chance, The Pride of the Yankees, Lifeboat* . . . a big talent. He was a fifty-six-year-old Russian who had done a lot of work with Frank Capra, and his presence alone lent weight to the project. He was gentle and Jewish and had a soft sense of humor.

Ernie and I began to work with him at his splendid beach house in Malibu where he smoked cheap cigars and wrote, in time, a book for the show. There was, however, something still not quite right about it, and Ernie and I suffered over this problem while Jo sat in the sun, content with what he had done. Finally, Ernie cracked the problem. He came in one day and said, "There has to be a bet."

"Of course," I agreed, seeing in a blaze of understanding what had been lacking and what Ernie had solved. "And it has to be over a dame!" Ernie had diagnosed the problem and I had fleshed it out.

Swerling, however, was totally in the dark. What bet?

A bet that involves a doll. It's crucial to the drama. The stakes have to be important. We're writing about gamblers and they have to gamble with something important.

Swerling was unconvinced.

"Look, we are talking about crap shooters," Ernie said. "These guys bet on cheesecake, for Christ's sake! This whole thing, the whole show, cries out for a bet."

"Give me an example," offered Swerling.

"I have it," I said. "It's an old plot, but they use it in *Sailor Beware*. There's this one dance hall beauty who never gives anyone in the fleet a tumble. Finally, one of the sailors—a real ladies man—bets that he can break the ice. Everyone in the fleet gets in on the bet."

"So?" asked Swerling.

"That's the bet," I said. "Sky Masterson makes a bet that he can get into Sarah Brown's pants. That's how he gets all the gamblers to come to the mission!"

We loved it. Swerling was highly indignant. "You want me to steal a plot, somebody else's work! I will not do it. I have my reputation, my honor . . ."

He went on and on about his honor while we were trying to convince him about something pretty basic. We argued all day, but he wouldn't budge. He wouldn't even agree to find his own variation on the plot or see that a bet was essential to the characters of the people who inhabit the world of *Guys & Dolls*.

And that's how we saw that Swerling was the wrong guy for us. It was basic. Irreconcilable differences. We finally had to fire him, although he insisted that he still receive first billing in the credits for the play and retain some small percentage of the royalties. This in spite of the fact that not one of his words ever appeared in the show. This from a man who was so touchy about his reputation and his honor, although how his reputation would be protected by first billing is a real brain twister.

*   *   *

This presented another problem. Before moving to California we had already gotten the financial backing for the show. *Guys & Dolls* was going to be a little more expensive than *Where's Charley?* but given our track record, we had no trouble raising about two hundred thousand dollars. The shares were divided into fifty units, worth about four thousand dollars each. We didn't have help, as we did in the first show, but we were a proven team, and with only one or two of Frank's songs and a title, we quickly sold out the shares.

Most of the investors from *Where's Charley?* came back onboard; they would stay with us for all of our shows. It was March of 1950 when we parted with Jo Swerling, and we were obliged to inform the backers that the show would have to be placed on hold for at least six months until we found another author. We were obliged to give them a chance to pull out, now that the timetable had been broken. Well, they all stayed with us, with one exception: Billy Rose. He was always very careful with his money and didn't risk long-term investments, even though he only had one unit sunk into the show. For the rest of his life, however, he would complain that we locked him out of *Guys & Dolls*.

Chapter Thirteen

*A*fter the California fizzle, New York felt colorfully creative. I needed a place to get down to real work after all that West Coast nonsense. Posy and I rented three floors of a brownstone on East 64th Street, and I began again the ditch-digging toil of putting the show back together.

We were under tremendous pressure to get *Guys & Dolls* moving. After all, the financing had been arranged, the backers were waiting (except for Billy Rose), and we had just thrown out the whole book. The first thing we had to do was to find another writer.

Fortunately, I knew the perfect guy: Abe Burrows. He had everything I wanted. Not only had he been a New Utrecht High School classmate (which counted for something, although I couldn't say what), he had a very down-to-earth yet erudite wit. I had seen it firsthand at all the show-business parties. With great gusto, Abe would break into song parodies: "The Girl with the Three Blue Eyes," or "I'm Walking Down Memory Lane Without a Single Thing to Remember . . ." Although he was a terrible piano player, Abe was very popular at parties. Come to think of it, the bad piano playing added to the effect of his humor. The other thing was that

Abe was also very well read and highly educated, but he kept that hidden under the surface glaze of a street-wise, Brooklyn mug. Furthermore, I knew that I could work with him. Abe was a real sweet man. I never saw him get mad. But I also knew that there were many more layers of untapped depth.

My problem was how to lure him away from a very well-paying, steady job to work in an extremely speculative and entirely shaky enterprise. At the time—spring of 1950—he was the chief writer on a very popular radio show, *Duffy's Tavern*, which was the *Cheers* of its day. (Incidentally, his son, Jimmy, used to hang around the theater while we rehearsed. Jimmy Burrows would later produce *Cheers* and *Will & Grace* and directed lots of episodes of *Frasier.* There was another kid hanging around backstage and he, too, later drifted into show business: Robert Klein, the future comedian. The last kid I'm gonna mention—because it's starting to depress me, how much talent I failed to spot—was Alan Alda, the son of the star of our show, Robert Alda. I didn't know they were gonna grow up into big-time celebrities.

Meanwhile, Ernie and I launched our campaign to enlist Abe as our writer. We told him that he'd be crazy not to give up this very large paycheck in order to write the book for our foolproof future smash hit *Guys & Dolls*.

"I got families to support," he argued. (Abe had been divorced and was about to marry Carin). "This is a very risky thing you're asking me to do."

"Perfect," I answered. "*Guys & Dolls* is a show that is about gamblers. Risk takers. You'll know just how it feels. See, you're already ahead of the game!"

He had another strong argument: "I've never done a show."

"Don't worry," I reassured him. "We'll guide you through all the mine fields. We've done this before, you know."

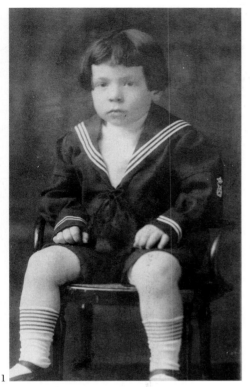

Cy at four years old in Brooklyn, 1915.

The mysterious Herman Feuer,
Cy's father.

Cy working as a lifeguard for the Echo Lake Tavern in the Adirondacks, 1930.

3

Posy in her twenties.

4

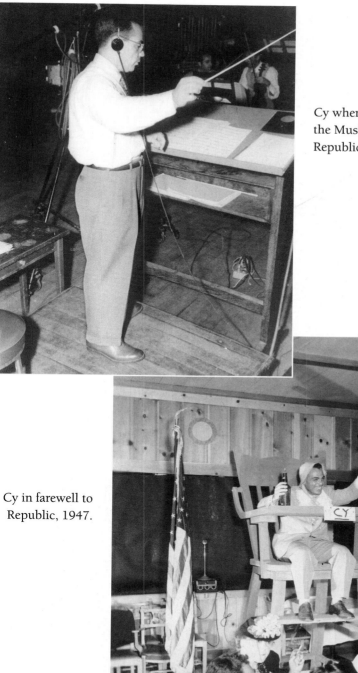

Cy when he was head of
the Music Department of
Republic Pictures, 1941.

5

6

Cy in farewell to
Republic, 1947.

Captain Feuer of the Army Air Force in 1943.

Posy and Cy at a party at Abe Burrows's house, late '50s.

Posy poses with Robert, twelve, left, and Jed, five, in 1953.

Straight Line

Joke!

George S. Kaufman, Cy, and Ernie Martin at the 46th Street Theatre during rehearsals for *Guys & Dolls*.

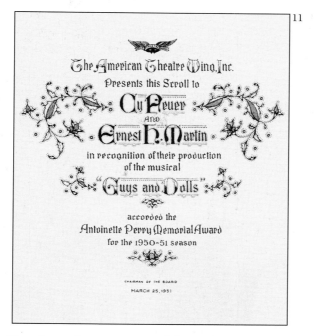

The plaque that accompanied the 1951 Best Musical
Tony Award for *Guys & Dolls*.

Abe Burrows, Cy, and Frank Loesser working on *How to Succeed
in Business Without Really Trying*, 1960.

Taking a break in Paris while shooting the film *Cabaret* in Germany, 1970.

Posy at the helm
of the family boat,
the *Posy Lee*.

Posy, in a picture
taken by Warner
LeRoy, 1970.

Feuer & Martin wearing
their game faces, 1969.

The 1962 Tony Award ceremony for *How to Succeed in Business Without Really Trying*.
From left to right: Ernest H. Martin, Cy Feuer, Robert Morse, Willie Gilbert, Charles
Nelson Reilly, Jack Weinstock, Abe Burrows, Elliot Lawrence.

Cy suspends hostilities with Bob Fosse to conduct "Tomorrow Belongs to Me" from the beer garden scene of the film *Cabaret,* 1971.

Cy exchanging a few words with HRH Princess Anne after receiving the British Academy Award for *Cabaret* (1972).

During the shooting of *A Chorus Line,* 1983.

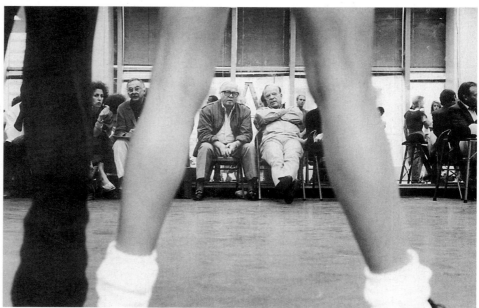

Rehearsals for *A Chorus Line* with Richard Attenborough, 1983.

In Sun Valley with Stan, 1980.

Amused, 1982.

Directing Liv Ullman in *I Remember Mama,* 1979, photographed by Jill Krementz.

25

With granddaughter Kate Feuer, 1992.

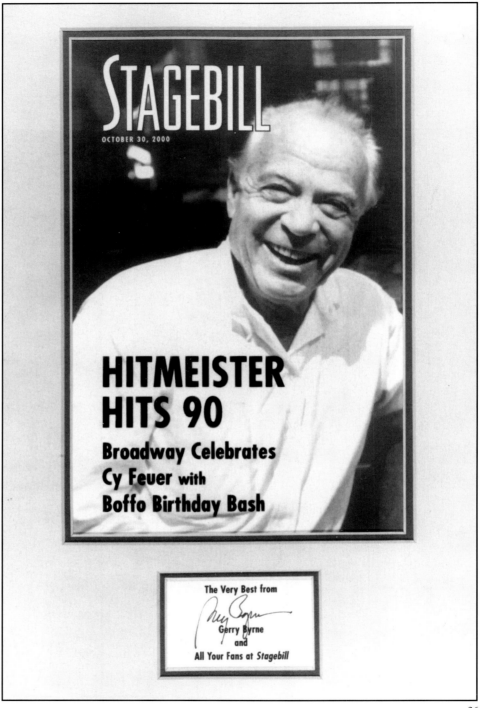

STAGEBILL

OCTOBER 30, 2000

HITMEISTER
HITS 90
Broadway Celebrates
Cy Feuer with
Boffo Birthday Bash

The Very Best from

Gerry Byrne

Gerry Byrne
and
All Your Fans at *Stagebill*

In retrospect, I'm a little ashamed of throwing out that particular promise. It is true that we stumbled our way to a modest success by producing *Where's Charley?* but it's not as if we had earned an advanced degree in theater arts. In fact, you could make a good case that we got by mostly on pure luck. Nevertheless, Abe bought it.

* * *

We went to work on the show in my new apartment on 64th Street. Abe was a night writer, having developed that habit from his radio days. We'd have dinner at Abe's place on York Avenue—he was a great cook—and then Carin and Posy would do whatever they did while Abe and I went over to my place and wrote in the den. He'd have a huge glass of bourbon and soda, which he would refill whenever the plane fell below the drought level, and write in his longhand fashion the brilliant start of *Guys & Dolls*. As we worked late into the night, it became clear to me that Abe had a great gift and understood exactly what we had been trying to convey to all the other writers who came and went. It was this: Damon Runyon was a genius for getting the sound of a Broadway hustler down on the page. It was wonderful to read. However, it did not translate into dialogue. I had run some of the movies based on his stories, "Little Miss Marker" and "Lady for a Day," and the dialogue didn't work. It worked when you read it, but not when it was spoken out loud.

When I analyzed it, I saw that Runyon wrote in the present tense and in the first person and used no contractions. He didn't use "-don't" or "won't" or "can't." It was "do not," "will not," or "can not." This gave his writing an internal punctuation that has its own punchy flow. But when the written lines were spoken, it didn't lay right on the ear. The exaggerated tone of the text simply couldn't be uttered with any credibility. It was a caricature of speech.

For example: "I am standing in front of Mindy's, minding my own business, when along comes Big Red from Philadelphia and says to me as follows: 'Have you ever been to Europe?' Not wanting to answer Big Red hastily, I say, 'Which Europe do you mean?' Big Red surprised: "Why, is there more than one Europe?"

Or: "She is the kind of doll who gets married any time she feels like it. To date she has felt like it four times and is now beginning to feel like it again."

That reads great on the page. I called it "Runyonese." Abe understood the problem and fiddled with the tenses and contractions and adapted the dialogue so cleverly that you were fooled into thinking that you were hearing Runyon.

Listen to Abe:

(Nathan Detroit, the "sole owner and proprietor of the oldest established permanent floating crap game in New York," starts to make his entrance. His two cronies are already onstage, being addressed by police lieutenant Brannigan.) I understand that Nathan is having a tough time trying to find a place for his game. Well, you can tell him for me that the heat is on. *(As he starts to exit the stage, Nathan enters the scene, not seeing Brannigan.)*

Fellas, I am in terrible trouble. That lousy Brannigan . . . *(His cronies shush him, indicating the policeman. Nathan, to Brannigan.)* Lieutenant, I hope you do not think I was talking about you. There are other lousy Brannigans.

Nathan, I understand you are having a difficult time trying to find a place for your game.

Yes, Lieutenant, the heat is on, as you must know from the fact that you now have to live on your salary. *(Brannigan exits.)*

What does that cop want from me? I have been running the crap game ever since I was a juvenile delinquent.

It was an uncanny adaptation because it caught the spirit of Runyon, it sounded like Runyon, and yet it was Abe's spin.

When we had three scenes of the first act, we decided to find a director to push the project along. It was still early summer and we wanted to open in the late fall. That meant we had to move quickly. Max Gordon, a friend, cabled George S. Kaufman, the dean of the American theater, who was vacationing in the south of France, and said he couldn't pass up this show. Kaufman was a fellow panelist with Abe on a very popular television show called *This Is Show Business*. George was fond of Abe who arranged a meeting.

It is hard to exaggerate the awe in which George S. Kaufman was held by the artistic universe. Not just for his two Pulitzer Prizes (*Of Thee I Sing* and *You Can't Take It With You*), but for a lifetime of pretty distinguished work in the theater. He was also a founding member of the Algonquin Round Table, where he traded quips with the likes of Alexander Woollcott, Franklin P. Adams, Dorothy Parker, Harpo Marx, Robert Benchley, et al. Once, when a publicist asked how he could get his leading lady's name in the newspaper, Kaufman, then drama editor of *The New York Times*, replied, "Shoot her!"

There is no doubt that Kaufman was brilliant, but I always had the feeling that he had a body of quips rehearsed and ready to pull out when the occasion arose, which is not to diminish his immense stature. All those Round Table knights worked on sharpening their quips. Except, maybe Harpo.

At the time, Kaufman lived in a penthouse overlooking Park Avenue with his second wife, Leueen McGrath, a woman of such delicate radiance that she illuminated even rooms crowded with movie stars. That she was twenty-five years younger than the sixty-year-old Kaufman seemed only an insignificant detail. After all, he was the legendary "swordsman" who conquered every leading lady on Broadway (not to mention some of the understudies, the chorus girls, and more than a few stray members of the audience). In her diary, the film star Mary Astor recorded a blissful day in 1936 in which they made love "twenty—count them, diary, twenty (times). . . ." Such fine detail was made public by her husband's divorce lawyers.

To look at him, however, was a whole other matter. He was tall and lanky and had a shrub of untamed hair growing north. He seemed to be in a permanent slouch, weighed down no doubt by the burden of having to speak, which was something he didn't seem to enjoy, unless he was delivering some deathless bon mot. Kaufman was aloof, but in a good way. He didn't waste words on polite greeting or insincere flattery or small talk. But when he spoke, it carried all the authority of a great concentrated effort. (On the other hand, maybe he was justifiably exhausted.)

He read the first four scenes of *Guys & Dolls* and said in his severe and laconic way: "There's something very good here. But we must be careful and not compromise."

I was thrilled. That meant that he took the job.

* * *

George had a long string of thoughts and suggestions, the most important of which was that the book needed a secondary story. Sky Masterson and Sergeant Sarah Brown were fine, but it was essential to have a parallel story going on at the same time. He came up with a fiancée for Nathan Detroit—Miss Adelaide. And in his ingenious fashion, he added just the right touch of whimsical evasion to the relationship: "They have been engaged for fourteen years."

With that simple stroke, George Kaufman expanded the story of *Guys & Dolls* to its proper proportions. It was magnificent.

He then asked Abe if he could come down to Bucks County where he had a country home and they could work on the book in peace. "When do you want us there?" I asked.

He turned and pointed at me and said in a stern, commanding voice, "Not you. Just me and Abe."

I must have looked confused. He explained: "Three cannot collaborate. It's not a fair fight. Two guys can fight it out. That's the way I work. So you're out."

That was fine. That was great. That was George S. Kaufman taking charge.

George snatched Abe and brought him to his Pennsylvania manse, Barley Sheaf Farm, which was suitably old and venerable and outfitted with a croquet lawn. He locked Abe in an attic room he called a study and would, from time to time, collaborate. The maid would be sent up with breakfast and lunch and dinner while George entertained us day visitors on the lawn with splashes of witty conversation and the occasional lettuce leaf. And while Abe was up there sweating over George's suggestions and criticisms, George and Moss Hart and company would all play croquet, a game that seemed completely pointless to me. Polo without horses.

During my visits to the farm, I noticed something almost human about George Kaufman, whom I had mistakenly taken for a Jewish Abe Lincoln. He was an extremely jealous man. Every time some young, handsome actor/dancer/writer/companion came by, George kept a close eye on Leueen. She had been an actress and was still quite a dish, and she was by nature a flirt. This didn't help George's disposition, but it did add a lively undertone of latent drama to the atmosphere.

Because of the crush of time, we were also casting the show. We were in a panic because we could not find a suitable actress to play

Sarah Brown. Three days before rehearsal, Ernie called and said he had found the perfect candidate; her name was Isabel Bigley. He would drive her down to the farm so that she could audition for Kaufman. They were expected for dinner. Ernie was bringing her down in his Jaguar. He was a car buff.

While we were waiting for Ernie and Miss Bigley, I told my famous Jaguar story. After *Where's Charley?* opened, Ernie and I somehow got into an English mood. We both bought Jaguars. Mine was an old classic model—prewar—very low slung. One day I was driving down Second Avenue to a rehearsal hall when I was stopped by a red light. One of the Bowery derelicts happened to be crossing the street and was fascinated by this unusual automobile stopped for a light in his territory. He bent down to try to read the name, which was embedded in a disc on the hood. Obviously it was a difficult thing to do, given his unsteady condition. The traffic light changed and he was still there, weaving back and forth in front of the car, trying to bring the name of the car into focus. Meanwhile, the cars in back of me began to honk to get him moving. The derelict stood up straight, gazing ahead at the line of cars impatiently honking in his direction, and held up his hand. "I'm reading!" he said with all the dignity of a duke.

The light had turned red again and was about to change back to green when the derelict, bent into his task, began to slowly slide down into the gutter, exhausted by all that reading effort. He had fallen asleep. The street was a very noisy place and tempers were getting red hot, so I got out and lifted the man, dragging him over to the sidewalk.

At that instant, a policeman happened by. "What's going on here? Did you hit him? We better call for an ambulance."

I explained the situation to the skeptical policeman, who saw that the derelict was not injured, merely sleeping. Still, he took down all the vital information, then said to me in that New York cop style of plain common sense, "What the hell kind of car is that to be driving down here?"

It was the only time I ever saw George Kaufman reduced to tears from laughing.

When Ernie and Isabel Bigley arrived after midnight, he said that they got lost in his Jaguar. By the way, she got the part.

* * *

George and Abe worked well together. That is, George told Abe what he should do and Abe did it. George did not do much writing. He was a collaborator. He was more pensive, more the godlike presence who decided what worked and what didn't. And his instincts were exact.

When we had the book, which didn't take too long, we moved into the 46th Street Theater, which is now the Richard Rodgers Theater. It was ideal. It had stadium seating, which meant that the seats rose gradually so that no one was blocked from seeing the stage. And we had tagged a label onto the title. The show was now called *Guys & Dolls, A Musical Fable of Broadway*. This gave us some license in stretching our story and letting the audience know that we were not there to be judged literally.

Ernie and I quickly decided that we were going to break some rules in the casting. First, the chorus boys would have to display a certain amount of machismo so that no clearly effeminate dancers or singers would be laughed off the stage. We hired Michael Kidd to choreograph the show. He was very talented and immediately understood what we were after. He was also very young, which led to an embarrassing evening when we were in Hollywood. We were invited to Johnny Green's for dinner. I brought along Michael Kidd. Johnny Green was head of the music department at MGM and a terrific pianist, and when we arrived, I introduced "Mike Kidd." We spent the whole evening there and Johnny never spoke a word to Mike. When we were leaving, I said something to "Michael," and Johnny Green's mouth dropped. "Hey! You're Michael Kidd?!" He thought I had brought along "my kid."

Michael Kidd, who had choreographed *Finian's Rainbow,* solved some really tough dance problems for the "crap-game ballet" and gave us believable dancers. He could improvise and whip things together overnight.

One of our great contributors was Alvin Colt, the costume designer, who was slightly straitlaced when it came to the girls in the "Hot Box" chorus. (Alvin was also very tall, six feet five. I once got into an argument with him and noticed that we were eyeball-to-eyeball. When I looked down I saw that he was on his knees.) His big trouble came with Ernie who made him shorten the chorus girl costumes.

"Their belly buttons will show!" Alvin protested.

"Now you got the idea," cried Ernie. "Also, I want you to cut away the sides on their shorts."

"But that will show their fannies!"

"Exactly!"

That provoked a chorus-girl revolt. They didn't want to show their belly buttons or their fannies. And they had a strong reason for such tender modesty: "My mother will be in the audience," a delegate from the chorus complained. "All of our mothers will be out there."

I was a little astonished—Broadway dancers with such modest demands. "Look, it's not really dirty," I explained. "It's a joke. The whole show—it's not meant to be taken literally. It's an exaggeration of Broadway. There's not a single dirty word in the whole thing."

They looked skeptical, so I offered a deal. "Listen, have your mothers call me. I'll explain it to them." A couple of the chorus girls' mothers actually called. I described what we were trying to do, and they were fine with it. Thus, we won that great navel battle.

*   *   *

Our biggest concern was to find authentic "characters" who would look like Runyon gamblers. This was not as easy as it sounds. We would have to search far outside the regular eight-by-ten head-shots to come up with brand new craggy faces to fill the stage. But from the first, it seemed that the gods of Broadway had smiled on this show. Everyone was inspired. We couldn't seem to do anything wrong.

The most important casting choice was Nathan Detroit, the lovable scoundrel who keeps Miss Adelaide waiting for fourteen years while he runs his floating crap game. There was no contest as far as I was concerned. Sam Levene was born for the part. Sam was a lonely, lopsided, pugnacious forty-five-year-old character actor with bristly hair and a thin mustache who lived in a single room at the St. Moritz Hotel. He had a long string of movie credits, ranging from small-time urban crook to vaguely embittered cop. But in whatever part that he played, he exuded a kind of knowing, big-hearted, and woeful fortitude. He was a universal, archetypal Jew, with all of the implied baggage and forbearance. An Americanized, vulcanized, secularized, world-weary, wise unmistakable Jew. Nathan Detroit.

When we had him signed, we sent him a recording of a song Frank Loesser had written with him in mind. It was called "Sue Me."

All right, already,
I'm just a nogoodnik.

All right, already,
It's true, so nu,
So sue me, sue me,
What can you do me?
I love you.

After he learned it, he came down to the theater to sing it for us so we could find out which key he sang in. There we were in the front row—Frank, Abe, Mike, Ernie, and I.

The pianist played the first two notes and then came Sam with "Sue Me." Not even remotely near the proper key.

The piano player tried to help him out. He sang, "Sue Me" on key.

Sam sang "Sue Me" too high.

The piano player tried it again: "Sue Me." Correct key.

Sam: "Sue Me," too low.

Sam continued his futile search for the right key until Frank had an idea. "Instead of hitting the note cold, try sneaking up on it. Use the words, 'Call a lawyer and sue me . . .'"

Sam: "Call a lawyer and sue me . . ." Not even in the same neighborhood.

We all five turned to each other and said, "Holy shit, he's tone deaf!"

Frank had written four songs for Nathan Detroit and we whittled them down to two. Sam got offended when Frank told him not to sing when he was onstage and the chorus was singing. He would throw them off.

"What should I do?"

"Move your lips," said Frank. "Just don't sing."

It was no use, but not even that could hurt the show. Eventually we realized that Nathan Detroit should be unmusical. It wasn't wrong. It was charming. If he suddenly burst forth in glorious song it would have been out of character. His rotten sound juxtaposed against Adelaide's (Vivian Blaine) professionally sweet voice was just right. When they arrive at the end of the song and he croaks,

> *Sue me, sue,*
> *shoot bullets through me,*
> *I love you.*

It was ridiculously moving.

Chapter Fourteen

For two years Ernie and I had been obsessed with a tricky problem that was at the root of *Guys & Dolls*—the casting. We knew that we couldn't use regular actors. It wouldn't look right. They were too neat and clean. We wanted rough angles and odd shapes on that stage.

"We want people with bumps," is the way I put it.

George Kaufman had that same vision for our Broadway lowlifes. "What we want, gentlemen, is a kind of geometrically interesting ensemble."

Different and complementary configurations. Short, tall. Skinny, fat. Neat, sloppy. Mugs. Together they would form the distinctive skyline of the show.

Fortunately, there was a quirky loophole in the Actors' Equity rules that allowed us to go outside of the regular casting circles for our Broadway denizens. The union did not allow exclusive contracts between Broadway agents and artists. That meant that any agent could hijack any performer, as long as he had a job to offer. So agents acted like talent scouts.

In our case, we sent Marty Baum and Abe Newborn to track

down our "bumps." Marty and Abe had gone into the agency business at about the same time that we went into the producing business. They reminded me of us. They were very hungry and willing
to go to any lengths for the sake of the show. When we said that we
needed a big eater to play the part of Nicely-Nicely Johnson, Marty
and Abe went after the tubbiest tenor around, which is how we
discovered Stubby Kaye.

Under ordinary circumstances we never would have found him.
Stubby was strictly a Borscht Belt singer. He had never appeared
on the legitimate stage. In fact, he seldom came down from the
Catskill Mountains. But Marty and Abe heard about him, and
somewhere between Grossingers and the Concorde, he fell into
their clutches. The moment I saw him I knew he was perfect for
the part. Nicely-Nicely Johnson is a genial character sporting a
loud bow tie and a bulging sports jacket and a perpetual cheery
disposition. (He was given his name by Damon Runyon because
whenever someone asks how he is, he invariably replies, "Nicely,
nicely, thank you.") Nicely is intended to anchor Nathan Detroit's
odd band of faithful sidekicks and would be paired with the
diminutive and tightly formal Benny Southstreet (he always wears
a homburg), played by little Johnny Silver.

The Borscht Belt performer with the sweet disposition also had
a golden voice. For a couple of years on Broadway, Stubby Kaye
would stop the show when he sang "Sit Down You're Rockin' the
Boat."

A lot of our troupe came our way through that same kind of uncanny piracy.

Harry-the-Horse was a one-time longshoreman named Tom
Pedi. He retained the homegrown, deep Italian-American rasp in
his voice that made that character come to life: "Hey, do not make
Big Jule hafta do somethin' to ya!" They were conjured up, as if
sensing that something unusual was being put together at the 46th

Street Theater. Even our stars—Vivian Blaine, Robert Alda, Isabel Bigley—had never appeared on a Broadway stage. Only Sam Levene had legitimate stage experience.

But of all the "bumps" who were crucial to convey Damon Runyon's cartoon view of the Broadway hustlers, Big Jule personified the species. It was a role that called for someone who combined menacing size with comic balance in a way that was ultimately endearing. If cast right, Big Jule would embody the essential joke that was at the heart of *Guys & Dolls*. That is, there was nothing really mean-spirited about the show. Like the "Hot Box" girls and their exposed fannies and belly buttons, it was all in fun. We wanted the audience to get it immediately, so the sight of Big Jule had to signal the right message.

We auditioned a hundred actors, but found no Big Jule. There was either a detectable nastiness to the interpretation, or else they lapsed into a coy burlesque of a tough guy. Marty Baum said he had someone who was perfect for the part, but we'd have to wait a few weeks because his potential client was temporarily unavailable.

"Where the hell is he?" I asked.

"In jail. A minor offense. He'll be out in fifteen days."

It sounded promising. One day, during the frenzy of auditions, a comic actor named Gene Bayliss came in cold looking for work. He was telling some jokes onstage when we heard a rough, growling roar coming from the wings. It could have been someone trying to encourage Bayliss. A friend, no doubt. On the other hand, it could have been someone laughing, or coughing—the sound he made was so gruff and meaty that it was impossible to tell. I yelled up to the stage manager to bring out whatever creature was making that terrible racket, and he led out onto the stage this refrigerator-sized character who announced in a gravel-pit baritone his name: "B. S. Pully. Guess what B. S. stands for."

"Mister Pully," said George Kaufman, whose standard courtesies never failed, "do you happen to know anything about shooting craps?"

Of course we were looking at Marty Baum's client and could tell instantly that this was no dancing master. B. S. Pully worked as a very blue comedian in the more lowdown dives of New York City. His act was so rough that he drove out the more sensitive members of the audience with an opening barrage of foul language. And now there he stood on a Broadway stage, a gnarled smile on his face, addressing the legendary George S. Kaufman. "Do I know anything about shooting craps!?" he growled as he extracted a pair of dice from his pocket and held them out for us to see. Then he shook the dice and tossed them onto the stage and snarled: "You're faded, ya bum!"

Before the dice came to rest, George S. Kaufman, as astute a judge of raw talent as ever worked in the American theater, turned to Abe Burrows, Frank Loesser, and me and said, "Gentlemen, we have found Big Jule."

Unfortunately, by the time Kaufman turned back to the stage to inform him that he had landed the part, we lost him. B.S. vanished. Abe and Marty had to launch a citywide search and eventually found him working in a cheap Greenwich Village dive. He was so accustomed to rejection that the possibility of acceptance did not enter his mind.

*　*　*

Once we had the cast, we held the first reading of the play. It was a nightmare. Very few of our bumps could remotely act. George Kaufman threw up his hands and started to walk away. "I didn't take this job to run an acting school," he muttered.

"These guys were very hard to come by, you know," I said.

"They are perfect physical casting. They can all perform musically. Your job is to get the book out of them."

He heaved a deep sigh. I was right and he knew it. There was work to be done, but he could coax some kind of performance out of them. The important thing was that we were all delighted with the look of the mugs. This was confirmed in a very conspicuous manner. One afternoon a group of our principals—Big Jule, Harry-the-Horse, Benny Southstreet—was hanging around outside the stage door grabbing a smoke when a mounted policeman came by. He rode his horse onto the sidewalk, scattering the mugs and barking, "Break it up! Break it up! No loitering!"

Our first review!

And so the casting and fussing continued. There is no better architect at staging and constructing a play than George S. Kaufman. He knew all of the secrets of the stage. He knew where the story lagged, where it spun out of control, where to introduce new plot elements, and, perhaps most important, when to leave things alone and simply allow them to settle. The earlier business about introducing the secondary story of Nathan and Adelaide was a master stroke.

This is how he solved one problem that baffled me: the set for the Save-a-Soul Mission seemed impossibly stiff to me. The audience was always looking at a profile of the players who had to face each other. The lectern for the missionary had to face the sinners and vice versa. George simply turned the lectern and the seats of the sinners forty-five degrees toward the audience. Now it appeared as if they were facing each other, but they were, in fact, facing—for the most part—the paying customers.

George was not infallible. His unrelenting courtesy and respectful manner was threatening to sabotage the show. It was always "Mister Kaye," or "Mister Levene," or "Miss Blaine." It made the

actors nervous. After his first line, Stubby Kaye stepped down-
stage, leaned over the footlights, and asked, "Was that all right,
Mister Kaufman?"

"That was fine, Mister Kaye. You don't have to check with me after every line."

Nevertheless, the general decorum went to their heads. They
began to think of themselves as members of "the theater," performing on Broadway, being directed by the great George S. Kaufman. They became very impressed with themselves and suddenly
turned into actors. Rotten actors. It was alarming. I went to
George and asked what he was going to do about it.

"Don't worry. I'm going to have a meeting. We'll put a stop to
this right away."

So George called a cast meeting. "Gentlemen, you've all been
hired because of your odd shapes and the great way that you look
and the terrible sounds that you're capable of making. We don't
want you to change anything. We love you all exactly as you are.
There's just one thing—a fundamental rule—which we will observe from this moment on. Just read the lines and get off. Above
all, no acting!"

This cured part of the problem, but there was a certain amount
of stagecraft that had to be roughly taught. Sam Levene, a real actor accustomed to working with professionals, was determined to
teach his crew, who knew nothing about picking up cues, listening, or even appearing spontaneous, how to behave onstage. For
example, there is one scene:

Nathan

Nicely (*he grabs Nicely's elbow*), run over to
Mindy's and find out if he sold more cheesecake
or more strudel.

At the next rehearsal, after Nathan said, "Nicely," Stubby Kaye obligingly offered his elbow. It drove Sam crazy. "Don't do that! You don't know I'm going to grab your elbow."

Still, Nicely, being nice, always offered his elbow. Sam decided to take matters into his own hands. He stood on a staircase that led from the stage to the basement (acting rehearsals took place below the stage, in the ladies' lounge; the stage belonged to the dancers) and held a rolled-up newspaper. All the mugs were below him. If they anticipated a piece of business or missed a cue, he would hit them on the head with the rolled-up newspaper. He was like a lion tamer circled by cringing beasts.

If his method was unusual, it was also effective.

*   *   *

Ernie had his own crazed fixations. He wanted everyone to look right, or, in this case, wrong. He insisted that Nathan Detroit wear a dark suit with prominent stripes—the uniform of a shady gambler. It was not as easy as it sounds, getting just the right outfit. All the ordinary striped suits could not be seen from the back of the theater. Finally, Alvin Colt came up with an idea of using appliqué stripes that could be seen from the balcony.

When he brought in the suit, Sam Levene was appalled. He reluctantly tried it on and then proclaimed, "If you think I'm gonna wear this stupid suit you're outta your mind."

Ernie, who had a short fuse, was right back in his face: "You're gonna wear that stupid suit and if you don't wear that stupid suit I'll see to it that you never work in this town again."

I wondered: How is he going to do that? I was standing nearby, astonished at the escalating scale of this ridiculous argument.

They were eyeball to eyeball for ten, twenty, maybe thirty seconds. The whole population of the theater—cast, crew, musicians, everyone—was frozen, waiting to see how this was going to play out. Finally, Sam shrugged and said, "What are you getting so excited about? I'll wear it. I'll wear it."

Ernie came over to me in a mild sweat. "Boy," he said, "that was close."

"You don't know how close," I said. "If it came to a choice between you and Sam Levene, you would have been outta here like a shot."

* * *

Maybe it was the speed with which we had to get it done; maybe it was the tight budget; maybe it was our own tempestuous nature or the combustible force of Frank Loesser; maybe it was all of those things in combination, but there was an atmosphere of high-pitched intensity that hung over the rehearsals and production of *Guys & Dolls*. (This excludes Abe Burrows and George Kaufman who were by nature mild-mannered, gentle men, never speaking above an arched eyebrow.)

Ernie and I were called tyrants for our determination and hot style. We accepted that. It was the price, we believed, of quality work. If there was some other way to enforce our will on temperamental artists, we didn't know it. We took a simple brute stand when we believed that we had no other choice. The application of aesthetic muscle could be difficult. For example, early on in the production I had to fire Irene Sharaff, the famous Hollywood costume designer. She was famous for designing the outfits in such films as *Girl Crazy, Ziegfeld Follies,* and *The Best Years of Our Lives*. She just didn't get the look right for *Guys & Dolls*, and when Ernie and I saw the sketches, we both knew that she had to be fired. Ernie said, "This one's on you." I took her to my office and waffled around, and finally she said with suppressed horror, "Are you firing me?" I said, "Yeah, I am," and she burst into tears. I didn't know what the hell to do. "I've never been fired before," she cried. But she was wrong for the job and that was that.

This direct attack was also the same tactic that Frank Loesser used. He also wanted his way. For example, he demanded full lung power all the time from the singers. He had a trick of using "Happy Birthday" sung higher and higher, louder and louder to test the singer's strength. He could get pretty carried away if he didn't think you were going all out. In fact, at one point, when Isabel Bigley couldn't seem to get her song right ("If I Were a Bell"), Frank actually stood on a small step in order to slap her (she was taller than he was). If that seems unforgivably barbaric now, bear in mind that this has always been an emotionally unstable industry, and this incident took place more than half a century ago. If that's not enough to convince you, Frank, though explosive, was also very close to being a genius. Such things came and went in the theater without much fuss. It was not a big deal. Flowers were sent, apologies were made, groveling took place, and the show went on.

It was inevitable, given the temperaments, that Frank and I had our share of showdowns. While working on the second act, Frank wanted a reprise of a ballad from the first act, "I'll Know When My Love Comes Along." It was a conventional thing to do in Broadway musicals, reprising numbers that were expected to become hits. It was also something that bothered me, since it interrupted the flow of the plot.

George, Abe, and Ernie were not interested in this argument. Or, rather, they did not engage in the actual dispute. They sat on a sofa, as if watching a tennis match, turning from one opponent to the other as the battle shifted.

"It's sappy," I said. "Romantic crap."

"I'm in the romance business," yelled Frank, who had a habit of physically jumping up and down when he was frustrated, which was often. "I'm in the romance business!"

"You're in the storytelling business," I shot back.

Romance. Story. This went back and forth, with the group on the couch not wanting to interrupt such a delightful impasse. Finally, George Kaufman cleared his throat, which could be a very loud statement.

"I'll tell you what," he said, addressing Frank, "we'll agree to a reprise of a first-act song in Act II, if you'll agree to let us reprise a few of the first-act jokes."

Frank paused and then laughed. He knew he was beaten. The crisis was over.

When we were walking away, he said to me, "Don't think Kaufman's gag got you off the hook. I'm not finished with you yet, you son-of-a-bitch. How about dinner?"

This was Frank Loesser—a genius with a bad, but erratic temper. "Tell you what," I suggested, "if you can find a spot that doesn't hurt us, you can have your reprise."

"I'll find it."

He never did.

Chapter Fifteen

I can hear the music now. I shuffle through the apartment and hum the tunes and murmur the lyrics. It's funny. I'm half deaf and half blind, but I can hear it all perfectly, and I can see us all in our prime, half crazy with worry as we brought the show to Philadelphia more than half a century ago.

*   *   *

It was late October of 1950 and we were booked for a four-week run at the Shubert Theater. George Kaufman and I were sitting in the parlor car of a train heading south from New York. We went around a long, lazy curve and you could see the whole train coming after us. George pointed to the last car, which was a freight car carrying all of our scenery.

"You know what's in there?" he asked.

I shook my head.

"Trouble," he said.

Nothing we couldn't handle. The Shubert Theater was a step up from the Forrest Theater in Philadelphia. In the Shubert, the dressing rooms were in the same building. At the old Forrest Theater, you had to run across an exposed alley to get to the dressing rooms. Abe and Carin and Ernie went over to look at the take-in while I checked into the Warwick Hotel. This was Abe's first show, plus it was sort of his honeymoon (he and Carin had gotten married on October 2, which was, coincidentally, the first day of rehearsals in New York).

I remember that heady atmosphere of very high excitement, plus the dread that surrounds a show in its birthing. Not that I ever caught that emotional overheating. I knew that a lot of stuff was right about the show. That wasn't important. I was interested in the parts that didn't work.

This business of taking a show on the road is a little like the trial runs of a brand new ocean liner. It looks like a ship. It's beautiful to behold. But until you get it out in the water, you can't tell how it'll behave. You don't even know for sure if it'll float. And once you are afloat, things happen. Engines quit, the boat yaws in a heavy sea; things that never show up on plans or in dry dock appear out of the blue and must be fixed, attended to, dealt with.

Our boat had a slow first act—a matter of pacing. This was one of the problems we came to Philadelphia to fix. Trouble in the first act is better than trouble in the second act. The reason is simple: you have the momentum and structure in the second act; you're just sliding into home. In the first act you're getting the engine going, setting up the premise—all details that can be repaired with some tinkering.

With a little help from Abe, George came up with a nifty solution to the first-act doldrums. It was also a way to silently signal the winner of the crucial bet (whether Sky Masterson could lure Sergeant Sarah Brown to Cuba). The Save-a-Soul Mission band would nightly march past the window of Mindy's, with Sergeant Sarah bringing up the rear, shaking her tambourine. On the night in question, all the mugs gather in Mindy's window to witness

Nathan's triumph, with Sarah bringing up the rear. No one believes that Sarah Brown will actually go to Cuba with Sky. However, when the band passes by, the smiles in Mindy's window fade as they realize that Sergeant Brown is not bringing up the rear. The stage lights go out and a big sign goes on that says, FASTEN YOUR SEAT BELTS.

Sky has won his long-shot bet.

That bit of staging not only moved the action along, it was a delight for the audience. Now they were in on it.

There was another dead spot in Act One. It was a song called "Travelin' Light," which was performed by Sam Levene and Robert Alda. This really stopped the show, but in a bad way. As someone told Abe Burrows, Sam Levene may not be able to sing, but he sure can't dance. However, solving this problem was touchy. Almost all of Sam's songs had been cut and he was only allowed to mouth the words when the chorus was on the stage; he was starting to take it personally, and I would have to wait for the right moment before attacking the problem.

We still had to find a spot for the horseplayers. We were unable to find a comfortable home for "The Fugue for Tinhorns," that amazing contrapuntal ode to horseplayers.

Someone argued that it had no business even being in the show since *Guys & Dolls* was a musical about crapshooters, and "Fugue for Tinhorns" was about the ponies. On the other hand, there was that magnificent song.

No one in his right mind would give that away. We jammed it into the second act, we plugged it back into the first act, but no matter where we put it, it stuck out. We were at sea, sitting at a lunch counter, unable to solve the placement of a great song. Feeling a little stupid, as a matter of fact. George Kaufman, that celebrated aesthete, stuck his hand inside one of those clear plastic domes and pulled out a piece of stale Danish. "How can you eat that filthy thing?" I asked. He didn't even look at me, just bit into it and ate the whole thing.

Then a lightbulb flashed on over Ernie's head: "Okay. I got it. We open the show with it," he said.

"What?"

"'Tinhorns.' Nobody knows at that point what the show is about. Horseplayers. Crapshooters. All they know is that it's about gamblers. So we open with this big, rousing generic gambling number."

Of course he was right. It worked. It has worked for fifty years. And in all the years that *Guys & Dolls* has run, in all the revivals and road companies and amateur productions, no one has ever questioned this fundamental logical inconsistency—a show that opens with a song about horseplayers, then drops the idea and spends the rest of the performance playing craps. We suffered over dirty Danish in a Philadelphia diner until Ernie got it right. The generic gambling number fit perfectly.

Sometimes a piece of business can work too well. A wonderful moment can throw off the rhythm and timing of the show. For a greater good, it has to be cut. Most of the time, the job of executioner fell to me. As in the case of a sweet old man.

One of the unusual bits of casting was Pat Rooney, Jr., who played Sarah's grandfather, Brother Arvide Abernathy. Pat Rooney was an old vaudeville trooper who was at one time famous for his waltz-clog dance routine. In the early part of the twentieth century, Pat was a headliner. And so during the second act we let him perform his waltz-clog dance to a sentimentalized version of "The Daughter of Rosie O'Grady." Pat, who had been complaining about his small billing and low salary, figured that if he got a big reaction, he'd renegotiate. During the first performance of the number before a live audience, the crowd went wild and he thought he had struck gold. He even got a standing ovation. Only it was the wrong kind of standing ovation. A lot of it was pure nostalgia. But worse than that, the number was completely wrong for *Guys & Dolls*. It was out of place and out of synch with the show. Ernie and I were in the back of the theater watching, and after all that applauding and standing died down, we turned to each other and I said, "Gotta cut it." He nodded agreement.

When I went backstage to tell Pat, I heard him in his dressing room talking to his agent, Marty Baum. They were still pumped up by the reaction of the audience.

"They're gonna have to pay me what I'm worth now," I heard from behind the closed door.

I not only had to inform Pat that his salary was staying the same, but that we were cutting "The Daughter of Rosie O'Grady." If it seemed pitiless, it would have been worse to hurt the show. That was our primary obligation—the well-being of the show. That's why we were in charge, to maintain that essential priority.

* * *

After that first performance, there was a meeting in the hotel room of George Kaufman. Ernie and Frank and Abe were all there. That initial optimism had been replaced by the certainty that the show had gone flat in several crucial stretches. We were in trouble, but that's why we were in Philadelphia. Of course, we were not seeing this thing in a vacuum. Marlene Dietrich came to see the show, no doubt because she had once had some kind of fling with George. She spit on my shoulder, claiming it was an old traditional gesture to wish me luck. Noël Coward came down for one of the early previews. He was a friend of Kaufman's. He came backstage afterward and said, "George, don't touch a thing," which meant, "I hope you go on your ass."

The first spot to attack was a void in the first act that cried out for a defining moment, something that would tell the audience what it was that made this particular band of desperate gamblers so appealing. We wanted them to be seen as we saw them—quirky and lovable aristocrats of the gutter. Frank had written a number called "Action," but we all agreed that it didn't work. It was bland.

During an idle moment, Abe and Frank were picking at the problem, circling around and talking about it, when, as he recalls in his book, *Honest, Abe,* Abe says: "You know, in the dialogue I have Sam introducing himself as Nathan Detroit, sole owner and proprietor of the oldest established permanent floating crap game in New York. So maybe the guys could . . ."

That's the way we all remembered it: Abe delivering his own lines of dialogue and Frank's head snapping up and his eyes glowing because he had just heard a lyric. They repeated the line together: "The oldest established permanent floating crap game in New York." It was a beautiful line. It even scanned.

Frank asked Abe to remove it from the libretto and spent all night in his hotel room, chain-smoking Camels, writing one of the great songs of the show. That's how Frank worked, in the middle of the night. And, as in almost everything we touched, it worked. The song lifted that first-act slump into something amusingly reverential. A hymn delightfully saluting Nathan Detroit's holy calling of being the "sole owner and proprietor of the oldest established permanent floating crap game in New York" was rendered harmlessly charming.

The love song in Cuba was still not working. Isabel Bigley was just too dignified and high-minded to bring off "If I Were a Bell," and at some point Frank gave it to Vivian Blaine. Vivian already had her own showstopper in "Adelaide's Lament," which, to this day, I believe is the most brilliant piece of musical comedy material ever written. It is the anguished cry of a woman who has undergone a fourteen-year engagement with no sign of relief and has, as a consequence, developed a permanent cold:

The average unmarried female, basically insecure
Due to some long frustration, may react
With psychosomatic symptoms, difficult to endure
Affecting the upper respiratory tract.
In other words, just from waiting around
For that plain little band of gold
A person can develop a cold.

There have been many Adelaides over the years, some very good, but no one could duplicate that angelic vulnerability of Vivian Blaine. In recent years the show was revived on Broadway with Faith Prince in the role, and while Faith Prince is many things (including large and brassy), she is definitely neither sweet nor vulnerable.

None of this helped "If I Were a Bell," which was stuck in a rut. Finally, we all concluded that it had to be Isabel who sang that song. Frank had done everything in his power to bring it out of her (including the slap, for which he was only partially forgiven), but nothing worked. Finally, I had an idea. How about if she sings it when she's drunk? After all, Sky has been feeding her liquor, disguised as flavored milk. If she's drunk, she can unleash the hidden passions and feel like a bell.

And that was the key to the song.

*   *   *

By the end of the run at the Shubert, we needed another week. So we moved into the Erlanger Theater for eight more performances. The male chorus had to go over "The Oldest Established Permanent Floating Crap Game in New York." Frank had rehearsed the singing for two days, which, as I was aware, was always at the highest pitch. Then Michael Kidd had to stage the number. I was fearful that the chorus boys were going to blow out their voices, so

I tried to make it easier for them. "We're gonna have a long morning and a performance tonight, so save your voices while we block this," I cautioned them.

They were walking through the routine when Frank came tearing down the aisle. He seldom arrived at any other pace. "What the hell is going on here?" he is yelling. "Goddammit, we rehearsed all day yesterday and now what do I hear? Nothing!"

He was on fire. Mike started to explain, but Frank cut him short. "You stay out of this. You take care of the dancing." Then it was my turn. He pointed at me: "And you're Hitler!"

I laid low—he was hot. "I want to hear the goddamned song the way I rehearsed it. And I want to hear it now!"

The poor guys in the chorus sang their hearts out. Mike stayed down and so did I. Frank started to back out of the theater, listening to the chorus boom out his song, which lends itself to a loud, throat-threatening treatment. He made it to the lobby and turned and left. I followed him. He turned right and disappeared into a candy store. When he came out he was holding a vanilla ice-cream cone. He was heading back to the hotel, eating the cone and listening to the male chorus, which you could hear very plainly from the street.

There was one other reason we needed an extra week. We were waiting for the costumes for the "Take Back Your Mink" number. They arrived on Friday and we only had three performances to test them out: Friday night, Saturday matinee, and Saturday night. After that it was Broadway.

The breakaway costumes arrived and the girls performed the number, which was a very sweet piece of business. The girls come out onstage, swaddled in expensive gifts, which have been given to them in return for implied favors. The honorable chorus girls then sing in their screechy sweet voices:

Take back your mink,
Take back your pearls,
What made you think
That I was one of those girls . . .

And as they sing, they fling away the furs and hats and pearl necklaces, and it was a slight bit of chaos. Pearls landed in the pit. Fake mink stoles went awry. Afterward, backstage, the "Hot Box" girls were desolate. They were openly weeping, thinking that the number failed. It hadn't. I had been sitting out front and I saw all the chaos, all the mess, but also something else: it was a sensation. We could always fix the messy parts, but you don't turn away from a sensational number. It had a big impact on the audience, which is the true gauge of what works and what doesn't.

There's this thing about shows that is amazing but true. Some things work and some things don't and sometimes you don't know why. You fiddle with something and it affects something far down the road. You're doing the same business that got a huge laugh the night before and the next night it is gone, affected, maybe, by that slight change you made somewhere else. And the thing is, you never know what change has made the difference.

The unpredictability is so tricky that it's almost impossible to know how things will eventually turn out. For instance, in Philadelphia, Sky Masterson and Sergeant Sarah Brown were the protagonists—theirs was the main storyline. In New York City, the leads were Nathan Detroit and Miss Adelaide. The explanation for that one was simple. New York City is Jewish; Philadelphia is mainline gentile.

When we brought the show to New York, we opened on November 24, 1950. There was one more piece of unfinished business before the curtain went up. I called a meeting in the afternoon, and as the cast stood on the stage I placed myself in the aisle, near the exit.

"There's just one change in tonight's performance," I announced. A certain stiffening on the stage. "'Travelin' Light' will not be performed. I repeat, 'Travelin' Light' will not be performed." Sam Levene's jaw dropped. He was momentarily speechless. That's when I made my escape. I ducked out of the side exit and into the cab that I had waiting.

Posy and I were sitting there when the show opened. Three guys walk up to a newsstand; each picks up a copy of the racing form, comes down front, and studies it. A trumpet suddenly plays the famous "Racetrack First Call." The audience burst out laughing. Without a bit of the show in their laps—just that upbeat call to attention—the show was alive. The crowd fell wholeheartedly into our Broadway-Runyon universe. I turned to Posy, squeezed her hand, and said, "They were waiting for us."

Then I went to the back of the theater and paced with the boys. A woman rose out of the fifth row in the middle of the first act. She was a friend. I had gotten her her seats. "Where the hell are you going?" I demanded.

"I have to call the baby-sitter."

"Get back in your seat," I commanded.

The critics were called "the seven butchers of Broadway," no doubt because of their high standards and sharp judgments. However, on that night there were only lambs in the audience. We received seven rave reviews. "A work of art," wrote Brooks Atkinson of the *Times*. Richard Watts of the *New York Post* was so overcome that he ate crow: " . . . Mr. Loesser has long been recognized as a bright and resourceful songwriter, and, with the scores for *Where's Charley?* which I didn't at first properly appreciate, and now *Guys & Dolls*, there is no doubt that he is a valuable addition to American musical comedy . . ."

The show went on to win a lot of awards and is counted among the classics in musical theater. It was even picked for the 1951 Pulitzer Prize, but there was no Pulitzer that year for the theater. I am told that the trustees of Columbia University refused to endorse the selection. They cited no reason publicly, but word came back through indirect sources that it was because *South Pacific* received the prize the year before (1950) and they couldn't cheapen the award by giving it to a musical comedy two years in a row. I was told another reason, which is that they wouldn't honor Abe Burrows because he refused to cooperate with the House Committee on Un-American Activities.

I didn't like either version.

Part III

Coping with Success

Chapter Sixteen

We were stuck in a broom closet. I was suffering from jet lag and a bad cold and we had the worst room at the Ritz Hotel in Paris. There was a water pipe running down the middle, and the window faced Rue Cambon, which everyone knows is the wrong side of the Ritz. Not that I was in any condition to raise a stink. I was so sick and so hungry that we simply ordered up room service. A huge cart was rolled in with great silver domes and platters of fantastic food, and a fine bottle of wine, and Posy and I sat on the edge of the bed and wolfed it all down. It was the fanciest meal I had ever eaten.

And then I went to sleep. In the morning, I was feeling better, but awoke in the same hovel. Posy went down to the manager to complain and they moved us into a beautiful suite that faced the gardens. There were flowers and fruit on the tables and a wood-burning fireplace in the sitting room. Apparently you had to complain before they took you seriously at the Ritz.

It was February and very cold; this was Posy's first trip to Europe and in the winter of 1952 Paris was extremely beautiful. It was also extremely foreign. The money was French, the people spoke in long musical passages, they looked great, and the food was full of terrific surprises. A plain tomato could stop the show.

I hadn't been back to Paris since the war, but I knew my way around in general and it was fun showing Posy the sights. We went to museums, took in the open-air food markets, the fancy pastry shops, the designer clothing stores, and the ordinary street traffic down the Champs-Elysées, which is never ordinary. We ate big platters of garlicky potatoes and unborn lamb at Chez L'Ámi Louis and were both caught up in the spell of Paris.

I had two hit shows under my belt and was feeling pretty good about myself. I called my friend Irwin Shaw, who came over to the hotel for tea with his wife, Marian, and the baby, Adam, who was about eleven months old. I knew Irwin from Hollywood and Broadway and Brooklyn. He was my kind of guy: a skier, plain-spoken, unsentimental, street tough, no nonsense. And a terrific writer.

We went to a party at his home, which was on the island between the Left and Right Bank, and then we went to see a few shows. One of them was a show called *Le Chanteur de Mexico* in a huge theater called the Chatelet. It originally was a seventeenth-century prison, but had been converted into a vast theater. The show lasted almost four hours, which is about average for the French, but this woman who was the star took over the show. Her name was Lilo. She had one of those personalities that dominates the stage, pushes everything else out of the way. A slighter version of Ethel Merman. When I saw her a notion began to move around inside my head.

Sometimes an idea gets up in the wind and everyone has a crack at it. That season the air was filled with Henri de Toulouse-Lautrec, the short nineteenth-century artist. The John Huston *Moulin Rouge* motion picture was in the works, and several books about Lautrec and the fin de siècle were just being published.

Lautrec's posters of Montmartre at the turn of the century caught the spirit of the Belle Epoque with its stiff men in high hats and its garish women in long skirts. Posy and I went up to Montmartre near Sacre Coeur and prowled around the shabby streets with its shady nightclubs. She posed in front of Le Chat Noir, which was the name of one of the more wicked nightspots of the period. It was very suggestive, very tempting, very close to something I had wanted to turn into a musical.

However, I was in Paris on other business and I turned my attention to that. We were to meet a Monsieur Van Clair, at least that's the way it was pronounced—Monsieur Van Clair. He was the agent who represented a property called *The Baker's Wife,* a 1938 French comedy based on a novel by Jean Giono and adapted by the great French cinema artist Marcel Pagnol. The movie is a poignant love story, truly French, in which the baker in a small village is cuckolded by his wife who runs off with another man. The baker is so grief-stricken that he is unable to bake bread, which is a very large catastrophe in a small French village where everyone depends upon their daily baguette. The citizens—great and small—toss off all petty quarrels and unite to reconcile the couple and get the bakery going again. The beauty of this story is that the important love story is not between the baker and his wife, but between the French and their fresh bread. A simple plot with complex human emotions. The ingredients, I believed, for our next musical comedy.

The agent turned out to be a nice, dapper little man whose name was spelled "Winkler," but pronounced "Van Clair." He agreed almost immediately to our terms—2 percent of the gross profits for the property. Of course, he would have to consult with lawyers for both parties.

While we waited for an answer to the offer, we had dinner with the film's director and author of the screenplay, Marcel Pagnol, who was a fabulous character with a dozen kids and women of various and ill-defined roles hovering all around him. He claimed that his primary residence was in Monaco to escape French taxes, but the French government provided a financial incentive for more children, so their citizenship was French. It was all very thick with devious Gallic innocence. Pagnol, himself, was a wonderful man who enjoyed food, wine, and regaled us with spellbinding stories.

The next day I went to see Winkler who had the answer from the lawyer for Jean Giono, the author of the novel from which the movie was adapted. A mere formality, I thought; everything was very straightforward. I had not counted on the dense subtext of pride and ego that attended such transactions in old, spiteful cultures. The offer was that Giono would receive an even split with Pagnol, 1 percent each of the gross profits. Oh, no, the lawyer told Winkler. My client provided the earth for this plant to grow. Without the novel there would be no movie, and so on. M. Giono demands one and a half percent to M. Pagnol's half percent. Unfortunately, Pagnol's lawyer also balked at the terms, with an almost identical reservation. Without the movie, there would be no interest. The movie was the fertile soil. No, no, no. M. Pagnol demands one and a half percent to Giono's half percent. They were both entrenched, Winkler said. I raised the offer to 3 percent—one and a half percent for each. Again, no deal if it was perfectly balanced. I went up to 4 percent before giving up.

It was, in the end, a matter of principle. One guy has to win, but more important, the other guy has to be humiliated. In the face of this standoff, the project had to be abandoned, to the complete satisfaction of both Giono and Pagnol who could now blame each other forever for sabotaging a surefire Broadway hit. I came to see that they would rather have the grudge than the deal. It was more satisfying.

Later, in spite of the spite, the rights would be sold and *The Baker's Wife* was turned into a David Merrick musical that never opened on Broadway, but remains (thanks to the cast album) a cult classic.

It was frustrating for someone like me, who goes headfirst after what he wants and is intolerant of people who don't see it my way.

I still had Toulouse-Lautrec rolling around in my head and I believed that there was something we could do with that idea. Ernie agreed. He liked the image of La Goulou, Lautrec's principal model who is seen doing the can-can in his most celebrated posters. La Goulou (which means "glutton" in French) was a famous dancer who was arrogant and proud of her debauched life, and although she entertained royalty and was bedecked with expensive gifts from admirers, she died alone without a sou.

Such a musical risked being dark.

One day in the early summer of 1952, while I was visiting Ernie in California, we came up with the title, *Can-Can,* and that seemed to lift the cloud. It sounded bright, cheerful, and full of energy. Cole Porter should do the music, we decided impulsively.

Maybe I should have thought of Frank Loesser. We'd done two shows together and had a social history and were friends. But I was bullheaded, charging head down, and thought of Cole Porter, and I did not give Frank the courtesy of a call.

"Where do we find Cole Porter?" I asked Ernie.

"He lives here. On Rockingham Drive."

In fact, Cole Porter had four homes, all kept in a state of perpetual readiness for his visits. All were equipped with his linens and silverware and clothing, and each was fully staffed. Cole traveled frequently and without luggage. He had an apartment in Paris; a suite at the Waldorf Towers in New York City; a fancy country house in Williamstown, Massachusetts; and a house in Brentwood. Ernie said that he was, at the moment, living in the Brentwood house. I picked up the phone book, found his number listed, and dialed. He answered the phone and I introduced myself.

"Where are you?" he asked.

"About a mile away."

"Why don't you come over."

Which is how we came to know Cole Porter. Ernie and I piled into his Jaguar and drove over to Rockingham, and Cole met us on the patio in his immaculate style. There was a flurry of butlers and attendants. Refreshments were offered. Cole was, in all things, a perfect host, a perfect gentleman. He had heard of us, had even seen *Guys & Dolls,* which he liked.

I told him the title of the next show, and when he heard *Can-Can,* along with the idea of using Toulouse-Lautrec, he said, "I'm in." We offered to tell him the story (which, at that time, we didn't have, just a jumble about La Goulou and turn-of-the-century Montmartre); he said that he wasn't interested.

"I'm not very good at it," he said in his soft, easy manner. "You just tell me what you want and I'll write it. Let me stick to what I can do."

I was not going to argue with Cole Porter. These legends all had their idiosyncrasies—George Kaufman wasn't interested in the music, and Cole Porter didn't care about the story—but they worked their miracles anyway.

Ernie had one admonition for Cole Porter. No songs about Paris. It's really a tiresome cliché. "Songs about Paris are so stale," is the way Ernie put it.

One of the first songs Cole wrote for the show was "I Love Paris." It wasn't malice; he was inspired. It simply poured out of him. He called me over one day and played it. It started off in a minor key and was astonishing.

> *I love Paris in the springtime,*
> *I love Paris in the fall,*
> *I love Paris in the winter, when it drizzles, . . .*
> *I love Paris in the summer, when it sizzles,*

Then an amazing thing happens. The song bursts out into a major key. It is like the sun coming out:

> *I love Paris ev'ry moment,*
> *Ev'ry moment of the year.*
> *I love Paris,*
> *Why, oh, why do I love Paris?*
> *Because my love is near.*

As Posy said when I played it for her, it's a Jewish song. And the tonal shifts were Jewish cantorial tradition. Cole said that he loved Jewish music.

Ernie was horrified when I told him about the Paris song. "Oh, Christ," he moaned. I told him to behave himself until he heard it. Then, of course, like everyone else, he fell in love with "I Love Paris."

*   *   *

I was interested in the story, even if no one else was. When we found out that Abe Burrows was in town, staying at the Ambassador East in Beverly Hills, we decided to track him down. We found him walking on Sunset Boulevard. He describes the encounter in his book: "About five seconds after I started out, a zippy Jaguar came tearing along Sunset Boulevard and suddenly the driver slammed on the brakes and blew his horn. It was Ernie Martin, and with him was Cy Feuer. Ernie, who doesn't often waste time on the amenities, said they had something important to tell me: it was time we did another hit show and they had a great idea for one. . . ."

That version sounds about right, if a little soft-peddled. We were lions on the prowl and poor Abe was in our hunting ground. We wanted a writer and he was it. He wanted to know what this sensational new show was about and that's when I got creative. I said it was terrific. Paris, 1890s. Toulouse-Lautrec. It's called *Can-Can*.

Ernie: "That's it, Abe. It's gonna be a great show. All it needs is a little paperwork."

That's what Ernie called writing the book, "a little paperwork."

Abe was a little hesitant; he had another commitment. The thought of writing about Paris during that golden age was a little daunting, and we hadn't even given him the bare outline of a story. Just a name, an era, a "look," and a locale.

I was persistent. "Burrows, don't think about it. Do it." How could anyone resist that kind of charming offer? And still he hesitated. Standing on the sidewalk of Sunset Boulevard, his escape blocked by Ernie's Jaguar, Abe Burrows refused to commit.

That's when I really got tough. I told him we had Cole Porter. He broke down and took the job.

*   *   *

The next time we saw Abe was in New York in November of '52. He was sick in bed. After reading the reviews for his new show that had just opened, *Three Wishes for Jamie,* anybody would've taken to his bed.

We barged into his sick room with material. Research stuff about Montmartre and Paris and the 1890s and Toulouse-Lautrec. He protested. He said he was still sick. I said, "Get to work, read this stuff, you'll feel better."

We mentioned that we had Michael Kidd for the choreography and he began to recover.

"It's all here," said Ernie brightly. "All you need is an idea for the show."

Chapter Seventeen

I operate on a simple law of physics: two projects cannot occupy my brain at the same time. Therefore I was thoroughly riveted to the enterprise in front of my face, which in this case was *Can-Can*. My concentration could not wander. This doesn't mean that life did not proceed without me. That's the thing about life—it has a way of pushing you aside and moving on.

Children went in and out of school, wives complained, friendships ended or started. And marriages ended. For example:

Sidney Kingsley had an apartment on 59th Street facing Central Park South. We exchanged dinner appearances from time to time. He was also a playwright and had written a new drama, which had opened on Broadway to high praise. It was called *Detective Story,* a pretty good piece of work. Posy and I went to see it early in the run and fortunately had seats on the aisle, because in the middle of the first act—at some moment of great drama—I felt a powerful tug on my sleeve. It was Ernie. "C'mon," he whispered. There was shushing all around. "Into the lobby."

Posy and I duckwalked back into the lobby where Ernie was waiting. "I just left Nancy," he said. "The marriage is over." He led us out of the theater and into the nearest coffee shop where this news could be absorbed without disturbing the audience.

If Ernie seemed a little too composed, considering the circumstances, that was his style. He was a cold fish. Posy and I, however, were stunned enough for all three of us.

"We went shopping this afternoon," said Posy, as if that contradicted what he was telling us. That's the way you talk about people who die; I just saw them—alive. Only this was a dead marriage.

"She's at the hotel," said Ernie.

They were staying at the Ritz-Carlton.

"You gotta go talk to her."

He meant me. I don't know why he picked me and not Posy to go over there and talk to Nancy. Maybe it was because I was good at handling trouble. In any event, he and Posy stayed behind in the coffee shop while I went to the Ritz-Carlton to put out the fire.

It was one of those awkward moments when you might as well be a lamp. You just sit there and listen to the outpouring of grief and then offer consolation. At least, you swat at it, like a fly. I don't know what I said, beyond the usual idiotic stuff like, "It's gonna be OK," "You can count on me and Posy," but whatever it was, it was inadequate to the job. The woman was completely distraught, crying, saying, "He just walked out and left me."

It was apparent that this was not one of those periodic spats in which couples issue threats, make false starts, and then reconcile. This was a real breakup. Eventually, Nancy ran off to England where she stayed with Amy Brandon-Thomas, the owner of *Charley's Aunt*. We'd all become friends since the play opened, and Nancy spent some weeks in that beautiful twelfth-century cottage in the English countryside mending her wounds. There were no children to worry about, so she could lose herself in the medieval English countryside.

It was funny, because, as I heard it from Amy, Nancy went

through a real Cotswold country detective mystery while she was visiting. Someone broke into one of the homes in the village and the police laid a trap for the intruder. A constable hid under the bed, windows were left ajar, and a lot of tweedy rustics stood ready to pounce. Only, as I recall, the villain never returned. Nevertheless, the whole thing shook up the sleepy village and kept everyone awake for a while. And it had a therapeutic effect on Nancy, who recovered her balance while staying with Amy. She came home reconciled to the end of the marriage and remained our friend, even when Ernie went on to marry another Nancy, Nancy Guild, whom we naturally called Nancy Two.

Nancy Guild was a nice woman, who had a shot at becoming a movie star. One of the studios went all out, tried to build a following, put her in a movie with Glen Ford. I remember the publicity releases: "Nancy Guild, rhymes with wild," trying to drum up excitement. But she lacked that essential something that makes a star and never went beyond the buildup. However, there's an old poster of her in that movie—a full-body picture—that was showing at the Museum of Modern Art. She was a knockout, and nice.

The impact of the breakup was not confined to Ernie and Nancy. The ground under me was made a little unsteady by the suddenness of the abandonment. I had no inkling of trouble in the marriage. And I had to ask myself, How much did I know about Ernie? Obviously, not as much as I thought. We were not the type of people to confide our deepest secrets to each other. That was not our nature. We were bred to reticence. If you asked me, I would have called him a friend, but it was a surface relationship, and that was sufficient. Maybe we would have damaged the partnership if we went too far. It was not something upon which I would dwell, only now, half a century after the fact, it leads me to believe that we kept each other at arm's length for a reason.

*   *   *

At about this time, I decided to become a country gentleman. This is a perfect demonstration of how partial attention and impulse can lead to disaster, or, in this case, White Plains. Everyone was moving to the suburbs, buying station wagons, extolling the virtues of nature over asphalt, escaping urban blight. So without consulting anyone, including my more sensible self, I bought a house in White Plains. I bought a station wagon to go with it, in my ridiculous attempt to country gentlemanize myself.

The house was nice, a big stone château on a hill with a separate smaller house for a married couple hired as domestics. We even bought a dog, a hound of some mixed breed. We called him "Dudley." Dudley the dog.

When I set out to do something, I went whole hog. We brought a prominent decorator up to Westchester County who outfitted the house in French Provincial style and introduced us to period furniture. I actually studied the subject, but could not plunge into it very deeply. There was that other thing on my mind—*Can-Can.* Posy would later take up acquiring antiques as a small profession, which is probably the only good thing to come out of it.

Nevertheless, I tried to fit in and become a commuter. I joined the Jewish country club and went ice sailing on a frozen pond, and I did some portage of the children—that is, I drove them to school and play dates, but most of that business fell to Posy. The boys were always fed, invariably in some school, and usually present at the dinner table. I noted their increasing height, but my primary job was in the city. I would drive to York Avenue in Manhattan where I would work with Abe Burrows on the libretto of *Can-Can.* I was essential to Abe's writing because he needed an audience. He would write and I would laugh. Then, after a full night's work, I would drive back to White Plains where I felt unbelievably out of place. I drove back and forth in my vintage Jaguar. It took about an hour, if the traffic was light. I enjoyed the driving. It was kinda like an activity, and I'm always happy to participate in an activity.

Progress on the show was pretty good. We had abandoned the idea of using La Goulou or Toulouse-Lautrec as the protagonists. Abe couldn't find any dramatic push there. Instead, we focused on the battle that went on between the puritanical reformers and the libertine performers in Paris during the early 1890s. Our research indicated that the city was torn between the nightclub operators and the French Victorians who wanted to clean up Montmartre in time for the 1889 International Exposition of Paris. That's when the Eiffel Tower was officially unveiled. The reformers did not want the out-of-town tourists to be shocked by the rough antics of the can-can dancers; they didn't realize that the rough antics of the dancers is precisely what the tourists were coming to see.

The story had some pretty interesting twists. The girls who danced the can-can were not professional entertainers. They were plain laundresses during the day, slaving over tubs of soap and lye. After ten or twelve hours of that backbreaking work, these young girls were out for a good time. So they went into these clubs, like The Moulin Rouge, and started doing these pretty wild and racy dances—all on their own, nothing coordinated—which was very appealing to the paying customers. The great scandal was that these can-can dancers would often wear no underwear. Or at least after a few turns around the floor they ended up without underwear. This caused the men in the audience to sit up and pay close attention.

We even had a made-to-order antagonist, the president of the League Against Licentiousness of the Streets, a French senator named Rene Berenger. He tried to close down several of these dens of depravity. There were even a few public trials featuring very funny testimony about the extent and exact nature of female nudity at the shows. All of this gave us the basic structure for the show: the uptight judge, whom we would call "Aristide Forestier," versus the lustful owner of a nightclub featuring the can-can, a beautiful woman we called "Pistache." This would introduce the crucial element of sexual tension, plus the dramatic catalyst of trying to corrupt the upstanding judge.

Cole, who told us that he preferred to stay out of the story conferences, needed some guidance about the music. As he wrote the book, Abe mailed his requirements for a particular love song, which Cole Porter would have to cut like a tailor: "Our hero (the judge Aristide) is going to fall in love with the girl (the nightclub owner Pistache) and he is going to be astounded by the fact. I should think it would be a good idea if the lyrics would contain, in addition to the hero's happiness, something about the fact that he is surprised by all this . . . He'll be frightened, happy, chilled, warmed, ecstatic, puzzled, upset, shocked, and delighted."

And, perfectly tailored, back came "C'est Magnifique."

> *When love comes in*
> *And takes you for a spin,*
> *Oo-la, lala, c'est magnifi-que.*
> *When, ev'ry night,*
> *Your loved one holds you tight,*
> *Oo-la, lala, c'est magnifi-que.*

It seems so inevitable and perfect now, the exact melody, the correct mood, the right lyrics, but then, in late July of 1952, Abe was sending out rough measurements and getting back a classic piece of work.

Cole was in Peru, Indiana, that summer where his mother, Katie, had suffered a stroke. She died on August 2 and Cole stayed there settling affairs for a few weeks. While in mourning, sitting on the porch of the family home, he wrote the breezy, buoyant lyrics for "Can-Can."

> *There is no trick to a can-can,*
> *It is so simple to do,*
> *When you once kick to a can-can,*
> *'Twill be so easy for you.*
> *If a lady in Iran can,*
> *If a shady African can,*
> *If a Jap with a slap of her fan can,*
> *Baby, you can can-can too.*
> *If an English Dapper Dan can,*
> *If an Irish Callahan can,*
> *If an Afghan in Afghanistan can,*
> *Baby, you can can-can too.*

There were endless variations. It became a game to tack on clever refrains:

> *If Debussy and Ravel can,*
> *'Twill be so easy for you.*
> *If the Louvre custodian can,*
> *If the Guard Republican can,*
> *If Van Gogh and Matisse and Cézanne can,*
> *Baby, you can can-can too.*

* * *

By late summer, we had the score and we had the book and were starting to cast the principal players. Allan Jones came in to audition for the part of Aristide Forestier, the judge. A group of us sat in the dark of the theater listening to Allan trying to sing "I Am in Love," a song that builds to the climactic, "For I am *wildly* in love with you." Allan began singing and climactically built to "For I am *mildly* in love with you." He was promptly dismissed from the running. He was too concerned with his singing to pay attention to the words. Due respect has to be paid to the lyric.

Nothing distracted Cole Porter from his work. In spite of the fact that he was in constant pain from a leg mangled in a riding accident twenty years earlier and was obliged to hobble into auditions and rehearsals with a cane or on crutches, he remained a master craftsman. A singer who did not respect his lyrics and paid too much attention to his singing was unacceptable.

Cole did not need the money or acclaim. He was born rich and he had achieved high rank in the musical pantheon as a young man. He was driven by a workman's pride.

Before we ever began *Can-Can,* Cole told me what his reviews would be. "Not up to Cole Porter's usual standards." It didn't matter how good the show or his score.

I didn't understand the critics. They expect this guy to be great and the fact that he was great was taken as a given. Too much familiarity with magnificence.

The part of the judge went to Peter Cookson, who was only mildly adequate for the role.

I wanted Carol Channing for Pistache, but she was committed to perform in *Gentlemen Prefer Blondes* in London. And then I thought of Lilo, the French singer. Abe and Ernie went to Paris and caught her act at the Theatre du Chatelet where they were also impressed by her bawdy presence and gutsy voice. She couldn't dance, but we could find someone else for that. They flew her to New York, then to Los Angeles where she auditioned for Cole, who seemed to be more impressed by her husband, Guy de la Passardière, a French marquis, who was also her manager. I called him the managing marquis. He was a very charming guy, or Guy, and it pleased Cole to speak to him in French and to introduce him, with all his titles, to his friends.

Lilo was acceptable as a singer and the manager of the nightclub. But she could not dance. Therefore a lead dancer had to be found since this was a show about dancing. I had seen a young girl in a Chicago club who had impressed me. She was a member of the Jack Cole dance troupe. He was a Svengali who had all his dancers under his spell, none more than Gwen Verdon. At the moment, she was under contract to 20th Century–Fox, coaching Marilyn Monroe for *How to Marry a Millionaire,* and was reluctant to take on the role.

We flew her to New York for an audition and she sang well, but the dance sequence exploded. We were out front, watching this kid, astonished at her pure ability. She was agile and graceful and lit from within with the joy of what she was doing. And I can say without fear of contradiction, that in her youth, no one had a better behind. She was terrific. For her boyfriend, we found an elegant comedian, Hans Conried.

The show had come together by the end of the winter of 1953. Normally, we would wait until the fall to open on Broadway. But a technological advance had changed the seasons. Theaters were now air-conditioned. Broadway theaters used to be air cooled in the summer. Theater owners would bring in great slabs of ice and huge fans would blow cool air across the audience. This was fine, except at the end of every performance the audience went home very wet. But air-conditioning made a spring opening possible.

We were shooting for early May.

*   *   *

Meanwhile, it was apparent that I had made a terrific mistake by moving to White Plains. I was not cut out for the suburbs. We had been living there for a year and the driving was starting to get on my nerves. Posy was sick of it before we even moved in. She had no friends, missed Manhattan, and was bored by the quiet. The kids were not enthusiastic about it, either. Apparently, even Dudley the dog hated the place. He ran away.

We were all out of our element. So we moved back to Manhattan. In fact, I actually bought George Kaufman's old house, a brownstone at 158 East 63rd Street. He had since moved into a penthouse. Maybe the old house retained the stench of greatness. The truth is I liked being able to walk to work. I liked playing tennis on the courts at Grand Central Station. I liked going out to dinner at night with friends who wouldn't come up to White Plains.

I knew that I had made the right choice when Posy reported with glee a conversation she overheard when escorting twelve-year-old Bobby and another friend back from a Manhattan public school.

"Your name is Bergman?"

"Howard Bergman."

"Do you have a sister named Ingrid?"

Clearly, our kids were show-business brats, spoiled by the proximity to fancy restaurants and big stars and the glamour of a life in the theater.

I, too, felt the peaceful frenzy of my systematic life back in place. I could put the suburbs out of my head and keep my brain focused on the single idea: *Can-Can*. While Posy fixed up the house and attended to the domestic front, Ernie and I got the show on its feet. Suddenly, we were booked into the Shubert Theater in Philadelphia for the middle of March in 1953.

Chapter Eighteen

Gwen Verdon had a mild shock when she arrived at the Shubert
Theater in Philadelphia on the day of the take-in, March 16, 1953.
There was a guy up on a ladder, holding a ruler, measuring the size
of the name Hans Conried. He was comparing it to the size of the
other stars, Lilo and Peter Cookson. The surprising thing was that
the guy holding the ruler was Hans Conried.

This was a pretty good omen. You got the feeling that everyone
thought that *Can-Can* was gonna be a great big hit and wanted the
full measure of being part of it.

Not that Hans Conried had to worry about credit. He was a tall,
thin, and quirky comic actor who played a mad Bulgarian sculptor
named Boris Adzinidzinadze; he gave the show a very rich offbeat
edge. Gwen Verdon was cast as Claudine, his lover, and she got
about half his billing. But that would change. She'd come out of the
show with a bigger name than all of them.

Except, of course, for Cole Porter, whose name was on top of
everything, including the show. That's who the public came to see,
the unseen man whose invisible hand guaranteed a high degree of
quality. There is a silky sense of security that attaches to everything
he touches. Nothing can be too bad when Cole Porter's name is

over the marquee. We were sold out for the full four weeks of the Philadelphia run because of his brand name.

Of all the out-of-town openings, this one was probably the smoothest. Usually, you limp into Philadelphia with a sick show and take the vital signs by reading the audience reaction. Then you get under the show's skin, perform the necessary surgery, juggle the bones, or just stand back and let it heal itself. Only there wasn't much wrong with *Can-Can*.

Of course, nothing is ever that simple. Problems did emerge, though not structurally. That was fine. The headaches concerned personalities.

Gwen Verdon didn't like Michael Kidd. It was a question of loyalty. She thought that Michael was a lesser talent than her Svengali, Jack Cole. Dancers get like that; they belong to a dance troupe and they surrender to it completely. Anyone else seemed puny to her, not that she was insubordinate. She did what Michael told her to do, but she did it without any show of respect or real appreciation. There was a coldness in their relationship that was completely undeserved. All he did was turn her into one of the greatest stars on Broadway, with her picture on the cover of *Life* magazine. But at the time she didn't recognize his strength. Only later, when she worked with Bob Fosse, did she change her opinion. Fosse set her straight, made her see that Michael Kidd had transformed her life with his choreography, and even forced her to apologize. Of course by that time she was under Fosse's spell.

In his own modest way, Michael Kidd gave us dramatic answers to riddles that had us completely baffled: how to stage a dance number that appeared lewd enough to provoke an arrest without actually offending the audience or being lewd. That was the point of the drama, these laundresses—these can-can dancers—were performing an immoral act. In the play, the judge attends a performance, along with a photographer who is ready to flash pictures of the illegal dance; his intention is to obtain evidence in order to shut down the nightclub.

Michael Kidd's brilliant solution had two pairs of four girls, facing each other, standing with their legs wide apart. The audience sees them in profile. The male dancers rush the girls, fall to their knees, slide underneath the open legs, and come up on the other side holding a pair of panties. Each girl reaches under her, grabs the back of her skirt, and pulls it through to cover her exposed bottom. That's when the flash goes off. The audience never saw anything bawdy, but the illusion was perfect. It was one of those rare and ideal moments in the theater when the audience sees the trick, understands the dramatic intent, appreciates the art that went into it, and feels a conspiratorial part of something terrific. It never failed to elicit a roar of approval and glee. And nobody got hurt.

* * *

The biggest problem we had with *Can-Can* was with the behavior of our star Lilo. She became a little too enthusiastic in her efforts to win over the American audience. She overplayed the part with an abandon that was frightening: gestures, eye batting, unscripted moves. It drove everyone crazy.

"You gotta talk to her," I told Abe Burrows, the director.

"I have. Then she goes out and does the same thing again."

Abe was a gentle director, not a screamer. He tried to reason with his actors, but in my opinion, a show in trouble is not a time to be reasonable. You have to be able to tell the actors when it doesn't work and what to do about it. First, however, you have to get their attention. And then they have to listen. But that's my technique. George Kaufman had a quiet approach. He could command attention with a reproachful gaze over his eyeglasses. I've actually seen him do it by sarcastically closing his eyes. But no matter what he did, Abe could not get Lilo's attention.

Not that Abe's approach was wrong. A lot of the actors misjudged him, took his easy warmth for weakness. He could usually get the job done. Sometimes it took a whole bag of tricks. There was the problem of getting Hans Conried unstuck from the stage. No one could pry him off the stage after his exit line. The guy just stayed there, waiting for more appreciation. Burrows took him aside, spoke to him gently, but that didn't work. Then he used sincere firmness. That, too, fell on deaf ears. Finally, he tried pleading. It was no use. Abe hadn't counted on the awesome power of the unleashed ham in an actor like Conried, who lingered on the stage, as some actors do, hoping to be rediscovered. Abe became so frustrated with his loitering actor that he got a flashlight and waited in the wings backstage for the exit line. When Conried finished his turn and was supposed to go away, Abe flashed the light on and off. Conried finally got the message that he was going to get upstaged by a flashlight if he didn't scram. It worked.

Lilo was a tougher nut. First of all she had a gritty French urchin quality that was like spit in your eye. Second, she was the marquess and Cole had a weakness for fancy French titles. He invited Lilo to dinners with the duke and duchess of Windsor and Millicent Hearst—all of his society friends.

Her husband, the marquis, was easier to deal with. There was something very pleasant and charming about Guy de la Passardière. Maybe it was that endearing hapless quality that he had. No one could forget the night he arrived in Philadelphia and accidentally washed his title out of the bathroom window. He was washing his hands when the baronial ring squirted off his finger and flew down an air shaft. The hotel staff spent a whole day searching, but they never found the ring. The poor guy, or Guy, was afraid that he wouldn't be accepted as a true aristocrat without evidence.

Ring or no ring, Guy, too, fell under Cole's protection. They spoke aristocratic gossip together in French, two things that Cole loved—gossip and French. He could forgive Lilo's bawdy side. But there were limits to Cole's forbearance. One day he ruthlessly cut her off completely, told her in so many words never to return to his home. There was never an explicit reason given for her banishment, but it came after she had encouraged a rumor that she and Cole were having an affair—a story too ridiculous to be given credence, and yet unforgivably wounding to a man of Cole's ultrasensitive sense of decorum. It called attention to the unspoken though universally accepted fact that he was a homosexual. His marriage to Linda was a gesture to social decorum, as well as something rooted in true chaste affection.

There was a definite anointed court that surrounded Cole, and I was one of the chosen. I had something he admired and he had something the whole world idolized. He respected my musicianship and training and I appreciated his musical genius. That gave us common ground and gave me some standing in his eyes. I once told him, "Cole, the terrible thing is that I know more about music than you do. Except that you write music and I can't."

He also had an unreasonable affection for Posy. He enjoyed her company, respected her taste, appreciated her sense of humor. He even left her some things in his will. While I was out of town, he took her to dinner. He sent his driver, took her to El Morocco for drinks, then dinner at Pavilion where they kept his table perpetually at the ready. They also kept fresh his private silverware, as well as his plates and napkins and even his own personal menu on standby.

That's the way he lived—a splendid world of familiar fineries. Just the grand way he arrived in Philadelphia for the out-of-town tryout of *Can-Can* was a reminder of an imperial style that seemed, in his hands, justifiable.

There were two hotels in Philadelphia. Most of us stayed at the Warwick. It was utilitarian, serviceable, but not fancy. The Barclay, however, was elegant, devoted to luxury and dainty rituals, and, of course, very expensive. Cole moved into a suite at the Barclay preceded by a flurry of attendants who were acting with the feverish urgency of installing a king. First he had his man bring his personal items down from New York City in his Bentley. The hotel removed the cheap print pictures in the suite and replaced them with Cole's Van Goghs, Utrillos, and Cézannes. Photographs of his friends were scattered on tables and on the piano he had sent ahead. He also sent his own personal bed linen, tablecloths, linen napkins, porcelain napkin holders, crystal, silver trays, dinnerware, flatware and cutlery, flower vases, and wastebaskets. He even had his own dinner table and breakfast table, card tables, and an ironing board.

The hotel was given a list of seventy-five essential items that had to be stocked for his needs, including: "American Store Cheese—sharp, 1 can Water Chestnuts, 1 Smithfield Ham, 3 Lux toilet soap bars, six cartons of Chesterfield cigarettes, three cartons of Camels, six cans of Pard dog food, and fruits of every variety."

Cole arrived by train, like George V.

It was not simply a rich man pampering himself. Cole was able to endure the lifelong pain from his riding accident, consoled by his own personal objects and the vast inventories of art and trimmings. It was little enough solace, and sadly disproportionate.

*   *   *

Meanwhile, Lilo was screwing up the show and Abe had run out of gimmicks. Talking did no good. She would go to Cole and complain about Abe; she would write him passionate letters in French complaining about me. Her desolation over the lack of appreciation was endless. But Cole was savvy enough about the theater to stay out of the battle. He even read us her letters, translating the French. Ultimately, it was up to us to rein in our star. We increased the pressure on her, but she continued to defy us.

In fact, she kept pushing it, going further and further, until during one performance, she grabbed the head of Peter Cookson and rubbed it between her breasts. She was apparently attempting to make the emphatic point that her character, Pistache, was earthy and had the weapons to defeat the crusading judge who was trying to close her nightclub. We were horrified. It was a vulgar and an intolerable piece of stage business.

"She has gone too far," I told Abe.

"Two too far," said Abe.

"What are you going to do?"

"I'm going to speak to her."

"No," I said finally, "let Ernie and me handle it."

And we did. The next day we went to her hotel suite and handed her an envelope. In it were two airline tickets back to France.

"What is this?" she asked.

"You're fired," said Ernie.

Naturally we did not really intend to fire her. We didn't have a replacement. Just throw some fear into her. And it worked. She stopped all the vulgar business and became almost meek onstage. We had gone too far. Her next performances were almost inaudible. Abe was ready to kill us.

"What the hell did you guys do to her? I had a lion and you turned her into a mouse."

"I know," I said, "but she's not vulgar."

"Gimme back my lion," said Abe. "Pistache has to have some fire. Fix it!"

So we went back to Lilo and told her that we didn't mean to curb her enthusiasm, we wanted her to ignite the stage, to have life, to play a bold and bawdy Pistache. We just didn't want her to rub Peter Cookson's face between her breasts.

Eventually, we reached a happy medium and she played the part with fire and without offending anyone. Upon reflection, I think, maybe she knew something that we didn't recognize. She was in a real fight for domination of the show with Gwen Verdon. Not that Gwen lit up the stage in Philadelphia. She was only mildly received there. Neither the critics nor the audiences paid much attention to her.

It was in New York, at the opening on May 7, that she stopped the show. I had never before seen a show truly stopped. I've only seen it twice in my whole life in the theater. The other time was over a clever bit of staging. But this was different. This was a star emerging, recognized fully by the audience. It is a pretty impressive thing, when the audience takes over and refuses to allow the performance to continue. The audience outburst came after Gwen's Apache routine in the second act. They rose from their seats and applauded and cheered with such determination that it left the actors for the coming scene standing there, unable to continue the show. The set had already changed. Gwen was in her dressing room getting into her next costume, but the crowd wanted her back for a bow.

And they wouldn't stop. I was out front and recognized that this was not going to subside, so I went backstage and dragged Gwen back to the stage. She was in her dressing gown. She didn't want to come. I insisted. And so she finally came, clutching her gown, grinning awkwardly, standing there while this appreciation washed over her. And the show was stopped while the audience, just for fun, continued applauding. They took over the show.

" . . . With Gwen Verdon leading the ballets with impudence, recklessness and humor, the dancing is spectacular."

That was Brooks Atkinson in *The New York Times*.

Lilo was right to be worried about possession of the stage.

Chapter Nineteen

I can't do what I once did. The desk is not so neat. The dresser is not so organized. The shoes are not so polished. It's age. The personal routines shift, or they're shed. I used to shave my face every morning like a soldier going on parade. But I can't do that anymore. For one thing, I can't see it. I accept the fact that I'm old and have a daily loss of function. It's a bitter pill, but I swallow it.

I didn't always have such elasticity. When *Can-Can* opened we had three hit shows on Broadway. Soon we would have five. Shows, like people, get old and sloppy. They drift. Actors who start out on stage left move an inch or two every night and soon, before they're even aware of it, they're starting out on stage right.

It's a natural tendency. And it has to be corrected. Someone has to come in and reposition the players, put them back in place. Someone with a clean eye and fresh ear has to remind them of the staging and hitting the marks and delivering the lines the way they did when they were fresh. A running show is a living thing. More often than not, I was the guy who came in and lit a fire under a tired show.

It is one of the reasons we ran so high for so long—this devotion to detail and quality. Ernie and I believed that this exertion, this enormous amount of attention and effort, was the explanation for our success—and the price. We called ourselves ditchdiggers because it felt like that. People asked what we did as producers, and we'd say we dig ditches.

Naturally, this is a very exotic form of manual labor. We were in pretty lofty company. I sat at the feet of Charlie Chaplin at a Hollywood party. I sailed home from England on the *Queen Mary* with Groucho Marx at my table. I chatted over the back fence with P. G. Wodehouse on Long Island. I was friends with John Steinbeck. So I am not whining about the suffocating work load, although what I did required a level of activity and attention that robbed the other facets of my life. I assumed that Bobby and Jed were growing up all right. They seemed to get taller and stronger. I had no complaints from the police—yet. I assumed that Posy was satisfied with her life of lunches and friendships and shopping excursions, not that I ever asked her or really wanted to know if there was a problem. If she was a show in trouble, I could have taken her to Philadelphia and straightened her out.

This was the single-minded, narrowly focused, all-inclusive ditch-digging season of my active, professional life. I believed completely that I had no choice but to immerse myself up to my eyebrows in my work.

* * *

The national road company of *Guys & Dolls* was assembling, which would open in San Francisco, and once again the great challenge was casting. B. S. Pully had a friend whom we all thought was just right for the part of Big Jule. His name was "Slapsie" Maxie Rosenbloom and he developed a successful comic personality by playing a punch-drunk ex-pug. He did it so well because he was, in fact, a punch-drunk ex-pugilist. Slapsie was a former world light heavyweight boxing champion. His comedic gift was good enough to carry him through sixty-three movies. Nobody looked more like an ex-pug than Slapsie Maxie Rosenbloom. He wasn't big—a little under six feet tall—but he had a conspicuously busted nose and a cauliflower ear, and he spoke as if he was drowning. A terrific natural version of Big Jule.

His friend B. S. Pully offered to help Slapsie Maxie learn the part and coached him on the stage. Pully, with his gravel-pit groan, and Maxie, with his punch-drunk gargle, were going at it as Ernie and I watched from the audience.

"God dammit, Slapsie, how come you talk the way you do?"

"I've had thirty-five fights. What's your excuse."

"I got this way from bettin' on ya!"

We were listening to an improvised duet from two genuine *Guys & Dolls* mugs.

On opening night, Ernie and I made our customary rounds of the dressing rooms before the curtain, wishing everyone well. Slapsie motioned to us; he wanted to let us in on a secret. He made us close the door. "I want youse to know how loyal I am to youse guys. I just turned down an offer to throw the show!"

I wouldn't swear he didn't take the short money. In the first scene he "went up." He stood there, frozen, then went down to the edge of the stage and leaned out to the audience: "I'm really sorry. I forgot my lines. Don't go away. I'll start all over again."

After that Big Jule owned the house.

*   *   *

A show like *Guys & Dolls* demanded constant attention. The line between the gorgeous fable and a ridiculously absurd distortion of the show was thin. The movie version is a perfect example of how things can go wrong; attempting to turn Frank Sinatra into a Broadway wise-guy Jew was a fundamental and fatal mistake. A true ethnic identity was crucial to the story. But I had nothing to do with the movie and, in fact, was ignored by Sam Goldwyn who thought that Sinatra's marquee value was more important than a faithful rendition of the show.

If I was shut out of the movie version of *Guys & Dolls,* I was still responsible for our road companies and I monitored them closely. I could always drop into a Broadway house, but the national company was on the road. It was doing well, but being a hawk, I stopped in for a routine checkup in Omaha. The show was fine, but the stage manager took me aside. He was having a problem with Benny Southstreet, or, at least he was having a problem with the actor who was playing the part, who for purposes of this story, I'll call Benny. He had fallen in love with one of the Hot Box girls.

"What's the problem?"

"She won't have anything to do with him."

"So?"

"He will not take no for an answer."

Benny was so persistent—calling her hotel at all hours, leaving notes everywhere—that it was beginning to disturb the company. The stage manager had run out of arguments, and still Benny would not leave the poor girl alone.

"Would you have a go?"

I liked Benny, and he was a valuable part of the company. But this was silly.

"I understand there's a problem with you and the girl?"

"It's a problem for me. I'm really taken with her."

"Listen, it's apparent that she doesn't want to have anything to do with you. Benny, you have to control yourself. You can't let this govern you. You're an adult."

"Well," he said, "I just can't, but I've got a solution for the whole thing."

"What is it?"

"Fire her."

"Fire her?"

"Yeah, if you fire her then I won't have a problem because she won't be around."

"I can't do that. I'm not going to fire the girl because you can't control yourself. It's ridiculous! You're just going to have to cut it out and behave yourself."

I went to the stage manager and told him what happened. "I spoke to him, but I don't know if it's gonna do any good. Call me at the end of the week."

I returned to New York and at the end of the week the stage manager called.

"As bad as ever."

"Fire him," I said. "Give him two weeks' notice and I'll come up with a replacement to take over."

That afternoon the phone rang and it was Benny.

"Cy, it's Benny."

"Yes, Benny."

"I want to know why I was fired."

"Benny, you were fired because you wouldn't leave that poor girl alone. You were acting like an unmitigated shit."

"Thank God! I thought it was my acting."

*   *   *

Between checking on the shows and hunting for the next project, I spent a lot of time in California. After all, Ernie lived there, and so did my mother and my brother. My mother was quite an impressive woman. She and a friend—a female—made a tour of Europe in a rented car. She was fearless. She went everywhere and climbed everything and had a terrific time. She was in her seventies. It was not until after she died that I discovered that my father had probably been married before. I made another astonishing discovery—my brother, Stan.

It was a moment of pure recognition. I don't know how else to explain it. Before that we were brothers, but not especially close—normal brother close.

It was my habit to call him when I came for a visit, and one day I came in from New York and called Stan. I wanted to meet for lunch. "Okay," he said, "we'll meet at the club." He belonged to the Beverly Hills Tennis Club, which was the Jewish club in Los Angeles and had by far the better cuisine. By now, Stan had had his own success in the air-conditioning business. He was an engineer, but he wanted to be his own boss. So he launched his own company. He started out in a truck, going door-to-door down Melrose Avenue, offering to air-condition all the stores. Soon he had a fleet of trucks running up and down California installing air-conditioning. Apparently he had an entrepreneurial gift.

On this particular day—a bright, beautiful, clear California day—I was waiting for him to finish his game. I was sitting on the terrace and I saw him come out of the dressing room. Suddenly, I realized that coming toward me was this very attractive man whom I really liked. And as we sat and talked, I thought, He is really a very nice man. This nice, attractive man happened to be my brother. There were no more sibling rivalries, no hidden agendas, no unsettled grudges—just someone I truly enjoyed being with.

From that moment on, he was my friend. We talked about this later and he said he felt the exact same thing at that exact same moment, although it was nothing that he could put into words at the time.

I haven't completely given in to sentimental delusions. My guess is that part of the reason we were able to become close was the fact of the separation. We lived three thousand miles apart so there was no chance of getting on each other's nerves. And when we did see each other it was an occasion—skiing or playing tennis or at an opening.

I enjoyed skiing, but Stan was really a great skier. We'd go up to Sun Valley in a foursome—Stan and Margo, Posy and me. Skiing was a better sport on the West Coast. In the east the snow is too thin and there are always patches of ice and it gets too cold. On the other hand, in Sun Valley, the snow is deep and packed and you don't have to worry about running into ice or a stretch of rocks. It's also more comfortable in the West because it doesn't feel as cold. That can be a little deceptive; you can't tell if you're getting frostbite until your nose falls off. You have to keep your eye on the temperature. We had wonderful vacations in Sun Valley, the whole family. I remember them as idyllic, but then strenuous activity was always my ideal. Not that there had been any kind of overt break, or even coolness, but the reconciliation with Stan was a bonus.

* * *

It was during one of my periodic business trips to California that I got a call from Ernie. I was noodling around with Cole Porter over a new musical, which was still in the very early stages of gestation. I was determined to produce a musical version of *Ninotchka*. But here was Ernie on the phone. "Drop everything," he said. "Get right over here." He was calling from London.

"What is it?"

"I just saw our next show."

Chapter Twenty

If there is such a thing as a Broadway confection, *The Boy Friend* was it. Only it was too much trouble for a confection and it didn't start out on Broadway. Apart from that, everything I said is totally accurate.

In the spring of 1954 Ernie was over in England making deals for productions of *Guys & Dolls* and *Can-Can*. He was staying at the Savoy, enjoying himself, which, in his case, was looking for work. And he found it. It was playing at the Wyndham's Theater in the West End and it was called *The Boy Friend*.

I was, at the time, in the middle of trying to turn *Ninotchka* into a musical with the assistance of Cole Porter. It was a big project that required a lot of work and would, in the end, become *Silk Stockings*. Ernie knew how important it was to keep going on the *Ninotchka* enterprise, so I assumed that he wouldn't pull me away from Cole Porter with something pointless. Ernie had a nose for our kind of material.

"There's something great on the stage," he said of *The Boy Friend*. I trusted him enough to put *Ninotchka* aside and get on a plane.

It's hard to classify what *The Boy Friend* was, exactly. It was a lampoon of all of the fluffy musicals of the 1920s, but done in such a way that it wasn't cruel.

The show was written by Sandy Wilson, a guy who was definitely sending up that syrupy and overblown style of romantic fairy tale, but not without affection. Even the title was an echo of the airy Rodgers and Hart comedy *The Girl Friend*. As soon as I got to London I went to see the show and had the exact same reaction as Ernie. I was charmed.

* * *

We made a quick deal to buy the rights to make an American production of the show, only it had to be an exact reproduction to retain that delicate flavor I saw on the London stage. The London producers insisted on a faithful rendition of the show. We cast the eleven principal players in London and I even arranged to have a 16-millimeter film of a performance so we could have a reliable reference point. We were going to bring the director Vida Hope, the author Sandy Wilson, and the choreographer John Heawood to Broadway to make certain we got it right. Our backers swung into action for the quarter of a million dollars needed to put the show on the stage.

The story of *The Boy Friend* is simple. Polly, the most popular student at Madame Dubonnet's girl's finishing school on the French Riviera, falls in love with a poor bellhop, which is totally unacceptable in her social class. But he turns out in the end to be a rich bellhop with a title. It was so ridiculous it was moving.

But the English show was in the middle of its run and while I could get a lot of the principals by holding auditions, I had to find another leading lady to bring to America. Anne Rogers, the London Polly, was not willing to walk away from her triumph. Vida Hope said that she knew of a girl who could play Polly. The girl was in a play in Yorkshire and couldn't come down to London for an audition, so Vida and I took a train to Leeds to see an English production of *Mountain Fire,* which was a Cockney version of a backwoods' American tale of the Ozarks and the Ku Klux Klan. The accents and drama were hilarious, in a horrifying way.

The only good thing about the play was this girl who would, from time to time, come down front and begin to sing. The first thing that I noticed was that she had perfect pitch. There was no piano lead-in, no instrument to guide her to the right note, but she hit the note dead center every time. The music followed her. That was pretty amazing. But even more impressive was her voice. She had a glorious soprano voice that filled the theater. On top of that she was cute.

It was Julie Andrews. She was seventeen years old.

We took her out to dinner after the show and I was struck by her poise and that fine quality of dignity she had even then. And there was something else, which is surprising: she was a little shy.

When you run across raw talent like that it sorta takes your breath away, and you make whatever accommodations have to be made to get them to participate in your show. Like with Frank Loesser and Bob Fosse—I accepted their quirks and demands because it was part of the package. Maybe the genius was part of the eccentricity. Take away one and you lose the other. Not a smart gamble.

In Julie's case, it was a modest condition. She simply refused to sign a standard two-year commitment to do a Broadway show. She was afraid to be away from her family for that much time and I understood. I didn't fight her on that. Incidentally, that one-year deal would, indirectly, make her available to play the lead in *My Fair Lady,* a part that came up during the end of her run in *The Boy Friend.*

Meanwhile, we were booked to open at the Royale Theater on 45th Street at the end of September. There was no need for an out-of-town run since the show was a proven hit and we weren't going to fool around with the content. But unbeknownst to me, there were problems brewing. There was an underlying suspicion on the part of some members of the London company that we were taking their intimate little show, which had cost a mere eight thousand dollars to produce in England, and bloating it up with a big budget and fancy gimmicks into an ugly American Broadway monster.

The whole business got ugly, but not in the way the company expected.

First came the minor headache of what I call "overdirecting." Vida Hope had the idea that Julie Andrews had to duplicate the identical stage movements and gestures of Anne Rogers, the London Polly. The rehearsals were painful to watch. There was Vida telling Julie to move her head to the right and her hands up and to the left, in a gesture that was supposed to look coquettish but was making Julie dizzy. At the same time, she had to sing. Julie was baffled and confused by the contortions. These were not her normal gestures and movements and it was causing her attention to stray from the play. I did not say anything at the time, not wanting to interfere. But I didn't like it.

The real trouble surfaced in the second week of rehearsal. I came into the theater one day and saw Vida Hope rehearsing a whole new scene with a brand new number that I had never seen before.

I took her aside. "What's that?"

"Sandy wants it in the show. ."

"No, no. The show has to be identical to the London production. No new numbers."

"Sandy wants it in."

Then Sandy Wilson joined in. "Those heavy-handed producers in London took out this very crucial scene. I want it back."

"Listen," I said, "I don't have a deal with you. I have a deal with the English producers and they want the show produced exactly as it was in London. So it stays out."

He said that as the author he had the right to insert a number into the show, and that I didn't have any right to meddle.

I voiced my disagreement in unmistakable terms. "It's out."

"I'm putting it in," insisted Sandy.

"Vida, take it out!"

Her head went back and forth between Sandy and me. She didn't know which order to obey.

I reminded Vida that she worked for me, not Sandy, and ordered her to drop the number from the show. She said that she couldn't do it; her first loyalty was to Sandy Wilson.

"Be sensible," I said. "The scene is out. I'm not going to allow it in. It ruins the rhythm of the show."

I could see that she was caught between the two of us. The author and the producer. But her first loyalty was to Sandy Wilson. She was a nice woman and I really liked her. I understood her dilemma completely.

So I fired her. I would direct the show. I'd seen it ten times in London, and I had the 16-millimeter film. I knew it cold.

This didn't end the trouble. The company had witnessed the battle and was shaken by the abrupt change of command. I was the new director and they were uncertain about me. The presence of a sullen Sandy Wilson in the theater during rehearsals was not making it easier. He was loud and outspoken in his opposition to my staging. He made it very clear during the rehearsals that he didn't agree with my direction. I asked him to cut it out, but the next day he was back and complaining. I asked him not to come to the rehearsals. He showed up anyway. So I kicked him out of the theater and hired a Pinkerton detective to stand at the stage door and bar his entry.

This episode contributed to a bad rap that was spread through the usual Broadway virus of whispers and nasty gossip. Feuer and Martin were, according to our enemies—and there is a mathematically proportionate number of foes you accumulate with each hit—tyrants. We were high-handed, cold-blooded, heartless fiends. And, to back it up, they pointed to the well-known factoid that I handed return-trip tickets to France to the unruly Lilo during the out-of-town run of *Can-Can*. Furthermore, we were famous for firing people for refusing to do what they were hired to do. On top of that, we watched our budgets and enforced fiscal discipline as if the money belonged to us and not the backers. There were people who considered us the bad cop and worse cop of Broadway. We were gruff and unshakable in our opinions. But, in most cases, we were right.

* * *

While I was aware of the grumbling in the company of *The Boy Friend,* I nonetheless took charge. It was actually a relief to get my hands on the show. The problem with Julie's performance needed attention. She was floundering, making all those disjointed moves that didn't come naturally. So on the day of the opening, September 30, 1954, I took her out on the fire escape of the theater and we had a talk.

"I don't know how to play this part," she admitted.

"Don't worry about it. Just think of it this way. You're the most popular girl in the school, totally in control—until a boy comes along. Then you get flustered. And then you meet this bellhop who puts you at ease. That's all you have to remember. And forget all this nonsense with the hands and the eyes and the head. Just do what the hell you want with your hands and head. Act natural. Believe everything you say. Be Polly. If you don't, you'll be a disaster."

She had innate stage presence and wisdom beyond her years, plus she had the gift for acting. Beyond that, she had that magnificent voice. A teenage Julie Andrews played Polly brilliantly, once she got rid of all of that semaphore crap.

*   *   *

There was one other important piece of business: the band. The London company played with a three-piece band: a piano, drums, and a violin. This was supposed to duplicate the full sound of early jazz. I wanted something more ambitious. I had a fondness for that style of music. As a kid I was a fan of Paul Whiteman and Gene Goldkett and that kind of frisky music. I thought it would look great to have a big, old-fashioned jazz band in the pit, which was shallow and visible to the audience in the Royale Theater.

I also wanted to duplicate that twenties' jazz sound. Only I thought it would take a larger band.

Ted Royal was the orchestrator. He knew just what I wanted. I laid out an arrangement that we would use instead of an overture. To get the sound right, I wanted three saxophones, two trumpets, a trombone, five pieces in the rhythm section—drum, banjo, bass tuba, and two pianos. I put these guys in orange and black blazers and had moving spotlights on them. When one section performed, they stood and the lights were on them. Then the lights would move to another section when it performed. The musicians would go up and down, just like an old 1926 jazz band.

On opening night, you could feel the excitement during the over-ture. The guys in the band popped up and down and the audience got it. They started to laugh and applaud. At the end of the overture, the audience refused to stop clapping. The curtain went up for the play to begin. There was an actress on the stage—a maid who was supposed to talk on the phone—but she couldn't deliver the lines. The audience wouldn't let her. They wouldn't quit applauding. They wanted the orchestra Paul McGrane and his Bearcats to take a bow.

It was the only time that the overture stopped the show.

Chapter Twenty-one

*N*ow that we had *The Boy Friend* up and running, we went straight back to work on *Ninotchka*. We had bought the rights from MGM and were pushing for an opening in late 1954.

The phone rang at 4 A.M.

"Cy, it's me, Cole. Did I wake you?"

"No, Cole, Posy and I were just lying here waiting for the phone to ring."

"I'm stuck for a rhyme. The aurora borealis is not as heated as a da-da-da."

"The aurora borealis is not as heated as a da-da-da. . . . Yeah, uh, well, . . . I'll have to think about that."

"Oh, I'm sorry, I didn't mean to disturb you. Go back to sleep."

Cole was in Williamstown, Massachusetts, and Posy and I were in New York City. Technically, there was no time difference, unless you count the difference when you're working on a show and stuck for a rhyme. In that case there's no such thing as too late; the clock is always ticking toward opening night. So if Cole called me at midnight or noon, it's all the same.

Cole was writing the music and George S. Kaufman was writing the book. Neither had the slightest interest in what the other guy was doing. Each stuck to his strength. Cole just wanted to know what kind of song to write and George concentrated on the story. The music was out of his jurisdiction, in spite of the fact that he was the director.

It had been my intention for some time to make a sprightly Broadway musical out of the Billy Wilder, Ernst Lubitsch classic film, only we wouldn't call it *Ninotchka*. We didn't know what to call it and eventually I came up with the name *Silk Stockings*. Since no one could come up with anything better, that's the one that stuck.

Naturally, there would be a couple of plot tweaks to make it more musical. Instead of a trade commission, our three dopey Soviet commissars were trying to win back a renegade Soviet composer when they, too, are seduced by the splendors of Paris. Our Ninotchka—called Nina Yaschenko—is a special envoy dispatched to bring them all home to mother Russia. However, she, too, falls under the spell of tasteful materialism, wooed by a charming theatrical agent.

Cole wrote some terrific material, but he had trouble with some simple concepts. Like the life of the common man. For example, Ernie and I suggested a comic number about the three commissars' dread of being shipped off to Siberia after they are sent home in disgrace. The number would be a rationalization of life in Siberia. Maybe Siberia's not so bad. There are good things: unlimited ice cubes, winter sports all year, guaranteed white Christmas, no unemployment . . .

Cole was not enthusiastic. He said, "I can't write that."

"Why not?"

"Siberia's beautiful."

"What are you talking about?"

"Quite a few years ago Linda [his wife] and I were guests of one of the grand dukes at his estate in Siberia. It was one of the great experiences of our lives. We speak about it to this day. It was literally a winter fairyland. . . ."

"Cole, the average man thinks of Siberia as a salt mine."

"Well, it's not, you know. It's overwhelmingly beautiful."

"Yes, I'm sure it is, Cole, but believe me when I tell you that it is not regarded as such. It is not regarded as a nice place."

"Really?"

"Not to the average guy."

"If you say so."

It was a few days later that I received the 4 A.M. phone call from Cole, who was searching for that aurora borealis rhyme. The next morning I awoke with a dazzling solution. I couldn't wait to get to the office to call him.

"I've got it, Cole."

"Great. Let me hear it."

"The aurora borealis is not as heated as a palace is."

"That's the first one I threw out."

"Why?"

"You can't keep them heated, you know. When Linda and I had our palazzo on the Grand Canal in Venice, it was terrible. We froze to death. And it was summer."

"Cole, the average man thinks that a palace is a very nice place. Nice and cozy . . . and warm."

"But, Cy, they're really not. Some years ago Linda and I spent the night at Buckingham Palace as guests of the royal family. Same thing. Froze to death . . ."

"You must believe me, Cole; the average man on the street thinks that a palace is a wonderful place to live. . . ."

He ignored me. "How about, 'The aurora borealis is not as heated as Dallas is. . . .'"

"Stick to the palace."

"Well," he said with resignation, "if you say so."

Give him this, in spite of his aristocratic distance from the rabble, he caught the spirit and wrote "Siberia," which was sensationally on the money. This is what he did with the material:

> *When we meet in sweet Siberia,*
> *Far from Bolshevik hysteria,*
> *We'll go on a tear,*
> *For our buddies all are there*
> *In cheery Siberi—a.*
>
> *When we're sent to dear Siberia,*
> *To Siberi-eri-a,*
> *Where they say all day the sun shines bright,*
> *And they also say that it shines all night,*
> *The aurora borealis is*
> *Not as heated as a palace is.*
> *If on heat you dote*
> *You can shoot a sable coat*
> *In cheery Siberi—a.*

Maybe he moved around the world in highborn style and lived in palatial splendor, but Cole Porter had an artistic sensibility and could translate plebeian woe into music.

Now that the score was well in hand, the book was in two pairs of good hands. George Kaufman brought in his wife, Leueen MacGrath, to collaborate on the book. She had already written a play and had a pretty good—and pretty pretty—head on her shoulders. Not only could she write, but she could sort of keep George in line. Or so I thought. I have always found that George Kaufman functioned at his highest level when he worked with someone else, and I convinced myself that Leueen would bring out the best in him.

It escaped me, but during this time George was pretty sick. He'd already had a stroke, but I didn't know it; given his usual state of dramatic languor, it was impossible to detect. The man could be unconscious or bored. He looked about the same.

I think now that this was a terrifically hectic time in his life. He had taken on too much responsibility: a young, pretty, and ambitious wife; a big, important new show; and a new house in London. He had to be overwhelmed with aggravation.

All that new stuff required attention. George and Leueen hired Oliver Messel, a prominent English designer, to redecorate the house, which was located in St. John's Wood. Shortly before rehearsals began, Leueen suggested that Oliver Messel might be a good choice to design the sets for *Silk Stockings*. That sounded okay. We mailed him a script and then we sent Ernie and George to meet him in London and settle the questions about the design of the sets.

Oliver was a very proper English gentleman who had a very proper English gentleman's horror of bad taste. And so when they were invited to lunch at Messel's house, it caused some concern on George's part about Ernie's behavior. Ernie could be quite forceful and noisy when taken out in public. George suggested that Ernie behave himself.

"Please be calm and let me do the talking," instructed George. "Leueen and I are going to socialize with these people."

Ernie assured him that he would be a mouse.

Lunch was an extremely courteous affair, with all the silverware and crystal on display, accompanied by the customary English small talk. George Kaufman was famously impatient with small talk, even when it came from someone he was determined to impress. He wanted to talk about the script. Before he could get started, Messel said he was most excited about a scene that took place at the exterior of a château. What a great opportunity for a wonderful set! He knew just how he was going to do it.

George said abruptly, "That scene's been cut." He went to the top of the show, describing set requirements.

Messel was still thinking about the château.

"That château exterior was so beautiful."

"Yes, well, it's been cut." George pressed on about the show.

"The château exterior was what interested me most."

Ernie sat quietly, observing.

George was getting steamed. "And I've said it's been cut. Can we get on with the rest of Act One?"

"Why don't you restore the scene so I can have my beautiful set?"

"Are you seriously suggesting that I restore a bad scene in order for you to design a set? You must be out of your mind. Come on, Ernie, let's get out of here."

As he recreated the encounter in great detail and with much relish, Ernie pointed out that throughout he obeyed George's instructions and never uttered a word.

*   *   *

Meanwhile, the show progressed. In the casting, we found Don Ameche, who could play a charming agent, and had a pretty good comic flair. He was also one of the most professional actors I have ever encountered. Very pleasant. He went to mass every day and called his wife "Sweet Momma." It was quite endearing. One of his idiosyncrasies did put the fear of God in me. After every performance, he asked me to join him in his dressing room for a drink. He had a full bottle of Jack Daniels, and I sat with him, holding my one drink, while he emptied the bottle. He didn't get drunk. He just quietly, solemnly finished the bottle. When I first witnessed this I said to myself, "Holy Christ! We're out of business!"

But the next day he would invariably show up completely pressed and fresh as a daisy. Ernie said he must wear iron suits because he never seemed to wrinkle. It was astonishing.

His costar was someone Marty Baum found: Hildegarde Neff. She was German and maintained a slight accent, which added to the exotic flavor of her performance. She had the one ingredient I always admired—energy.

Marty also filled up the other parts with terrific performers: George Tobias, Julie Newmar, David Opatoshu, Gretchen Wyler. George Tobias was great in spite of one small defect. He played the big commissar of art who sends our Ninotchka—Yoschenko—to Paris after the three renegades. George had a complete inability to remember lines. This came from working in the movies where he only had to do one scene at a time, not memorize a whole play. He kept going up: "I am the new Commissar of Art. My name is . . ." And someone would have to feed him his name. His memory was so bad that I remember Ernie once admired his necktie and asked where he got it. Tobias replied, "Oh, my wife got it at Saks Fifth . . ." Someone had to feed him "Avenue."

I cast Leon Belasco as one of the three wandering commissars. It was an old debt. Leon was the bandleader who hired me two decades earlier when I had to escape New York and the falling pearls of my youthful dreams. He was a little older, but still the tall, elegant Russian. He no longer played the romantic violin or wore a swanky tuxedo; but acting suited him fine and he gave a great performance.

* * *

By the time we got to Philadelphia, we knew that we were in trouble. The show was not working and did not respond to treatment. Furthermore, George just dropped out. He took to his bed. No one told us what the trouble was, but he was clearly pretty sick. Finally, after we'd been out of town for a couple of weeks, he called a meeting in his room at the Warwick Hotel and announced that the show was dead. "Fellas, it's not working. We ought to close it."

I was not prepared to do that. You come to Philadelphia to fix a show, not to bury it. "Listen," I said, "we don't agree, and furthermore we're missing a member of the team. Cole Porter should be here. He's written an entire score and he's not even at this meeting."

"I think we should close," George insisted.

There were forty cast members and I don't know how many members of the crew who were gonna be thrown out of work.

"We don't have to close," I said. "We have to fix the problems. The idea is good. Cole's score is good. We have to keep working on it. What we need is that well-known play doctor George S. Kaufman."

He smiled, but shook his head. "Physically, I'm not up to it. I can't do the repair work that it needs."

I then suggested that we ask Abe Burrows to come down and work on the play.

"Yeah," said George. "That's a good idea. Ask him."

"No, you have to ask him," I said.

So he made the call and Abe came down and took over the script. We had Moss Hart—Kaufman's old collaborator and head of the Dramatists Guild—draw up the terms. George and Leueen would still get billing and some percentage of the royalties. Before he left, George said that he thought I should take over the direction of the show. I was already directing the musical numbers and was flattered that he thought I could handle it.

*   *   *

At first we thought that we would have a Thanksgiving opening, but we knew that we would be on the road for a while. Abe was rewriting the show. Christmas came and went and we were still on the road. In January, we moved to Boston and the show was still rough. Abe was polishing material, changing scenes, taking them out, putting them back in. Confusion was total, except for Abe and me. We were pretty well organized, but it didn't seem that way to the cast.

Boston audiences were very forgiving. They were accustomed to works in progress. They seemed to enjoy being part of the repair process. Everywhere we went in our strange odyssey, we were sold out. The Cole Porter name accomplished that, so traveling around on the road was not a financial burden.

Then, disaster. After a performance in Boston, Abe and I met in his hotel room to discuss some prospective changes for the next rehearsal when there was a knock on the door. It was George Kaufman. He had seen the show and had his notes and wanted to take over tomorrow's rehearsal. He and Leueen would begin with the first scene of the second act. Don Ameche was falling into some old habits that should be corrected. . . .

Abe and I just stared at each other. The thing had been settled in Philadelphia. George and Leueen were out. Abe had taken over. They couldn't just come back and take over.

I found Ernie. We knew that we had to act immediately.

We went down to George and Leueen's hotel room and found them in their bathrobes. I believe that Leueen was embarrassed by the situation. She understood that this was completely unseemly, that she and George should have stayed away, but she was unable to openly oppose him, or even join the discussion.

I hemmed and hawed, trying to avoid the obvious, but George knew where I was heading. "Are you asking us to leave?"

"Well . . . yes . . ."

He rose to his full, tall, dignified height and walked to the door, opened it, and ushered us out. The next day, with all the majesty that he could muster, he denounced us in the press as he boarded the shuttle back to New York. The Boston papers had pictures of him tragically getting on the plane with Leueen, as if he were being booted out of a Soviet bloc country.

We spent almost four months on the road. Cole had gone off to sail the Mediterranean with friends. It was the first time he missed an opening. But his wife, Linda, had died and he had nothing to hold him; so we sent him off with our blessings. In Detroit, I took the room above Abe Burrows because I knew he worked best under pressure. I locked him in the room as he rewrote the play and as time ran down I stomped on the floor.

Eventually, after six weeks in Philadelphia, six weeks in Boston, and a final four weeks in Detroit—with principals complaining about their long exile—the show opened in New York on February 24, 1955, at the Imperial Theater to rave reviews. But the triumph was bitter. Ernie and I would be tarred with the accusation of having abused and insulted one of the immortals of the theater—the great George S. Kaufman. The brute truth of it doesn't matter. We were technically right, and we got the show produced in spite of the inability and the unwillingness of George to go on.

The more sentimental truth is also somewhat accurate. We were rough and arrogant and went about our business as if we were on a sacred mission. At that time, under those circumstances, we thought that the end justified the means.

Both renditions are true. The second version, I have come to realize, has a longer life.

Chapter Twenty-two

*N*o one should have five consecutive Broadway hits, at least not when you're starting out. You take them for granted. You begin to think that it's you, and not some screwy combination of luck and timing and opportunity and effort.

That's what happened. I came to believe that we were incapable of producing anything but a hit. The very fact that we selected a project was a guarantee. I even told that to Dore Schary who was the head of MGM when we were in some kind of negotiations: anything we take on, whatever we put our minds to, we will make a hit.

The flops came as a shock.

*   *   *

Not that I neglected effort; I never neglected effort. The summer of 1955 on Long Island was a colossal blur of hard work along with lobster dinners, sweaty tennis matches, and sailing out into the Atlantic on my boat, which was aptly called *The Roc,* a mythical bird of prey, possessing enormous strength and enormous size.

I had bought this terrific thirty-two-foot sailboat, a beautiful wooden yawl built in Maine that could have slept four. But I didn't go out too far. I was a day sailor. I could have managed long trips, but I stayed near the coast. I had to keep up the work schedule. This was the summer when we went to work on *Cannery Row*.

John Steinbeck had a house over in Sag Harbor and in the past few years we had become close friends. We shared a certain gritty view of the world. And he was good company. We'd go out to the unsung places, restaurants like The Chuckwagon, and load up on unhealthy food, and I'd listen to John issue his vaguely pessimistic opinions, many of which I could not understand because his words were muffled by that underslung jaw and his gruff style.

I'd wanted to do something with *Cannery Row*, only I didn't want to use the story from the book. We wanted the characters—Doc and the bums and the whorehouse women. We had a great title, *The Bear Flag Cafe,* because the bear flag is the state flag of California and it just sounds so great.

I told John I wanted to extract the characters from the novel and build the musical around them and he offered to help. We'd use the same characters—Doc, the marine biologist, and the bums, and a vagabond girl who comes to town—to construct the musical.

So every morning John Steinbeck came over to my house to write a musical comedy.

In the morning, Jed and Bobby stood on the dock of the house we rented on Three-Mile Harbor in East Hampton, waiting for him. They'd spot him coming and yell, "It's John!"

Then they broke and made a run for it.

You have to picture it. If you were casting someone to play John Steinbeck, you'd pick John Steinbeck for the part. He was perfect. A big, impressive man. There he was, in his captain's cap and turtleneck sweater, looking like a man of the sea, put-putting in from his house in Sag Harbor with his thirty-foot power boat. He stood in his open boat, his hand on the wheel, his jaw thrust out in defiance, aiming for a smooth landing. And, then he'd crash into the dock. Every damn time. The man could not sail worth a damn. He was very macho, always willing to teach you how to hunt and shoot, but he couldn't land a boat.

After the initial bang, the kids went running back and grabbed the stern lines and the bow lines and tied up John's boat and then we went to work. We worked together and we worked separately. John was out there all summer, while Ernie and I commuted into the city during the week. Early on we gave him a tape recorder to get down his thoughts and record some dialogue, and he soon sent us a bunch of tapes, which we brought to our office on 52nd Street to be transcribed by one of the secretaries.

Ernie got the first batch of transcribed pages and he said, "Look at this; it doesn't sound like John Steinbeck."

It was Steinbeck, but the pages were flat. "Maybe that's how he works," I said. "Maybe it starts out this way and he redoes it."

So we sent the pages to John and he came crashing into the office, saying, "What the hell happened here?" He was writing dialogue like, "I and the boys are gonna throw ya a birthday party," and the transcriber, a recent graduate of a secretarial school that taught her to fix all errors of grammar and improper English, had translated it to "The boys and I are going to have a a birthday party for you." She took all of the "Steinbeck" out of Steinbeck!

After a while, John gave up trying to write a musical with us and made us a better offer. He was going to write the sequel to *Cannery Row* as a novel. That's what he did best—write novels. The novel presented itself to him during the course of writing the musical and we agreed with his decision. The novel would be called *Sweet Thursday* instead of *The Bear Flag Cafe*. I never understood why. I really liked that Bear Flag title. John promised to give us all of the dramatic rights to *Sweet Thursday*.

* * *

Meanwhile, we picked up where we left off on another project—
The Music Man. This came to us by way of Frank Loesser, who
published Meredith Willson's material. We spent six months
working on it and had a good start. The original idea—and it was
serious—was that there was a spastic boy in a small town in Iowa.
In those days they would put kids like that in an insane asylum,
not realizing that there was a captive mind trapped inside that
helpless body. There was only one person who got through to him
and he was this charlatan who came to town. Meredith had a real
serious point of view.

We were well into it and had some good material, including the
song "Marian, the Librarian," when Dore Schary approached us.
He was then the head of MGM. He wanted us to come to California for one year to make two pictures, *The Boy Friend* and *Stay
Away, Joe,* the latter a Dan Cushman novel about life on an Indian
reservation. I could not resist the chance to make two movies for
MGM.

I wanted Meredith Willson to come with us. I told him to put
this play aside, do the two movies with us, then we'll come back
and do the show. But he was dedicated to getting *The Music Man*
on Broadway. I couldn't blame him.

We then made one of our first blunders. And it was a beaut. We
gave up the rights to *The Music Man.* Turned the whole thing over
to Kermit Bloomgarten. We didn't even ask for 10 percent of the
producer's end, which we were entitled to, considering all the
work we'd already done. We just felt so guilty about leaving this
poor guy in the lurch that we walked away from the project. I still
regret that one—not that we lost the percentage, but that we lost
the show.

Nevertheless, we signed a contract for a one-year commitment
to make the two pictures for MGM. When we got to California,

they put us in a big office in the Thalberg Building, which was very nice, very grand, very Hollywood. We rented a house from Jane Wyman, Ronald Reagan's ex-wife, and settled in. It was a nice house, but maybe the most memorable thing about it was inside one of the desks. Posy found a letter from Jane Wyman written to Ronald Reagan when they were still married in the forties. It listed all of his marital flaws, enumerating his many indiscretions. It was sort of a plea and had a kinda sad, mournful quality, like someone trying to save a dying marriage. I don't think it was ever sent, and we threw it away, maybe losing a historically significant document.

* * *

I am not superstitious, but the decision to walk away from *The Music Man* seemed to jinx our Hollywood pilgrimage. The day we walked onto the MGM lot, the musicians went on strike. They stayed on strike for exactly one year, which was the extent of our contract. We made no musical movies, but we made a nice salary and, the truth is, it was nice just being out in California, away from the crushing deadlines of producing a Broadway show. I played tennis and went skiing with my brother, and I sailed one fine day to Catalina.

That was an adventure. I was friends with Harold Hecht, who was the partner of Burt Lancaster in a movie production venture. Harold started out as a dancer, but now he was a producer and could afford to buy a ninety-foot sailboat, which is a major vessel. Not that he could sail. As I recall, this was a boat that competed in the America's Cup. We were invited for a cruise to Catalina with about nine other people. Posy and I took Bobby and Jed for the twenty-five-mile overnight ride from San Pedro to Catalina.

A boat of this size required a crew and this one had a captain, a mate, and a cook who doubled as a second mate. On such a boat, they could always use more hands, so when we came aboard the captain asked each person if he knew anything about sailing. I had taken a Coast Guard course and had my own boat, so I told him that I had some experience. I could help out with the sheets, which are the ropes that raise and lower the sails, and could even man the helm and keep a steady course.

The captain let me take the boat out of the harbor, which is tricky because you're not allowed to go more than five miles an hour. You have to inch your way out under power because if you move at speed you create a wake; a big boat going twenty miles an hour creates a big wake that can knock all the little boats off their moorings.

When we got going, we started to raise the mainsail and I asked the captain, "What about a jib?" He looked at me and groaned. Oy! Like I was gonna be trouble with my amateur sailor fussing. It is a lot of trouble, but the fact is that when you raise a jib or a Genoa it makes the boat a lot easier to handle. To accommodate me, he raised the Genoa. We powered out of the harbor and then set the sails in order to let the wind take over. You bring the boat into the wind and the sails are luffing—fluttering—which means that the wind is blowing on both sides and there's no resistance. Then you turn the boat to one side, the sails fill with air, and the boat surges forward. You turn off the engine and the only sound is the swish of the water against the bow. Any true sailor is thrilled at this moment.

I set a course for Catalina, took that big wheel, and looked out over the great Pacific Ocean and felt a kind of exhilaration. Harold came up from the galley with a huge pitcher of some kind of unfamiliar drink. He might have said the name, but it meant nothing to me. I knew that it had ice in it. It was a hot day and I remember that he gave me the impression that it was just a pitcher filled with a soft drink. I began to sip at it as the boat sliced through the water. The drink was ice cold and had a really nice taste. I later found out it was consommé with vodka. I kept sipping at it all across to Catalina. It's a three-hour sail from San Pedro to Catalina and by the time we got to Avalon, which is the port of Catalina, I had finished the pitcher.

I turned the wheel over to the captain and then just lay down on the deck. It was one of the few times in my life that I have ever been completely drunk. Not one of those pleasant, drifting, buzzing drunks, but a very unpleasant, miserable drunk. When you close your eyes you feel like throwing up, and when you open your eyes everything's spinning. There's no relief. I was stretched out on the deck, wanting to die. When I opened my eyes, I saw Harold in a pair of red linen pants, heading for the stern to start a barbecue. Then I heard a splash. Even in my miserably drunken state I knew that he'd gone overboard and I yelled for the captain.

He was fished out and dried off, and in a little while he came back with a pair of yellow pants, heading for the stern to launch another barbecue. When I heard the second splash, it occurred to me that Harold must have had his own pitcher of iced drink. After the crew members fished him out again, they kept him away from the stern.

*   *   *

Before we went to California, Ernie and I went to see Oscar Hammerstein. He was a guy with a social conscience and we thought that he and Dick Rodgers should write the score for *Sweet Thursday*. Frank Loesser was trying to expand musically and didn't want to do any more "mug" shows like *Guys & Dolls*. He craved respectability.

Ernie, in his charmingly blunt way, told Oscar that he should take this on. After all, he was also a friend of Steinbeck. "You know, you guys are always doing shows with little girls running around with bows on their behind. It's time you did something a little more lusty."

It took some convincing, but they finally agreed to do the show, with one stipulation. "You know," said Dick Rodgers, "we produce our own shows. If we take this on, we'll have to be the producers. Of course we'll give you half of the profits."

I thought we were rich. This was Rodgers and Hammerstein. Only they ruined it. We had cast Henry Fonda as Doc, the marine biologist. He had a perfect stage disposition for the role, only he couldn't sing. "Don't worry," we told him. "We'll get a vocal coach. You don't have to have the voice of a singer. Look at Rex Harrison in *My Fair Lady*." He bought it and went around with a vocal coach for months until Rodgers and Hammerstein took it over and dropped Henry Fonda. Dick Rodgers wanted someone with a voice. That's all he cared about—the music.

That wasn't the only change made. They turned it into another show with girls with bows on their behinds. They changed the name to *Pipe Dream,* and instead of this gutsy cast of characters out of Steinbeck, they had "*Li'l Abner*" characters out of Dogpatch. The story had this homeless girl come to town and turn a water pipe into a cute little house with curtains. Hence the change of the title to *Pipe Dream.* They even cast Helen Traubel, an opera singer, as the madame of a whorehouse. This great big, dignified dame is supposed to be a madame? It was ridiculous. When it opened, it was a disaster and I wasn't rich because there were no profits.

Later on, we ran into Oscar when we were in California and he really let me have it. "It's your fault. You talked us into that show. Your enthusiasm was infectious. It made us lose judgment and try something we weren't equipped to do."

I tried to defend myself, saying that the material was there, but they handled it wrong. But Oscar was mad. "I blame you," he said to me.

He wasn't really mad at me, just at himself.

* * *

At the end of the year, with nothing to show for the effort, we left MGM. We took the Dan Cushman property *Stay Away, Joe,* which we made into an unsuccessful show, and MGM kept *The Boy Friend,* which was made into an unsuccessful movie.

Stay Away, Joe was a pretty funny novel, and we wanted Abe Burrows to write the book for the musical. But as Abe said at the time when he turned us down, "Indians ain't funny."

I was, as I have mentioned, besotted with my own gifts and ignored Abe's sage warning. Ernie and I wrote the libretto ourselves. It is the story—oh, what's the point. It didn't work. Even the title, *Whoop-Up,* was a miserable mistake. It's an Indian name for a wild party, but it sounds like what the critics would have been doing on opening night; we were spared their judgments by a newspaper strike. The show ran for only fifty-six performances, which was the extent of the advance sale, and then mercifully shut down.

Sometimes you have an idea and it may even be a good idea; but no matter how hard you try, it doesn't work. It can't work. You have to know when to walk away.

Chapter Twenty-three

I turned fifty. The world turned with me.

The buttoned-down, charcoal gray Eisenhower fifties ended with the election of John F. Kennedy. He came into office like a splash of cool color. Kennedy was witty and glamorous. One look at that guy and you knew that the universe had shifted. *Where's Charley?* would have been too corny for the Kennedys, but *How to Succeed in Business Without Really Trying* was just right. It was, like that whole sophisticated Kennedy clan, completely tongue-in-cheek, a touch cynical.

Originally, *How to Succeed* was a kind of comic handbook written by Shepherd Mead who was, of all things, an advertising man trying to write his way out of a job. In a winning manner, it made fun of the treacherous path to success in Big Business: how to wangle a job, how to kiss up to the personnel guy, how to impress the boss. . . . One of those not-quite books that doesn't require much thought, the kind that you read on the subway. The book's subtitle gave it away: *The Dastard's Guide to Fame and Fortune.*

How to Succeed had been a bestseller when it was first published in 1952. But it was ahead of its time. The scary depiction of "the organization man" hit its peak in the early sixties, so the sixties were the true home of this particular satire.

Two unlikely guys, Jack Weinstock, a neurosurgeon with playwriting ambitions, and Willie Gilbert, a legitimate playwright, had written an unproduced show based on the book. The story was weak but tempting. A ruthless imp battles his way to the top of World Wide Wickets, a completely immoral corporation devoted to greed and sex. The best part about it was that all of the characters were deliciously corrupt. It only lacked a love interest. But that could be fixed. The important thing was that we sensed a good musical in the debauched hive of corporate conformity.

Then we tried to get Abe Burrows to write the book. But he turned us down. He had legitimate complaints. The story line, the structure, etc. He couldn't see the humor until he attended a few dinners with the corporate sponsors of one of his shows. Every time he attended the dinners they sat him next to the head of advertising. And it was always a different guy. They kept firing the advertising guys. As Abe put it, if a guy gets tossed out of a job after twenty years, that's tragic; if he's fired after a week, that's funny. The other factor in his conversion was my persistence. Abe could not withstand my badgering. I knew that he needed this show.

On the surface Abe was a happy-go-lucky man, without a trouble in the world. I knew, however, that he was a secret sufferer. As a result, he had an indulgence problem. Food and liquor . . . and liquor and food. Once in a while he had to go to a "fat farm," or some other euphemistically disguised retreat to withdraw or dry out or slim down. Six weeks was the minimum sentence. He was never happy about it and would send me plaintive letters about his misery in lockdown. He once wrote and asked me to send him a file with a cake in it.

Abe needed work and he needed acclaim. What he needed most of all was a big hit. He hadn't had one in a few seasons. I convinced him that *How to Succeed* had all the ingredients for a smash. That's when he finally agreed to write and direct the show.

Frank Loesser was tougher to bring around. He was still trying to break into legitimate art. He had that enduring problem about his brother, Arthur, the Cleveland music critic and high-brow intellectual who regarded popular music with undisguised contempt, and so we all had to work on him—Abe and me and Ernie. We agreed to an added financial incentive, giving him coproducing credit. Frank was almost as shrewd a businessman as he was a songwriter. That he could make money by making fun of people devoted to making money was a nice, ironic twist.

Nevertheless, Frank had a good nose and he knew that there were no hit songs in this show. It was all what we call "material." We ganged up on him. We appealed to his loyalty. He made the sacrifice. And it was a sacrifice. He knew that in order to do it, he had to satisfy the show's demands, which didn't strike him as romantic, didn't appeal to his song-producing ability. But his integrity was at stake. What we got out of it was the pure best of a man who knew that he was laying down a bunt for the sake of the show.

He wrote a brilliant score, each song musically perfect for the job. There is one song, however, that never fails to astound me in its sheer musical acrobatic perfection: "I Believe in You." It is sung by the hero, J. Pierrepont Finch, to himself. This guy is trying to bolster his courage before going into a cutthroat board meeting and he sings a love song to himself in front of a mirror.

> You have the cool, clear eyes of a
> Seeker of wisdom and truth,
> Yet there's that up-turned chin, and the
> Grin of impetuous youth.
> Oh, I believe in you, I believe in you!

In chorus, all the other executives who are threatened by this ruthless upstart sing in counterpoint:

> *Gotta stop that man cold,*
> *Or he'll stop me!*

Frank had Finch shaving with an electric razor and for the sound of the razor, he had the orchestra play the melody on kazoos. It sounded just like an electric razor.

Frank insisted on high-quality work. And he had to deal with certain volatile members of the production staff—me. I was a powder keg. There was a problem with one of the musicians. A saxophone player named Henry Topper. The problem was that he was a really terrible saxophone player. Henry had been in the pit in every show I had produced and every musical director had the same complaint—he played so bad that he threw off the other musicians. However, in spite of all the pressure, I kept Henry alive and the rumor got around that he was my uncle. Why else would I keep such a bad musician on the payroll?

The truth was that I was paying back an old debt. Henry had gotten me work when I was just starting out. Uncle or no uncle, with Frank, the music came first and he sent the musical director Elliot Lawrence to do his dirty work. Get rid of Henry! Naturally, I blew up and started screaming and yelling, then realized that he was acting on Frank's behalf and that they were both right. Okay, so Henry wouldn't actually play in the orchestra, but I gave him a job as the librarian and contractor for the band—I wasn't going to let him starve.

*   *   *

Among all my other gifts, I was not so good at picking people. Ernie could spot talent with precision. I was more easily overcome by a momentary infatuation. For example, I went to see a trade show and was overly impressed by some kid who choreographed one number called The Pirate Dance. His name was Hugh Lambert. I went to the guys—Ernie and Abe and Frank—and convinced them to hire him as our choreographer on the strength of that one number. The trouble was that was all he had: one number. He came in and duplicated it for the show. It was The Pirate Dance. But that was it. He didn't have another number.

So I brought in Bob Fosse to save us. He only got credit for "musical staging," but he was, in fact, the choreographer.

It was during *How to Succeed* that I saw the full range and depth of Bob Fosse's genius. There are many negative things to say about Fosse—his lunatic paranoia, his wild self-indulgence—but no one can deny his talent. Above everything else, there was the talent. That forgave almost everything.

Needless to say, Hugh Lambert, a nice enough young man, stood around, a helpless spectator, watching Bob Fosse choreograph the show while he got the credit.

*　　*　　*

The key to *How to Succeed* was in the depiction of the characters as crafty and calculating buffoons. The show couldn't work if the cast was perceived as cruel, or even seriously sinister. These were all comic knaves in pursuit of ridiculous glory. Still, they would have to be appealing—the audience would have to like them, even grudgingly. The pathetic charm had to excuse their rotten behavior. But in the end, no one was let off the hook. They were all out for themselves. That's what made *How to Succeed* different. That's what made it possible to have a scoundrel for the lead character. J. Pierrepont Finch was forgivable only in the context of the other dastards.

Abe had worked with a young actor in *Say Darling* who, we all agreed, would be perfect as J. Pierrepont Finch, the ambitious and ruthless protagonist of the show. His name was Robert Morse and he was the sort of energetic puppy who could get away with murder. A great Finch.

Charles Nelson Reilly got the meaty role of Bud Frump, Finch's arch nemesis. We put him through an audition in which he was delightfully manic, singing, dancing, and giggling at his own mistakes. Since he, himself, was kind of cartoonish, he made a perfect cartoon villain come to life.

Bonnie Scott was the original love interest, Rosemary. In the show Rosemary seemed sweet, but she, too, in her own sweet way, was quietly remorseless. She set out to nab poor Finch. She sang about how she'd remain in the background while he was out climbing the corporate ladder.

> *I'll be so happy to keep his dinner warm*
> *While he goes onward and upward . . .*

As I have always maintained, this is a rather brittle parody of a corporate wife.

Bonnie Scott quit the show and the part was taken over by Michele Lee, who was a perfect fit.

For the devastating bombshell Hedy LaRue, we got Virginia Martin, who, I can be excused for saying, had terrific "blisters." That's what the part called for and that's what I called them and that's what she had. It made a delicious contrast with her secret lover, the repressed head of the company, J. B. Biggley.

Biggley's role was crucial. He had to be a total and complete WASP. Ivy League. Ridiculous golf outfits. An uptight martinet at the office. Later revivals would make a crucial mistake and cast crude, cigar-chomping, loud-mouthed louts in the role of Biggley. That missed the joke. When the utterly correct WASP carries on a secret affair with the completely vulgar Hedy LaRue, it's a funny surprise. When the lout does it, it's expected.

And the agent and talent scout Abe Newborne had the guy to

play Biggley. Rudy Vallee. Abe Burrows used to write for him in his old radio days, when he was a popular crooner and young girls went wild over him. There was a time when he was bigger than Frank Sinatra. We all agreed that he would, with his WASPY good looks, make the ideal Biggley. But where the hell was he? Abe Newborne tracked him down to London, Ontario. Where the hell is that? Canada, says Newborne.

"I'd like to see him."

"That's gonna be a little tough."

"Why is that?"

"There is no regular airline service to London, Ontario."

We looked at a map and it was in the Canadian wilderness. Well, we had no choice. We had to get a look at him. Ernie, Abe Newborne, and I flew up to Buffalo and chartered a Piper Cub with a bush pilot and flew off to find London, Ontario. We were flying over the Canadian wilderness and I looked down and I thought, if anything happens to this plane, I would have been killed in a Piper Cub looking for Rudy Vallee, for Christ's sake!

We landed at a tiny airfield and we got a cab into this miserable little town—some small industrial wasteland without any particular character. Nightmarish. And he was appearing at this second-rate little club called "The Silver Slipper." He was quite a shock. When he walked out onstage, there was J. B. Biggley himself. And then he did his act, which was one of the worst things I have ever seen in my life. It was filthy. Full of dirty jokes. Completely inappropriate for someone who was J. B. Biggley. I was offended. No one there had any idea who he was, but he had a screen and he would project bits from his old movies to remind them.

It would have been tragic had it been anyone else. Rudy Vallee had the ability to obliterate pity. For one thing, he was not broke. This was not a broken movie star fallen on hard times. No, this was a vain rich man. He was doing this out of ego.

He treated us with a kind of regal condescension. We signed him and he came down to New York and was a very big pain in the ass. He complained about his small salary, his small dressing room, the fact that his expenses were not reimbursed. He may be the cheapest man I ever worked with.

One evening, he announced that he was going to take the cast to dinner. Not the chorus, just about ten people in the cast. Rudy had a habit of giving out photographs of himself to crappy restaurants that would, in return, give him a free meal. So he took the cast to the restaurant where he had one of his photo displays and would therefore get no check. At the end of the meal, instead of a tip, Rudy donated three ballpoint pens with his name imprinted on them to the waiters.

One of the waiters, thinking that this was not equivalent to the expected 20 percent of the bill, called the syndicated columnist Earl Wilson and planted a blind item about a cheap Broadway star who stiffed three poor waiters. Well, the next day, when the item ran in Wilson's column, Rudy was furious. He wanted to call Wilson and complain. It was in the middle of rehearsal and he didn't want to telephone from the pay phone. He wanted to use the producer's phone, which was locked. He demanded that we unlock the phone so that he could complain to Earl Wilson about his not being cheap. Which he did. He told Wilson that the item was factually wrong. Not only did he give the three waiters three signature ballpoint pens, but he also gave each of them a lovely bottle of perfume.

Wilson, being a good reporter, called the waiters who said that the lovely bottle of perfume was really one of those free, small, sample bottles you get from people trying to promote a product. So Earl Wilson printed the correction, which made Rudy look even worse.

One night, during previews, an account executive who worked for *The Fleischmann Yeast Hour* came to see the show. Fleischmann's Yeast sponsored Rudy's radio program thirty years earlier. The account executive just wanted to say hello. But the minute he stepped into Rudy's dressing room, he was barraged with complaints—thirty-year-old complaints—about bad treatment from Fleischmann's: the old dressing room was inadequate, the pay was inadequate . . . every damned thing that he felt cheated out of, entitled to . . . Rudy stuff. The poor account executive says he just wanted to say hello. Rudy says fine, let's go and have a drink.

Rudy brings Eleanor, his wife, along and they wind up at a very pricey hotel bar. After a while, Eleanor says quietly, "May I have another martini?" And Rudy says, "Why are you asking me? Ask your host." He was determined to get something back from that account executive.

Rudy's biggest battles were with Frank Loesser. Rudy refused to sing the songs the way Frank wrote them. The most egregious example was "A Secretary Is Not a Toy," which Frank wrote in three-quarter time. A waltz. A great song. Rudy refused to go at Frank's pace and finally Frank comes to me and says that I have to talk to Rudy. He can't trust himself; he's run out of patience.

So I called Rudy and Frank and we all went into a small room off the rehearsal hall and I said, "What is this all about?"

"I'm trying to help this man," says Rudy, dripping with condescension.

"What do you mean?"

He turned to Frank: "Don't you realize that these are extremely simple songs? I can do them about as well the first time as I can the thousandth."

I could hear the steam coming out of Frank Loesser's ears. Rudy Vallee went on, in his oblivious and insulting fashion. "This is not a very strong piece of material," he says. He turns to me. "I'm trying to help the man. Do you know how many songs I've introduced in my career? I'm trying to help him out."

I do not know whether to throw myself on Frank or on Rudy. Finally, I say, "Rudy, just do it the way Frank wants it done." He scoffs and asks us to reconsider, taking into account his vast experience. And he says, and here I quote: "It's amazing that the man can't see that I'm trying to help him."

Frank is at the bursting point, no longer capable of speech. I command Rudy Vallee to sing it the way Frank has written it, and he walks out, convinced that he is dealing with a musically challenged production team.

Then Frank hisses at me. "You miserable son of a bitch!"

"Me!? Why am I a son of a bitch?"

"You didn't hit him, you son of a bitch!"

"What?"

"You didn't punch him out!"

Then he hurled himself out of the room. Quit the show. Sent a telegram of resignation. Refused to take any calls.

I sent him flowers and long telegrams of supplication. One telegram was five hundred words and filled with sappy sentiments: "The sun doesn't shine without you." Finally, I sent a telegram pledging to punch out Rudy Vallee the minute the show's run was over.

After three long days, Frank returned to the show and we still had a problem with the song. Rudy refused to sing it the right way.

*   *   *

We cut the song when we went to Philadelphia in September of 1961, but no one was happy about that. One night, two o'clock in the morning, after a very bruising meeting at the Warwick Hotel, we were walking back to our rooms and I hear Fosse mumble something into his chest. He was always doing that—muttering to himself. I thought I heard "giant soft-shoe," but I couldn't be certain.

The next day I asked him, "What did you mean by that?"

He says, "I've got an idea. Can you get me a large rehearsal hall? I need a large rehearsal hall, a piano player, and Gwen." Gwen Verdon was always there as his assistant.

I rented the Masonic Temple across the street from the Shubert Theater and told Bob to keep it quiet. If Frank found out he was fooling around with the number I'd have no choice but to punch out Fosse, too.

Frank was busy with the show and didn't even miss Fosse. On the third day, Fosse brought me over and showed me what he'd done. It was amazing. He changed the tempo from three-quarter time to four-quarter time. Instead of a waltz, he turned it into a soft-shoe routine. I was really impressed. But I wasn't the guy who hadda be sold. After the show, I grabbed Frank, practically by the scruff of the neck, and said, "You're gonna watch this and keep your mouth shut until it's finished. Not a word!"

When Fosse and Gwen began doing the number, Frank's head started to spin toward me and he began to lift out of his chair; I grabbed him by the thigh and said menacingly: "Not one word!" When they finished the routine, Frank shook his head. He said, "Jesus Christ, it's brilliant. I'm gonna have to rewrite the whole thing."

It became:

> *A secretary is not a toy,*
> *No, my boy, not a toy*
> *To fondle and dandle and playfully handle*
> *In search of some puerile joy.*

Frank worked through the night trying to get the music right. He had a piano brought in so that he didn't have to leave the room. He paced and worked and smoked. Everyone tried to get him to quit smoking—he was a two- or three-pack-a-day man. Camels. Unfiltered. The hard stuff. He hid cartons everywhere. Like the drunk in

The Lost Weekend. He kept promising to quit; all the while he was slaving away in his hotel room. There was a lot of rain that fall and the room upstairs flooded, then collapsed onto Frank's piano where, among the debris, they found a carton of Camel cigarettes.

* * *

Because we had no Cole Porter or George Kaufman, the advance sale for *How to Succeed* was not very good. Frank was appreciated by the theatrical world, but he didn't sell tickets. In fact, we were doing no business at all in Philadelphia. Noël Coward was at the Forrest Theater with *Sail Away,* which was completely sold out. Following us into the Shubert was a show called *Keane,* with Alfred Drake. That was a hot ticket. At the box office they had a window for advance sales. There was always a line for *Keane.* There was also a window for current sales, which was us. One day a couple of little old ladies came up to the current window and asked, "What time does the lecture go on?"

They wanted to attend the lecture that Rudy Vallee was going to give on *How to Succeed in Business Without Really Trying.*

Ernie and I were shaken. We wanted to change the title. Merle Debuskey, our press agent, said we were out of our minds. I never saw a guy so angry. He said it was the greatest title he'd ever worked on. He threatened to quit if we changed it.

Turns out, he was right. On October 14, 1961, we opened to rave reviews. The show got the 1962 Pulitzer Prize and a bunch of Tony Awards (except for Frank who lost out to Richard Rodgers for *No Strings* on purely sentimental grounds; Frank deserved it).

The show was such a great hit that it was very hard to get tickets. One day my son Jed wanted to get a few standing-room tickets and was told that he had to see Mr. Vallee. It seems that Rudy Vallee had a running order to reserve ten standing-room seats for every show, and while he couldn't legally charge more than the actual ticket price for the standing-room tickets, he did insist that the purchaser rent a seat-cane to go along with it. He had bought ten seat-canes, which he rented out to his standing-room customers.

But he gave Jed a break. He said because he was my son, he didn't have to leave a deposit.

*   *   *

It was all so lighthearted, that sunny season when everything we touched turned to gold. Of course it wouldn't last. Nothing does.

I was in Chicago rehearsing a road company of *How to Succeed* one cold day in the autumn of 1963. It was the normal rotation and replacement of cast members. I was at the Shubert Theater auditioning singers. They didn't have to just sing; they also had to be able to move around on the stage. They had to display some grace. Fosse had a routine to see whether or not they had any rhythm. It was very simple. He used a set of moves and poses and hand gestures—a test to see if they had two left feet or two left hands. He would have them move to "Yankee Doodle Dandy." They'd all sing, "Yankee Doodle went to town, riding on a pony, stuck a feather in his hat and called it macaroni . . ." And while they sang, they pretended to stick feathers in their hats, performing elementary steps in time to the tune. He called it moving, not dancing.

So there I was, all alone out front in this dark, big house watching the singers, and the piano was playing "Yankee Doodle" when I felt a tap on my shoulder. I was summoned to the box office. Everyone was huddled around a radio, listening to the reports from Dallas. And that's how I heard about the murder of Kennedy in November of 1963, hunched over a radio with the sound of "Yankee Doodle" in the background. That's how "Camelot" ended for me.

Chapter Twenty-four

We *spent another* summer in East Hampton. There I was, surrounded by show-business junkies—Neil Simon, Bob Fosse, and Gwen Verdon. I was bound to fall into old habits.

Ernie picked up a copy of *Little Me,* which was the fictional memoirs of a fictional celebrity, the creation of Patrick Dennis, the guy who wrote *Auntie Mame.* Once again, another Broadway musical dangled in front of our eyes. We couldn't resist.

Neil (Doc) Simon had just written his first play, *Come Blow Your Horn,* which was promising, a foretaste of his later brilliance. It was a new medium for Doc. He started out as one of the major talents in that gifted stable of writers assembled by Sid Caesar on the original *Your Show of Shows:* Mel Brooks, Woody Allen, Danny Simon, Mel Tolkin, Larry Gelbart, Lucille Kallen.

After reading *Little Me,* we went to see Doc in this small house in Amagansett, just down the road from East Hampton. He was there in the summer with his wife, Joan, and their two little girls.

Doc agreed to take on the show and had a terrific idea right off the bat. The book was about Belle Poitrine, a well-endowed woman who marries her way to fame and fortune by way of seven husbands, all of whom die conveniently and leave her their money.

Never mind the woman, said Doc, make the husbands the star. And make all the husbands one man. Furthermore, make him none other than Sid Caesar. He can play all seven parts.

Of course we had to convince Caesar. Ernie, Doc, and I met Sid in his office in Manhattan. The thing I remember most vividly was lunch. Sid was very particular about his food. He introduced me— he introduced all of us—to the hot pastrami sandwich topped with a sweet red pepper. It was a food revelation. The sandwiches came from the Stage Delicatessen and it was a time when pastrami sandwiches were still reasonable. Today they put five pounds of meat on the bread. No one can handle that much pastrami. Sid was a great big monster of a guy, with a huge appetite and a terrific sense of humor and a frightening sense of presence. If he told you to try something, you tried it. So we all cut the sweet pepper in half and put it on each side of the sandwich. Terrific. The man knew his pastrami.

The business about doing the show is not quite as clear as the sandwich, although I'm pretty sure that somewhere along the line he agreed to do it. I also remember that Sid was afraid of written dialogue. He'd never had to work within strict script limits before. Those guys on *Your Show of Shows* only approximated the script. They knew in a general sense the gist of a scene and ad libbed their way to the end. I explained to Sid that a Broadway show was different. Dialogue had to be memorized and performed exactly as written. Otherwise, the show flounders. Lighting cues, entrance cue, scene changes depend on adherence to the script.

Sid: "I have to learn every word?"

Me: "Every word."

Sid: "Oy!"

We hired Mickey Deems, who was a member of the cast and a friend of Sid's, but his principal job was to work as Sid's dialogue coach. He was also there to feed Sid a line if he went up.

The music was written by the terrific Cy Coleman with lyrics by Carolyn Leigh, and the one song they wrote that was hauntingly attached to the show was "Real Live Girl."

Fosse agreed to do the choreography, but he wanted to become a director, so I gave him a credit as a codirector. Bob had worked with Sid on *Your Show of Shows*, just performing some dance routines as an "act," not that Caesar showed any signs that he remembered him.

"I'm not a dancer," Caesar declared, "and I do not intend to become one."

He was also not a singer, which was apparent, and he declared that he would not sing more than three songs. "I have an aversion to lyrics."

This was not good news for Carolyn Leigh.

With all of Sid's zany idiosyncrasies, he was worth it. He was funny. He could mangle punch lines, cough during a joke, clear his throat when he had to speak—he was still worth it. There are people who are intrinsically funny. Like Sid. That is, when he had all his weight. He lost his funny when he lost all that weight. But back then, when he was whole, he was a whole vaudeville show. All that rolling rage and sweat had to be watched—you never knew where it was going. It was exciting. Zero Mostel was like that. Sid would drive us crazy with his wildness, but he would also split our sides. It wasn't doing seven roles that bothered him—he was in the seven-role business—what bothered him was any kind of constraint. He always seemed like he wanted to bite something. But when he was under the control of Doc's script, he was great.

One of the scenes had him as an actor playing Marc Antony who was being rejected by Cleopatra. He calls for the boy to bring him his faithful dagger. He takes the dagger and plunges it into his chest. Then he says, with that arch look of comic wonder, "You couldn't find a fake dagger?" Delivered by Caesar, Marc Antony was very funny.

The other side to Sid could be a little terrifying. One night I went backstage and mentioned that he should pick up the pace. I didn't say it mean—you wouldn't dare say it mean to Caesar. I just said it. He brooded about that. He kept muttering, "Pick up the pace!" "Pick up the pace!" He went back to his hotel room and paced . . . and brooded and muttered and, finally, screamed: "You want to see me pick up the pace?! Okay, I'll pick up the pace!" Whereupon he tore the bathroom sink out of the wall and threw it out of the hotel window.

"How's that for picking up the pace?"

So, knowing all this, everyone approached Sid with a certain ginger delicacy. You didn't want to make him mad. Still, this was a musical and there were scenes in which Sid had to perform some simple ballroom dancing. Nothing complicated. No running slides. Fosse stayed within Caesar's range.

There was one temperamental member of our company who gave me more trouble than Sid Caesar. Carolyn Leigh, the lyricist. She was a young woman in her thirties who had an unnatural attachment to her own lyrics.

We couldn't seem to find the right spot for her favorite number, "Lafayette, We Are Here," which was the closing number of the first act. It was a very nice song, everyone liked it, but, like so many of these things that defy explanation, we just couldn't get it to work. It was a spoof about World War I, all the Victory Girls coming to France to entertain the troops. It is a big, rousing number, played on a battlefield in France as the doughboys wait for the girls. We were going into our last ten days at the Erlanger Theater and I said we'd better get rid of this clunker while we still have the chance to replace it. Otherwise we're going to drift into New York with this junky first-act ending.

So I made the decision. I called a meeting onstage after the show. Fosse, Doc, Cy Coleman, Carolyn, and myself. I said, "I'm making the decision to cut the number." Everybody understood, shook their heads. Too bad, too bad. But they understood. Not Carolyn. She said that the number was very good. I said that I agreed, but it wasn't working and I wasn't going to waste any more time on it.

"Well, I refuse to cut it."

"Carolyn, I'm cutting it."

"I know my rights under the basic agreement of the Dramatists Guild and you cannot cut the number without my consent."

Technically, she was right. Under the Dramatists Guild agreement, you can't cut any material without the consent of the author or composer. However, this was real life and we were in real trouble, and I was cutting the number for the sake of the show. We went around four or five times—"yes, I will!" "No, you won't!"— she stuck to her guns and I stuck to mine and finally she just turned and stalked out of the theater.

Now, Carolyn was a very overweight woman and when she made an emotional exit, it was very dramatic.

"Where's she going?" I asked.

"I'm going to get a cop," she yelled back.

As I turned to watch her leave, I noticed a middle-aged couple sitting behind us. I assumed they were somebody's friends, just waiting to meet after the show. It turned out that they were malingerers watching the postshow show. "Very nice show," they said. Politely, we asked them to leave.

Outside every stage door in Philadelphia there is always a patrol car. Carolyn returned breathing heavily and dragging a bewildered Philadelphia patrolman. She pointed to me and says to the cop, "I want you to arrest him."

The cop looks around in a complete daze. "What for?"

"He's violating my rights under the basic Dramatists Guild agreement."

The cop blinks. This is probably not on his list of Criminal Code violations. Finally, he shrugs. "Lady, I don't know what you're talking about," then turns and walks out.

Carolyn was hurt, and while I understood her disappointment, the larger issue of the well-being of the show had to be the first consideration. Still, I may be the only producer almost arrested for song abuse.

Eventually, we made up and Fosse did another one of his magic tricks to save the first act ending. Instead of the brisk version of "Lafayette, We Are Here," he went the other way. He did a soft, sentimental, wistful reprise of the waltz "Real Live Girl." It was funny and moving when the doughboys performed it because the soldiers were dancing with imaginary girls. The news that the Victory Girls were coming over made the soldiers drift into this dreamy soft-shoe waltz. It was very effective.

*   *   *

The show opened on November 17, 1962, to pretty good reviews. Fosse won a Tony for his choreography. The show had a decent run because of Sid Caesar and Doc Simon's script. I still remember some of the very funny lines; they're scripted into my memory, the way you pick up and repeat something that tickles the whole family and becomes a kind of universal punch line. There's a scene in a restaurant when Sid as a young man declares his independence from his dominating mother. He says he's definitely going to marry the girl he loves no matter what his mother says, that there's no power on earth that can stop him, his mind is firmly made up.

The mother replies quietly: "We're leaving."

And Sid says, "I'll get the coats."

I can't leave a restaurant without thinking of that.

Chapter Twenty-five

M*arty Baum listened* to the pitch. He didn't have much choice. Marty was an old friend. He had practically come into the business alongside us, as a brand-new Broadway agent. When we were making *Guys & Dolls* and were desperate to find a Big Jule, it was Marty who delivered B. S. Pully to our doorstep. And now he was head of ABC Pictures—a big shot—hearing me out.

Strange how things turn out. Here I was making a pitch for my debut as a film producer to my old subordinate. A writer had come to me and Ernie—this was 1970—and said he had a story for Buddy Hackett. It's called "The Kicking Rabbi." Rabbi Hackett, on an outing with his rabbinical students, discovers that he is a natural football place kicker. Word gets out, scouts come down, and he is signed by the New York Giants. It's okay, because the games are played on Sunday.

It was a funny idea and we took it to Marty Baum who listened courteously and then said, "Fellas, put this aside. Clear your heads. I've just been offered the film rights to *Cabaret*. If you take it on, I'll go for it."

I hadn't seen *Cabaret* since it opened as a Broadway musical in 1966 and my opinions about it then were lukewarm. I didn't trust

my memory and wouldn't give Marty an answer until I was convinced it had a chance as a film.

Cabaret had a couple of incarnations. It started out as a story in
Christopher Isherwood's book *The Berlin Stories*. Then, in John
van Druten's *I Am a Camera,* it became a legitimate stage play, later
made into a movie. Harold Prince turned it into a musical with a
score by John Kander and Fred Ebb. It was the story of Sally
Bowles, a nightclub performer, who lives precariously in the heart
of debauched Berlin in 1931—the end of the Weimar Republic and
the dawn of Hitler.

The last road company was playing in Seattle so I flew up and
saw the show, which reinforced my initial reaction. The entire secondary story—that soupy, sentimental, idiotic business with the
little old Jewish man courting Sally's landlady by bringing her a
pineapple every day—had to be thrown out. I couldn't stand it. Besides, it was dull and uninteresting.

However, the part having to do with the Kit Kat Klub and the di-
abolical M.C. was terrific. I picked up a copy of George Grosz's
book, *Ecce Homo,* a magnificent depiction of the cruel decadence
of Berlin between world wars. I saw at once that this depravity had
a deep-seated heritage and I could do something . . . important. I
hesitate to ascribe importance to what I do. I have never devoted
myself to "art." I dig ditches. But there are occasional opportunities to dig a pretty good ditch.

I told Marty: "If you throw out the pineapples and put in a decent secondary love story—something that could appeal to young
people—I'll do it."

Another thing I meant to get straight (and this is no pun) was
the homosexual angle. In the earlier shows, the exact sexual inclination of Sally Bowles's admirer is either fudged or eliminated. The
guy is an English teacher and he avoids sleeping with Sally, prefer-
ring to observe her many trysts. My opinion was that if he wasn't a

homosexual he would have taken a crack at her. I wanted that dealt with in a forthright way. Berlin and the Nazis were all tied up in knots with sexual perversion and repression. The business of sex and violence was at the heart of their craziness.

There was one other thing—a generality—that bothered me a lot about the whole nature of movie musicals: people keep bursting into song in the middle of the street for no apparent reason. That couldn't happen in this story. I told that to Marty. There can be no unjustified singing on the screen. There's a reality about the movies that will not accept it. This is a show-business story and the singing takes place on the stage of the Kit Kat Klub. Period.

Marty agreed. He saw what I was getting at. Or, at least he trusted me to know what I was doing. And we agreed that I would do the picture. I would be the sole producer. Ernie would stay in the background on this project. For one thing, Ernie wasn't too interested in film. He was the money guy and the money was coming from ABC Pictures and Allied Artists. Besides, what this needed was a backup director. A whole script had to be developed. There was a lot that needed repairing and Ernie was never interested in that part of the business. Plus, and I'm not even sure that I was aware of it, the person I had in mind for the film's credited director would need the support of someone with my experience, someone who could help guide the thing if he got into trouble.

The first person I put to work was Jay Presson Allen, the screenwriter. Ernie suggested her. He was always good at picking writers. I told her my ideas about the changes in the story—that we use Sally Bowles from Isherwood's *The Berlin Stories* and the homosexual from Van Druten's *I Am a Camera*—and we keep the sexual tension high. I also thought we should have the secondary love story take place between a young Jewish heiress who cannot marry out of her faith and a gentile. The drama comes from the fact that she doesn't know that he really is not a gentile, but a poor Jewish schnook trying to pass.

Well, Jay is a really smart, tough woman and she agreed with me and we worked out both stories. The twist in the main story, we agreed, is that the English teacher who comes to Berlin is, in reality, a switch-hitter. That way he can have an affair both with Sally and the German baron who is romancing Sally. Ah, what a delightfully complicated triangle! She wrote a terrific screenplay. Kander and Ebb wrote three new songs for the movie, "Mein Herr," "Money," and "Maybe This Time." ("Maybe This Time" was what we call "trunk music." It was hidden away and pulled out when a song was needed. Kander and Ebb had it in their trunk.)

*   *   *

Now I needed a director. I knew who I needed, but I had to go about it delicately.

I was in New York when I started getting the phone calls from Bob Fosse. He knew that I was producing the movie and he wanted to direct it. He was kinda desperate. He'd just blown $10 million for MCA-Universal making the movie of *Sweet Charity* and was considered unemployable by the studios. He'd had a $3 million overrun and made some very basic mistakes in the filming. For one thing, he tried to make the movie too realistic and lost that abstract quality you get from a Broadway show. He didn't yet understand the difference between the stage and film. You can get away with suggestions and fake sets onstage; you can't do that in a movie. In the theater an audience can see a stagehand in the wings and it doesn't bother them. On the screen if they see a shadow of a camera, they lose interest in the entire film. It's a completely different set of rules.

My hunch was that Fosse had learned his lesson. We met for lunch. I had pasta, he had a pack of cigarettes. I explained the deal.

Manny Wolf, who was the head of Allied Artists, and Marty Baum at ABC wanted me to pick a big-name director—Joe Mankiewicz or Gene Kelly or Billy Wilder.

There was a wild, downcast look in Bobby's eye. That's how he was, always bouncing between unbridled enthusiasm and hopeless despair.

"I have to see the other guys," I said. "They expect it. If I don't see them, I'll seem unreasonable. But after I see them, I'll tell Marty that I've talked to everyone and I want Fosse."

He was grateful. For the moment.

I first went to see Billy Wilder. He was an old friend and he said, "I can't do this." It was the pain of Germany. He'd already seen too much of Germany. He had run away from the Nazis. He was cordial. He just wasn't interested. Not in the subject, not in the project.

Then I went to Gene Kelly, an old friend, and he was really interested and I felt bad. He could have made the movie, but it wouldn't have been the same picture. It would have been more . . . frivolous. It wouldn't have Fosse's dark side. These were only half-hearted interviews. My mind was made up on Fosse before I saw any of them.

"Listen," I told Marty after talking to everyone else, "we've got eight musical spots. They all have to work. I have a fifteen-by-twenty-foot playing area." That was the size of the Kit Kat stage. As I saw it, if one or two of the numbers didn't work, we had a flop. On the other hand, if all eight worked and the picture was a little short on dramatic direction, we could still have a hit. My bet was on the numbers. I had to protect the musical numbers. And there is nobody better on musical numbers than Bob Fosse. The picture could not have been done without him.

Marty was sensible. "You have to do it," he said. "It's your call. But you have to watch the budget."

Actors were going to be working for peanuts. Liza Minnelli was getting $100,000, Michael York was getting $50,000, Joel Grey was getting $35,000. Fosse was being paid $75,000. The reason we were shooting at the Bavaria Studio in Munich was to save money. The whole budget was $3.4 million. We were working with a very tight collar.

*   *   *

The issue of the cinematographer came up very early. Bob wanted his old cameraman from *Sweet Charity,* Robert Surtees, but everyone was against hiring him. Including me. Maybe Fosse felt comfortable with Surtees, but a European camera crew would avoid big union costs, and, even more important, we wouldn't have to worry about that arty tendency to overshoot that ruined *Sweet Charity.*

We went to Munich and Hamburg to check out locations and I hafta confess that Bob's eye was ingenious. When he looked at things, he saw them as if he was looking through a camera lens. He could picture it. For example, we needed a castle and we went all around Germany looking for one. In a little town called Eutin, which was just outside of Hamburg, we found a very nice castle. It had an enormous ballroom, sixty feet across, high ceilings, and great big fireplaces at both ends, and I thought, What the hell is he going to use this for? Of course, he used it for a famous scene in which the three principals—Sally, Brian, and the baron—stage a drunken seduction. It was a dance in which three people fall into an intimate swoon. But this was a huge, intimidating ballroom. It could hold three hundred people. I didn't see the possibility for anything intimate. Fosse did.

Being with Fosse was intense, but stimulating. I enjoyed traveling around with the guy. We were in London interviewing the cameraman Geoffrey Unsworth. I said, "I'm gonna show you something unusual." I took him to Moss Brothers, a famous old upper-crust equestrian outfitter in The Strand. Bob was wide-eyed, a bumpkin, which is surprising considering his great professional complexity. But that's the truth: he was kinda naive. The sophistication was something he picked up along the way. So we go to Mossbross (which is what we English gentlemen called it) and enter this bird-cage elevator and I say to the old retainer, "Gentlemen's swords, please."

The retainer takes us up to the third floor where they have a huge display of swords and breastplates and helmets. It was a little like a fairyland. Finally, a very well-turned-out fellow came over and I said, "Do you have anything in a short sword? Because I find at my height, being a short guy, the normal sword drags on the floor." The salesman didn't know what the hell I was talking about.

Then we went upstairs to the saddlery area where they have a full-sized wooden horse and when you buy your gear, they put you on the horse and you can test it. Among all the brown saddles, there was one black saddle and I said to Fosse, you know what that's for? He said, no. "That's for evening."

He really got a kick out of that.

*   *   *

The question of the camera crew hadn't been settled. Bob was still pushing for Surtees. We went back and forth to London, Paris, Stockholm, with Fosse interviewing cameramen. I insisted that he talk to other European crews. He agreed, but made me promise to keep an open mind about Surtees. And I didn't keep an open mind. I lied. But then, I never had an open mind about other directors when I talked to Gene Kelly and Joe Mankiewicz. I firmly believe that there are show-business promises that have to be made—for the sake of a fragile ego or to prop up an unsteady state of mind—but that do not have to be kept.

The truth is I didn't realize how deep this business of the cameraman went with Fosse. I thought that he would understand my tactical position. It didn't occur to me that our relationship was on such shaky ground that we would have a falling out over the cameraman.

* * *

The blowup came in Munich. We were staying at the Vier Jahreszeiten—the Four Seasons. Bob spent the day interviewing actors, and a scenic designer who didn't speak much English. The translator was a really cute woman named Ilse Schwarzwald, and before anyone knew what hit them, she and Bob had become a couple. Instantly. It was nothing that was hidden or secret. Even when Gwen Verdon, still his wife, came to Munich, she knew about Ilse. And about the others. I don't know how to explain this about Bob—or his women—but they all fell in love with him instantly and forever. And they all forgave him for all the other women; they all overlooked his reckless overindulgences. It was as if he lived in some other category of ethical accountability.

It was soon after that first meeting with Ilse that he demanded, again, Robert Surtees for his cameraman. I was getting tired of hearing about it. Surtees would cost us a minimum of $50,000 more than any of the European cameramen.

I was worn out. Maybe I told him that I'd try to get Surtees, maybe I didn't. He says I did. We both heard what we wanted to hear. I went to my room and the phone rang. It was eleven o'clock at night. It was Marty Baum from Los Angeles. He asked how things were going.

"We're still talking about cameramen," I said.

Marty suggested that we cut our losses, pay Fosse off, and get someone else. I wouldn't hear of it. Fosse was the right guy. I saw him in action. I heard the way he talked to actors. He was born to be a director. Then Marty said, "What about Surtees?"

"I'll tell you right now, I don't want Surtees and we're not going to have Surtees."

I know that I have a gruff, loud voice, but that's not what gave me away. Bob's room was right next door to mine and he was eavesdropping. He used a stethoscope or a water glass—something—but he was listening to my end of the conversation. I'm not being paranoid. Bob had done the same thing to Hal Prince in New Haven during the tryouts for *Damn Yankees*. He was famous for his paranoia.

That was at night. I went to bed, and the next morning at about nine, I was still in my bathrobe when Fosse banged on the door. The moment I opened it, I could see that he'd been up all night. He was like a bomb going off. "I heard your whole conversation with Baum last night. I heard it through the wall. You no-good son of a bitch!"

I sat down and he was looming over me. I was sort of caught off guard and didn't know what to say. He lambasted me with accusations, saying that I didn't think he could direct. I just hired him for the choreography. That I never intended to give him Surtees. I'm not sure how big a liar that makes me.

Weakly, I defended myself. "I never promised Surtees."

"That's a fucking lie. You're a two-faced shit."

I know now that he was insecure—very insecure—after the disaster of *Sweet Charity*, and that Surtees was a security blanket. Maybe even my little game about interviewing directors I had no intention of hiring was backfiring, making him think of me as inherently duplicitous. The fact that I did it in his favor when I was hiring a director didn't seem to count for much now as he was blowing and blasting me with everything he had.

But this had gone too far. I had to stop it. "What do you want to do about it, Bob?"

He was cornered. It was his move. If he wanted to quit, this was his moment. But he picked a middle ground. He said, "If you want me off the picture, you're going to have to fire me."

I didn't fire him and we settled for Geoffrey Unsworth for cinematographer.

It was bad. Marty Baum came to Munich to try to smooth things over. I remember we were in the back of a cab—Marty in the middle, flanked by Bob on one side and me on the other. Bob demanded that Marty fire me. Marty finally turned around and said, "Look, Bob, Cy is the producer of the picture so you might as well make up your mind to that. He's not being taken off the picture." From the studio's point of view, if anyone was leaving, it would be Fosse. Still, Marty tried to conciliate. He said that Bob should be grateful to me.

We were both waiting for Fosse to quit. If he had, I would have quit, too.

Fosse would later claim that he couldn't quit—he needed the money. But my guess is that it was more complicated than that. Fosse needed to prove himself and this was the perfect thing to do it with. He recognized the art of what he was about to do. He also needed an enemy. For that role he cast me.

And so we plunged into the making of *Cabaret,* not speaking, at least socially.

Whatever else we were though, Bob and I were professionals. We were able to work together, even talk, about the necessary details of making a picture. But it wasn't pleasant. And I took precautions.

In the beginning I was friendly with a first assistant director, a German guy named Wolfgang Glattes. We hit it off. We'd sit around and talk, very friendly. Finally, it occurred to me, I should have warned this guy. I called him into my office—I had an office at the Munich studio—and I said, "This is the last time I want to see you in this office. Or having anything to do with me. Because if you do, you're gonna be off the picture. Now, remember, not even hello, nothing when I come on the set."

Fosse was a hard man. He maintained a business relationship. He'd discuss the setups with me. We'd talk about lighting. We'd watch the dailies together. But beyond that, nothing. He wasn't just hard on me, he was hard on himself, working twelve, fifteen hours a day. Rehearsing endlessly. Liza Minnelli stood up to him. He tried to badger her about working late, and she just left. No one could ever accuse Liza of being lazy, and she had gone as far as she was willing to go on that particular day. She knew that if she stayed, they'd end up saying things that couldn't be fixed.

Liza was great. She worked her heart out. But she was dating this drummer in California and she was on the phone with the guy all night. The hotel manager came over to me and warned me about it. He said that her telephone bill was two or three thousand dollars a week. So I spoke to her. I said it would be cheaper to fly her boyfriend over, which is what she eventually did.

Posy also came over once filming started. She started taking art lessons with a former Nazi in Munich. Everywhere we went, Posy studied something. Art. French. Cooking. She was a pretty good artist, although she never took those things seriously. Maybe she was thrown off by her teacher who kept saying how much better things were in the old days, under Hitler. In most cases, the Germans were excessively friendly. And they all had relatives who were Jews. Long-lost relatives. Every one of them.

Meanwhile, the cast was assembled, the music was recorded, rehearsals were advancing, sets were being built. The schedule on a movie is very strict. Morning shoot, afternoon setup—everything is carefully prepared. And the Germans have their own work ethic. Every morning the German members of the crew would be issued six liters of beer. That was for the morning. They'd do the same thing for the afternoon. And every day there was a long lunch break. It's not like in America. The Germans take lunch very seriously. Nobody just grabs a sandwich. The food was sensational. I loved the bratwurst and the potatoes. It was the best food in Europe.

On Friday, if we had no weekend shoot, the grips would string these colored lights between the trees and bring out a huge table for a weekly wrap party. And every week somebody sponsored the food. One week it was Liza, then Michael York or Marisa Berenson, or Bob, or me. There was this one dish that was terrific—a big breaded loaf. You cut it into slices and inside the bread was frankfurter meat. It was delicious. The crew had its own bung starter made out of polished brass and they'd roll out a small barrel of beer. And there was the beer and the lights and all this food, and they all entertained. One guy showed up with a musical saw. We put him in the picture.

It became apparent some time early in the filming that something unusual was happening. The studio guys in Hollywood didn't necessarily recognize it, but it was better than good. Everyone was at the top of their form: Liza, Joel Grey, Michael York, Helmut Griem, Fritz Wepper, Marisa Berenson, and Fosse. Mostly Fosse. Not one of them would ever do better work. The attention to makeup—the garish, tawdry, corrupt look of the characters— was perfect; the transition between the musical numbers and the dramatic story outside of the Kit Kat Klub was flawless. The tone and texture and lines of the movie were exact.

When we filmed the outdoor scene, we had to construct our own beer garden. We found a perfect German youth of about twelve to sing "Tomorrow Belongs to Me." The kid is wearing a kind of Boy Scout uniform with a swastika armband. As he sings, he is slowly joined by the people in the beer garden—Germans of varying ages who had a rugged, outdoor look of great vigor. As they join in, the music gains in intensity until, finally, they are all standing and belting out this Nazi anthem. They don't actually sing, just move their lips to the words. We would dub in the voices later. But the lips had to move to the right words and none of them spoke English, so we put up huge blackboards around the tables so that no matter where you're sitting or standing, you were facing a blackboard. The lyrics were written in phonetic German.

The trouble was in getting everyone to take a haircut. This was 1971, and the youth of the world had long hair. We actually had "hair payments" in the budget to induce people to cut their hair. The twelve-year-old kid we got for the song had hair down to his ass. I knew that money wasn't going to buy him. But I was prepared. I parked an old army jeep in front of the stage. Then I sat him down in a makeup chair. The hairdresser, following my instructions, took a huge scissors and cut off a large hunk of his hair. The kid jumped out of the chair, yowling and crying. When he calmed down, I showed him the jeep. How would he like to learn to drive it? How would he like to drive it around on the set until we were finished filming? The crisis was over.

We had to find a voice to dub the boy into the picture. Posy and I went to Vienna and auditioned the members of the Vienna Boys Choir, but no one seemed to match the blonde in the picture. Much later, back in Hollywood, we heard a kid in a rock band who was perfect, and it was his voice we dubbed into the picture.

As we were getting down to the end of filming, we were running out of money. The insurance people came to see me. It was an English company that issued the completion bond. The arrangement is that when a company exceeds the budget, the insurance people take over. They bring in their own director, editor, whatever, and take over. So these two English guys came to me and I said, "Jesus, what am I gonna do? We're running out of money."

And they said, "We'll tell you what to do, if you'll do it. You've got to call Fosse in and say to him, 'here's the layout. We're closing on September 7. We have enough money until September 7, so, finished or not, the picture closes down then.'"

I did that and Fosse went into a frenzy and I said, "Well, what can I do?"

"What happens if I'm not finished by September 7?" he asked.

"They'll take over the picture."

He finished it on September 7.

The movie was released in 1972 and won eight Academy Awards, including Best Director for Fosse, Best Cinematography for Geoffrey Unsworth. We lost Best Picture to *The Godfather.*

Fosse maintained that if I had left him alone we would have gotten that one, too.

If I had left him alone we'd have gone three weeks over budget.

*   *   *

Having said all that, I still wanted to find some way to patch things up with Fosse. He was worth it, and there came a moment when I thought it was possible. It was the night of the Academy Awards, March 25, 1973. We were at the Dorothy Chandler Pavilion in Los Angeles, sitting neatly in a row. Joel Grey, Liza Minnelli, Geoffrey Unsworth, Fosse . . . me. We didn't actually sit side-by-side. Posy was between us, like a UN peacekeeper.

Although we were nominated in ten categories, I didn't think *Cabaret* had a chance of winning more than one or two, since we were up against *The Godfather.* And then the awards started coming down. Joel for supporting actor. Liza for lead actress. Unsworth for cinematography (a nice vindication of my side of the argument). But it apparently only made Fosse mad. When he got up to claim his own award for best director, he took one last crack at me: " . . . I'd like to mention Cy Feuer, the producer, with whom

I've had a few differences of opinion. But at a time like this you have affection for everybody."

I was still gonna say something appeasing when I accepted the award for Best Picture, which, given the fact that we seemed to be sweeping everything, was almost certain. Bob was Bob and he couldn't help his rage. That was what made him great. It was a creative rage. And I was gonna say something like that. I hadn't prepared a speech since I was so sure that we were gonna get wiped out by *The Godfather.* But so far we took eight out of the ten categories in which we'd been nominated. The last one was Best Picture, and by then I was unreasonably cocky and convinced that this was a fateful night. Then came that final moment and the Best Picture Award went to . . . *The Godfather.*

It was the most disappointing moment of my professional life. I missed winning an Oscar, but more important, I lost a chance to win back my friend.

Chapter Twenty-six

*A*fter *Cabaret* we spent a year in Paris engaged in a completely ridiculous project—making a movie based on the life of Edith Piaf. The early life. Not that it matters. Any part of her life would have been stupid for us to tackle. She was French, ultimately and completely French. We were totally and utterly American. What the hell did we know about French? I couldn't even speak the language.

But Ernie read a biography written by Piaf's kid sister and, with his usual gust of enthusiasm, swept me along into the project. We'd just come off a big hit and we were on top of the world and were a little arrogant. And a little dumb. However, like most flops, at the time it seemed a terrific idea.

Posy and I stayed at the Plaza Athénée while we looked for an apartment in Paris. The Plaza Athénée is a very fancy hotel and one night there was a jewel robbery and the police sealed off the lobby. The thieves had smashed some windows and the floor was covered with broken glass. This complicated matters since in their haste to make their getaway, the thieves had dropped a lot of diamonds, which were sprinkled among the glass. Posy and I enjoyed the comic splendor of watching the cops trying to keep the rich guests away from the broken glass and loose diamonds.

Eventually we found an apartment on the Right Bank and set up housekeeping. Posy took cooking lessons while I went to school researching Piaf's seedy world of Montmartre.

I was caught up in it. That's the exasperating thing about this whole project: there was nothing wrong with the story. Two half-sisters growing up in the sordid world of the Paris slums. Their mother gone, raised by a son-of-a-bitch father, a street acrobat, who screwed everything in sight. He used his kids to draw crowds for his sidewalk balancing act. Edith would sing and bang on a toy drum and her kid sister would play the harmonica. Afterward, the kids would collect the money and turn it over to this lowlife who would go off and spend it all on whatever conquest he'd made during the night. Finally, Edith had enough. She was plucky. She decided to start her own act, and she brought her sister along.

The story follows them through all the misery of life on the streets in Paris, right up until Edith auditions for a legitimate job. The audition is the final scene in the movie and it's a beaut. It takes place in an empty theater and there are a couple of guys sitting out there in the audience listening to this tremendous voice coming out of this skinny little waif. Then, when she finishes, we have a shot of her coming down off the stage, asking plaintively, "Was it okay? Was I all right?" And she's kind of looking out there in the dark and you can hear the great Piaf songs in the background; a stagehand comes around and turns off the bright lights and switches to the work light . . . and all the while we can hear this amazing sound: Piaf. The immortal Piaf! People I respect have told me that it was one of the best endings ever filmed.

If only the rest of the movie were that good. But it wasn't. And we had no one to blame but ourselves. We screwed it up. We shot the picture in French with a French director. The only thing missing was a French audience. It was a total flop. Nobody was even slightly interested in seeing it. Later, we figured out what went wrong. Imagine, we told ourselves, that we're sitting in our office in New York and one day a Frenchman comes in and says, "Fellows, I got a terrific idea. I want to make a great musical about Judy Garland." We'd look at him and say, "Yeah? Who gives a fuck?" See, we already know about Judy Garland. We don't need a French guy coming in and telling us about her. By the same token, the French already know about Edith Piaf. They don't need a couple of Americans telling them about her. What we should have done—the way to have handled this—was to make an American movie about Piaf. There was an English version of the film, which had a London opening, but even that bombed.

The fact that the movie did no business raised another problem. Our backer. We didn't have a studio. We had a single backer. Call him Al. My brother, Stan, played tennis at the Beverly Hills Tennis Club and he and Al played together. Now, Al was very rich and when Stan mentioned this low-budget movie that we were planning to make—something less than a million bucks—Al offered to finance the whole thing.

We should have sensed trouble. Al kept coming in late with the checks. We had to pay the cast and the crew and he was very slow. Finally, Ernie threatened to shut down the production unless he produced the money. That caused friction. And a grudge.

So, after the thing was finished and it was clear that we had bombed, and we were not going to make any money, Al sued us for fraud. He claimed that we stole money from the production budget. The charge was ludicrous, but the case actually went to trial. I didn't know it when we went into business together, but Al had a long record of suing people. He went from one case to the next. And it didn't cost him anything, since he had a lawyer on retainer.

I realized as we came to court in Los Angeles, when I saw Al lugging in those great accordion files that lawyers carry, that he was enjoying it. The man loved being in court. He carried the big briefs and he sat next to the lawyer and spread out the papers and I could see on his face that he was having fun. He enjoyed it more than tennis, more than making money, more than anything. He was probably glad the movie wasn't a hit.

It was a jury trial and it was six weeks of hell. They had us scared to death because if it went against us, he would have taken everything we had. However, they made the mistake of putting me on the witness stand without careful preparation. They did not do their homework. One of the chief elements of the case against us was that I had committed an act of nepotism.

Al's lawyer—a very tough Israeli—holds up a picture and asks me, "Do you recognize this person?"

"Of course."

"Who is that?"

"That's my nephew. Stan's son."

"What's his name?"

"Zach."

"Is it true that he worked on the picture?"

"Yes, he did. He wanted to learn the business."

"So, he was on the payroll?"

"No, he was not."

"He was not on the payroll?"

"No."

"But he was paid?"

"Yes."

"Who paid him?"

"I did. Or, rather, me and Ernie."

That was a particularly delightful moment. The faces all fell at Al's table. The lawyer was dumbstruck. Al was dumbstruck. The judge was probably dumbstruck. And I was savoring it. I had been caught doing the right thing. Call it foresight, call it intuition, call it an exaggerated sense of propriety, but when the whole thing started, I did not put my nephew on the payroll budget for the movie *Piaf*. He was, instead, on the Feuer & Martin payroll. His salary came out of my own pocket. And that was the end of the lawsuit. Or, at least, that took the teeth out of it. It never got to the jury. We settled the case by turning over all copies of *Piaf* to Al while he picked up all of our legal expenses.

From time to time someone will mention the movie—they've seen some bootlegged version in English—and I'm reminded that it wasn't all bad. There was the story. A good story. And there was that ending.

In fact, someone made a videotape of *Piaf* for me. One last copy. I had it with me, to show someone, when I went to the bank not long ago. I get confused at the bank, what with the deposit slips and the lines and the strain of getting it all organized and right. So I left the tape behind on the counter. A guard told me later that they must have thrown it out.

Chapter Twenty-seven

I don't believe that I suffered any loss of confidence post *Piaf,* but I was probably a little slaphappy. I needed a break after butting heads with the unrelenting Fosse and the litigious-prone Al. And so in 1975, Ernie and I became managing directors of the Los Angeles and San Francisco Civic Light Opera Association. It wasn't exactly a soft job, but it didn't have the high-octane pressures of running fresh shows onto Broadway. This was a subscription theater company that produced eight- and ten-week revivals in both Los Angeles and San Francisco. It allowed us to lightly keep our hand in the business while we licked our wounds.

When we were working in Los Angeles, Posy and I usually stayed at the Beverly Hills Hotel. In spite of the expensive cooking skills she picked up at Le Cordon Bleu in Paris, Posy preferred room service. And California was congenial. It didn't feel strange or difficult. One of our close friends there was George Furth, an actor and playwright who won a Tony for the 1971 musical, *Company.* George is a familiar face on the screen and in television; most people remember him as "Woodcock," the suicidally loyal custodian of the railroad safe in the movie *Butch Cassidy and the Sundance Kid.* He had a beach house in Malibu, and Posy and I would visit him and the Pacific Ocean, which was right outside his window. After a day in the sun, Posy would call the hotel and insist that before we returned, the housekeeping staff have the bed made to her strict specifications. The blanket had to be tucked in at the bottom of the bed, but not on the sides. The sheets had to extend exactly six inches beyond the blanket and be folded over at the top. It was picky, but she was shameless about the guidelines for our bed.

Needless to say, that's a dangerous quirk to advertise in front of a playwright. Everything is grist to a writer. And so when we were invited to the opening of one of George's new plays, I felt a small shock of recognition at the antics of one of the characters: a woman visiting a Malibu beach house. She gets on the phone with her hotel's housekeeper and starts laying out her demands for the makeup of the bed: the blanket had to be tucked in at the bottom and not on the sides. The sheets had to be precisely six inches beyond the blanket and folded over the top. So, as we were watching the play unfold, with the woman in Malibu making her wacky demands about the disposition of the bed, Posy jabbed me in the ribs and hissed, "See! I'm not the only one!"

Luckily the play was a flop so the world didn't get to see Posy in her full Marine Corps drill sergeant manifestation.

In spite of that particular dud, George was a strong playwright. He collaborated twice with Stephen Sondheim (*Company* and *Merrily We Roll Along*) and had a reputation for constructing a solid book to go along with musicals. He was pretty hot in the mid-seventies. One day he got a call from Liza Minnelli who was filming *New York, New York* in, of course, New York, New York. When she was done with the movie, she said she was going back on the stage. She needed someone to write the book for a musical. For the music she already had the team from *Cabaret*—John Kander and Fred Ebb. Come to think of it, she could also use a producer. It just so happened that Ernie and I were available. The show would be called *The Act*, and before we took it to Broadway, we had the perfect out-of-town venues to whip it into shape: the Los Angeles and San Francisco Civic Light Opera Company. We had four and a half months for tryouts.

George wrote a delightful story. Liza plays Michelle Craig, a nightclub singer who ruminates about her bumpy life during a series of engagements at the Hotel Las Vegas. It was inside show-business stuff, and it gave Liza a terrific platform to display her musical and acting gifts. When I went to see Liza in New York to talk over the show, I was a little startled. She has a tendency to gain weight, but this time she was really plump. I didn't say anything because I didn't have to. Liza is a pro and she told me not to worry about the weight. She promised to be in shape for the show. And six months later, when she showed up in Los Angeles, she looked terrific. When she says she's gonna take care of a problem, she takes care of it.

There was, however, one other problem, which she dumped in our laps. It was pretty late in the game—tickets had been sold, announcements made, theaters booked—when we met in our office in Los Angeles and Liza informed us that she had picked her own director: Martin Scorsese, the brilliant film director who had worked with her on *New York, New York*.

I tried not to fall off my chair.

Liza explained that she and Marty had spent a lot of time together while working on the film. Every night, after shooting, he took her back to his hotel room where he played old silent movies and educated her on the subtle points of great films. Marty is, after all, a very well-educated man when it comes to film. He even taught the subject at NYU. Apparently, he also gave private tutorials to film stars. As happens in such intense and intimate circumstances, there developed a wild and uncontrollable passion between student and teacher. So powerful was this emotional firestorm, that Scorsese abandoned his wife, Julia Cameron, and his brand new baby, Domenica Cameron-Scorsese, and followed Liza to California. Liza, herself, was in the meltdown stage of her own marriage to Jack Haley, Jr. Well, it was a crazy time, what with the rampant counterculture and the omnipresence of drugs. No one was behaving rationally.

Liza offered her own explanation for her demand: "Marty and I are in love and we're going to spend the rest of our lives together. We are together in everything that we do. Therefore, he is going to direct the show."

It didn't sound negotiable. Ernie and I were aghast. I spoke delicately: "Don't you think it's a little risky? He's never directed a stage musical."

She spoke categorically: "No. The man is fine. And that's the way it's going to be."

We were stuck. The shows were sold out, the cast had been hired, the music was ready, the audience was waiting. I had to submit. There is one overwhelming truth in the theater that transcends all others: you cannot force anybody to perform.

This is not the first time this sort of thing came up. Ten years earlier, in 1966, we were all set to go on the road with a show called *Walking Happy* when Mary Martin walked away. "Sorry, fellas, I'm not gonna do it. I'm going to do something else."

It was crushing then, and I was a younger man. *Walking Happy* was the musical version of *Hobson's Choice* and Mary Martin was the whole play. *Hobson's Choice,* a famous movie in 1954 that starred Charles Laughton and John Mills, is the story of the tyrannical owner of a bootshop whose daughter marries one of his employees to escape his domination. In the case of *Walking Happy,* the principal role was the daughter, a feisty part in which we depended upon Mary Martin for star power. But she declined. And I accepted it. What could I do? I had no real choice. It is that same basic law: You cannot force talent to perform.

Better to be graceful. "Of course, we understand," I told Mary Martin.

In the case of *Hobson's Choice,* we shifted the starring role from the daughter to the groom, the bootblack whom she marries. We brought in this British actor, Norman Wisdom, who was completely wrong for the play. He threw it off. There was something a little nasty about him and the audience could sense it. The run of the show was very short.

Liza's dictate didn't necessarily spell ruin. We weren't losing our star. We didn't have to rewrite *The Act* or change its emphasis. And, after all, Scorsese was a pretty talented director; maybe he could handle the material. He was also a pretty nice guy. I liked him. He was smart and he was dedicated to the success of the play. Maybe we'd get lucky.

However, I saw the problem as soon as he walked into the theater in Los Angeles and demanded a dressing room. I laughed, but he was serious. In the theater, I explained, directors do not have a dressing room. They're out front, watching the show.

On his movie sets, Marty always had his own trailer, his own retreat, so I guess he thought that he would get one in the theater. It is one of the differences between making movies and producing a show. Once the show gets going, there's no downtime. It's running. On a film set there are long gaps of time in which lights are being set up, cameras shifted. During that downtime, actors and directors retire to their trailers. To relax. It wasn't worth the fight. We gave Marty a dressing room, into which he vanished for long stretches of time. He had what appeared to be a permanent cold and required the privacy of his own room to recuperate.

There were other problems. He thought that he was going to be the boss, which is the director's role on a movie set. But in the theater, you have to rely on a lot of technical help. The stage manager has to be given his instructions and it has to be done with some clarity. The stage is controlled by one guy, the music by another, the sets by another. So we sort of surrounded him. Took away his dominance.

The biggest problem was that he didn't understand staging. He couldn't figure out how to bring actors on and off, how to set up a scene. The movies are different. In a funny way, the theater is easier. You get a second chance. You do a scene and it doesn't work and you rewrite and try it another way. You keep doing it until you find out how to make it work. You get a second chance, but you have to take advantage of that second chance and correct the flaws. You have to have an eye for it. Because eventually time runs out, and you're going to find yourself with a stage filled with all your faults.

Marty came in and started to direct and we always had someone around to bolster him up. I stood next to him during dress rehearsal, suggesting this and that. He was pretty amenable. He was smart enough to know that he was out of his depth.

It took a lot of sweat, but we put the thing together. However, no matter how hard we worked, there was one big problem: it didn't work. There was something clinky and rough about it. The first reviews in California were pretty tough. I didn't disagree. The trouble was still the staging. It didn't have an overall concept. This was the story of one woman who worked the Las Vegas nightclubs and that atmosphere had to be conveyed on the stage to the audience, and so far we didn't have it. We all thought that there should be a band on the stage, to signal the music and the nature of her universe, but we couldn't figure how to get them off when we switched to her dressing room.

Certainly Marty couldn't figure it out. He was either locked away in his dressing room fighting his running nose, or completely baffled about how to fix the problem. And he was missing shows. Finally, it was clear to me that he was the problem. *The Act* needed a real director. He had to go.

The only person who could fire him was Liza, and I had to tell her.

I took her aside and I said, "You know, we better fix this, because the next thing you know you're going to be standing on the stage at the Majestic Theater, facing a Broadway audience and Broadway critics. Liza Minnelli. Nobody else. You're going to take all the bullets. For Christ's sake, defend yourself. We have to get rid of Scorsese."

She understood. She's tough and professional and she worked it out. She went to Marty and convinced him to check into a hospital for a couple of days to cure his running nose. To save face, we announced that his good friend Gower Champion was standing by to help out and take over the job as director while Marty recovered from his ailment.

And that's what we did. Gower came in and restaged the play—he placed the band on a movable stage, which would separate and move off when the scene changed to the dressing room. He had very inventive ideas. At one point, a quick change was required and he didn't want to take Liza offstage and ruin the timing. So Gower had Liza surrounded by some dancers and a gown came down from the flys and draped itself over her waiting form.

It worked. The New York opening was a success. The show ran for a year. Liza and Marty got over each other. Liza got great reviews, and a Tony. George got another Tony. And I got blamed for firing Marty Scorsese.

Chapter Twenty-eight

Michael Bennett was hot. "I gotta get out of this place," he said. We were both staying at the Beverly Hills Hotel, but he meant Hollywood. "Those idiots are trying to ruin this thing." He meant that the studio executives were trying to turn his great hit *A Chorus Line* into a hack movie.

It was 1984 and he'd sold the fabulously successful *Chorus Line* to a major studio and they brought him out to California in order to torment him with their "minor" changes—not just a slight shift in plot, character, emphasis. The usual all-out assault on perfection. "They own it. They bought it. They can do anything. I can't work with these guys. It's just not my ball game. Who needs it?"

He didn't understand the nature of the beast. A movie is a big production and the studio is run by nervous executives who have a hand in everything. Broadway's different. The backers hand over the money and you produce a show. It's like running a small circus.

Michael quit and went back to New York.

Sometime later, Marty Baum got his hands on the property and he asked me to produce it. I went to see Michael in New York to tell him that I was going to produce the film and invite his blessing. He had a beautiful penthouse on Central Park South and he said that he was delighted that *A Chorus Line* "isn't in the hands of those damn people; I had a dose of them and they turned my stomach." He meant that mine were reliable, theatrical hands.

Then he said something of terrific importance. He warned me of a great danger to be avoided: "Don't make it the story of Zach and Cassie" (the director and the dancer in the story). The plot of *A Chorus Line* is the emerging vignettes of the dancers who are trying out for parts in a new musical before a cold and demanding director. On Broadway, the director is primarily a disembodied voice that comes from the dark. He is seldom seen. It is that unknown power in the dark that makes it frightening. The star of the Broadway show is the ensemble. The dancers.

There are three problems with getting advice. The first problem is getting good advice. The second problem is recognizing it. The third is acting on it. What I got from Michael Bennett was very good advice. What I did was ignore it completely.

Well, the truth is, I couldn't have followed it even if I wanted to. And I did sort of want to. I recognized that the charm of this play was the grit and bravery of the gypsies—the dancers who go from show to show like soldiers. It's a drab, grueling, and lonely life, but the audience only sees the bright smile of a synchronized chorus line. The backstage insight was the thing that made it so compelling.

However, the fate of the film had already been decided. Michael Douglas wanted to play the part of the Broadway director. He wanted to star in the film. He was even willing to do it without pay. Just his expenses, which, when you're dealing with a high-powered movie star, is not chicken feed. In his case, expenses were $150,000. When you have a big movie star anxious to work without any salary, it is my experience that movie studios are always willing to agree. It doesn't matter that the appearance of the big star will distort the movie, shift attention from where it's supposed to be—in this case, the chorus line. Studios are blinded by the stars. The film was doomed from the start. I had been warned, but I thought I could overcome the handicap.

Marty Baum suggested that we hire Richard Attenborough to direct the film. It might seem odd, given the fact that most people associate Lord Attenborough (as he is now known) with making large, weighty films, such as *Gandhi* (for which he won an Oscar), but he had a lighter side. He had directed the satirical musical *Oh! What a Lovely War,* and while he was criticized for being heavy-handed, he had one other encouraging asset: he, too, was Marty's client. I went to England to meet him. He lived in Richmond in a very wide house with a beautiful garden that faced out on a square. And I liked him immediately. He laughed a lot. And he was smart, in spite of being an actor. Of course he was an egomaniac, but an acceptable one. And, I thought, with a guy like Attenborough, I would have a certain amount of control because he was a musical neophyte.

So we went to work. We used the Mark Hellinger Theater on 51st Street as our studio and it gave us the authentic feel of a theater. However, I wanted to keep the audience portion of the theater dark, to try to salvage that claustrophobic feel of an empty theater and the disembodied voice. But without some lighting we wouldn't have seen Michael Douglas. And he was the star. I'm not even sure I fought so hard. You know, this was one of the great Broadway hits of all time and I wanted to make it as a film. I thought that it should be a little different. The apple had been stood on its head; now I tried to turn it over and stand it on the other side. That was dumb.

Stuff seemed to work. The scenes with the dancers seemed fine. The big scenes with all the actors seemed to work. The tryouts. The musical numbers. It was all very, very good.

We thought that we were making a decent film. But it wasn't.

When we made *Cabaret,* we took a second-rate play and made a first-rate movie. In *A Chorus Line,* we took a first-rate play and made a second-rate movie.

We released the movie during the Christmas season of 1985. We had a Radio City Music Hall opening. That's a big deal. A Christmas opening is supposed to bring in a lot of business. But after the reviews, after the audiences spoke, they pulled us out. Christmas is the major moneymaking season, and we were bombing. That's when I knew it was bad. If we'd opened in February, maybe we'd have gotten some attention, because there were some good things in the movie.

They blamed Attenborough unfairly. But then they blamed him before he did anything. Not Marty Baum. He was so pro Attenborough and pro me that we could do no wrong. Well, that's an agent. He likes his client's stuff. Someone once asked Swifty Lazar, the late agent, what he thought of his client's movie, and he said, "What kind of a stupid question is that? I'm the guy's agent, for Christ's sake. I love the picture. That's my job—to love the picture."

*　　*　　*

It is a completely mystifying thing, success. What works and what doesn't. You can apply faultless logic, work with geometric precision, allow for every single pitfall, have the perfect cast and the perfect story, and still turn out a dud. There are so many complicating intangibles. It's like the chaos theory. The miracle is that it sometimes works. Occasionally, in hindsight, you get some clarity. Take *Skyscraper.* It should have worked. We had a good story (a brave woman battles against big real estate developers to keep her home); I hired a terrific writer, Peter Stone, who amassed a staggering list of film credits: *Charade, Father Goose, The Taking of Pelham One Two Three, Who Is Killing the Great Chefs of Europe?* Peter, who became a lifelong friend, is funny and talented and he wrote a good play. We did everything right. We even drove to Long Island and climbed into a rented blimp and flew around Manhattan to get a sense of the skyline for the scenery. There we were, two Jews floating above the city, like something imagined by Chagall. I just made one big mistake, which is all you're allowed on Broadway: I put Julie Harris in the lead. It was dumb. She was a great dramatic actress and the lead in that show required someone lighter, someone who could sing, or at least give a reasonable rendition of a song. Well, in 1965, we were deluded into thinking that everyone could talk their way through the music. It was all Rex Harrison's fault. He did it so well in *My Fair Lady* that we were convinced that it was easy. He ruined a lot of great actors. I didn't even learn my lesson. Fifteen years later I tried to get Liv Ullman to sing in *I Remember Mama*. She worked her heart out—a real professional and a great sport—and she wasn't too bad. But the audience didn't buy it. Not in either case. They wanted serious actresses with great reputations to remain above that sort of thing. Their true talent should not be disrespected by being forced to sing badly.

Of course, by now, I'm probably no longer in a position to fairly judge the contemporary musical scene. I have outlived my time. Or maybe I just got stuck in the past. So when I say that I don't care much for a lot of the musical world now, it can be dismissed as the sour rantings of a codger. Still, I have always hated guitars, this is nothing new. It is not an interesting musical instrument. And the profundity of the lyrics that come out of Billy Joel and Bruce Springsteen kind of escapes me. While I'm at it, I don't like a lot of today's theater. Some of it I actively dislike. Like *Mamma Mia!* It's a big hit and it's a big mess. A lot of the American theater is influenced by the British musicals. It used to be the other way around. But Andrew Lloyd Weber, an excellent musician who's not big on story, took over. *Cats, Phantom of the Opera*. Not very deep.

I didn't even like *Rent,* a modern *La Bohème.* The audience wants sentimentality now—*Les Miz*—and I hate sentimentality. As I say, I prefer Loesser or Porter.

Of course, the economics are different than when we began. Hard to take big chances with fresh material when it costs so much. Broadway almost has to depend on revivals and cheap sentiment.

I know that people have said the same things about our shows. *Where's Charley?* seems touchingly dated now. Some things I have done stand up and some don't. You operate in the era in which you find yourself. But, still, at the time, when I was immersed in it, I thought everything we did was terrific. I saw the defects, too, but for the most part, I was blinded by the excitement of just doing it. I suppose I miss that part—the effort.

* * *

You know, in retrospect, when I think about it, I'm still not convinced about *A Chorus Line.* I can't remember the movie being *that* bad. It used to be that when I did stuff that was very bad, I acknowledged it. I didn't feel that way with this one. I wasn't ashamed of it.

Epilogue

I *get up in the middle of the night,* dress, and sit in an easy chair waiting for dawn. I don't remember doing it, but how else did I get here?

There's not much I can do while I wait. I can't read because my eyes are bad. I can't watch television because of the same excuse. I don't want to wake Posy. So I sit here and ruminate. The doctors have taken me off the pills that make me sleep. Apparently they interfere with the pills that lower my something or raise my something else. I can't keep track. A lot of my time is spent shuffling between doctors who wage ferocious battles over how to keep me awake or let me sleep or keep me alive. I'd settle for a good night's sleep.

There are times when I have to be alert. For example, on Wednesdays they send a car for me so that I can attend board meetings of The League of American Theaters and Producers, Inc. I'm the chairman of the board, which means that my presence at board meetings is essential. I'm the guy who says, "Can we quiet down?" And then someone else takes over.

* * *

I have adjusted to my somewhat distant and less urgent connections to the theater. That happens during the course of a really long life—you adjust. Posy and I sit here in our apartment on Park Avenue, adjusting. Her hearing aids get stronger and my eyes grow weaker.

It's funny, because while the various body parts wear out, our appetites are still powerful. We manage to get out and put away a big steak dinner. And we still get a kick out of each other. Our lives remain intact in that important way. And we have the kids . . .

* * *

The phone rings. It's Bobby. He's decided not to run for office. We're very proud of our son Bobby, a lawyer, who wages a brave but futile fight for campaign reform. He lives in Stockbridge, Massachusetts, with his wife and two kids (our grandchildren), Kate and Max. I am still a little stunned that he is a respectable member of the community. He used to be a hippie and live in a sleeping bag.

Jed is a different story (although he was no piece of cake, either). He's a musician. A truly brilliant composer. He has the great gift: he hears the whole thing in his head. Writing it down is just a formality.

* * *

There have been a lot of deaths lately. Not long ago there was a memorial for Gwen Verdon at the Broadhurst Theater. It was crowded. I slipped in unnoticed. I watched as best I could, remembering Gwen, Fosse, their daughter, Nicole (whom I had cast in *A Chorus Line*). Then I slipped out of the theater without having said a word to anyone.

Ernie died seven years ago. I spoke at his funeral. I have to look in the mirror to see if I'm still around. Things are slipping away. I fully expect to ask Posy one day soon, "Who was that guy I worked with for so long, the one who was my partner?"

She'll say, "Who wants to know?"

Acknowledgments

There are and were so many people who have played important roles in my life whose names, for one reason or another, do not appear in the body of this book.

Here are as many as I can think of. Everyone else, please forgive me. You'll all be in the sequel, *My Years as Power Forward for the New York Knicks*. Lawrence Bachman, Lauren Bacall, Milton Berle, Roger Berlind, Ira Bernstein, Patricia Birch, Mel Brooks, David Brown, Ralph Burns, Zoë Caldwell, David Carr, Guy Casaril, Jerome Chodorov, Marge Champion, Irving Cheskin, Alexander H. Cohen, Irving Cohen, Betty Comden, Lucy Cormack, Danny Daniels, Michael David, Robert Derecktor, David Dinkins, Phyllis Dukore, Sammy Fain, Joshua and Mark Feuer, George Furth, Margot and Leonard Gordon, Martin Gottfried, Robert and Rita Gottsegen, Robert Goulet, David Grossberg, Marvin Hamlisch, Sheldon Harnick, Jeffrey Hornaday, Rock Hudson, Bernard Jacobs, Ed Kleban, Kevin Kline, Marvin Krause, Rocco Landesman, Burton and Lynne Lane, Philip J. Lang, Alan Jay Lerner, Warner and Kay LeRoy, Paul Libin, Pia Lindstrom, Leonard Lyons, Donna McKechnie, Cameron Mackintosh, Shirley MacLaine, Elizabeth, Cecilia, and Polly Martin,

Thomas Meehan, Jo Mielziner, Robert Montgomery, William Moriarty, Barry Nelson, James M. Nederlander, Joseph Papp, Ron Raines, Robert Randolph, Chita Rivera, John Rodman, M.D., Gerald Schoenfeld, Eric Sherman, Ph.D., Keith Sherman, Herbert and Ann Siegal, Peggy Siegal, Philip J. Smith, Elke Sommer, Daniel and Madeleine Taradash, Nina Tisch, Gore Vidal, Mayor Robert F. Wagner, Tony Walton, Lew Wasserman, Onna White, Robert Whitehead, Gretchen Wyler, Jerry Zaks, and Al Zuckerman.

Special thanks to Jeffrey Borer and Ken Gross: Jeff, my cardiologist, dear friend, and the guy whom I credit with saving my life at eighty-nine: he introduced me to Ken Gross.

Thanks to Lew Grossberger for the title.

A big thank you to Jo Loesser, a wonderful talent and great friend for a long time.

Thank you, Chuck Adams. Editing is everything.

And my last two very special thank yous go to Jed Bernstein and Harvey Sabinson. Two of the greatest guys you'll ever meet.

Index